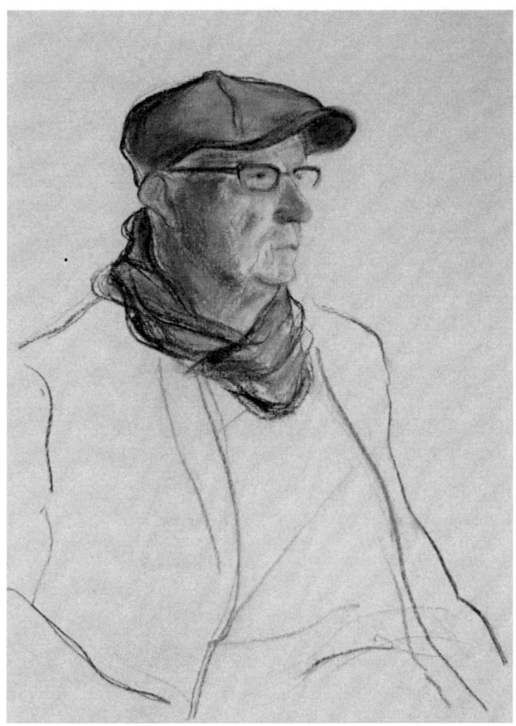

Portrait of Bill Hare (2018) Alexander Moffat.

BILL HARE was born in Edinburgh in 1944 and studied at the University of Edinburgh and the Courtauld Institute of Art, University of London, in the 1970s. Since then he has taught art history at the University of Edinburgh, Edinburgh College of Art and the Open University. In 1985 he was appointed Exhibitions Organiser at the Talbot Rice Gallery working with many Scottish artists as well as those from wider afield. Since 1995 he has concentrated on teaching and freelance curating, with his main focus on Scottish art since 1945. He has curated a number of important exhibitions both in Scotland and abroad, and has published books and catalogues on a range of different aspects of historical, modern and contemporary Scottish art. He is currently an Honorary Fellow in Scottish art history at the University of Edinburgh.

By the same author:

Contemporary Painting in Scotland, Craftsman House, 1992
Divided Selves: The Scottish Self-Portrait from the 17th Century to the Present, Fleming Collection, 2006
Barbara Rae, Lund Humphries, 2008
Facing the Nation: The Portraiture of Alexander Moffat, Luath Press, 2018
Scottish Artists in an Age of Radical Change 1945 to the 21st century, Luath Press, 2019

Scottish Art and Artists
in historical and contemporary context

BILL HARE

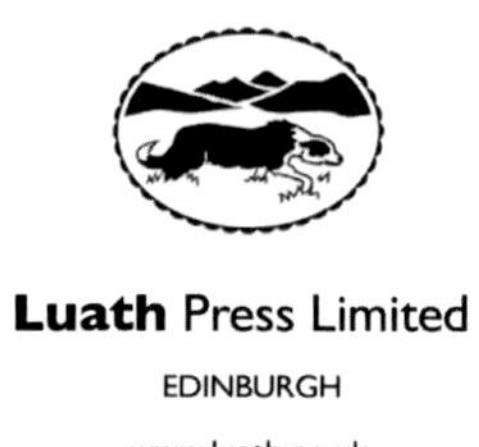

Luath Press Limited

EDINBURGH

www.luath.co.uk

First published 2024

ISBN: 978-1-80425-112-6

The paper used in this book is recyclable. It is made from
low-chlorine pulps produced in a low-energy,
low-emission manner from renewable forests.

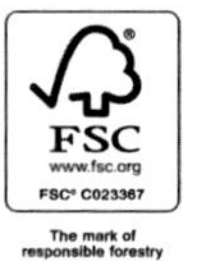

Printed and bound by
Robertson Printers, Forfar

Typeset in 10.5 point Sabon by
Main Point Books, Edinburgh

Cover image: Boyle Family – *Kerb Study with Metal Edge*, 1985
Mixed Media, Resin, Fibreglass
Collection of Glasgow Art Gallery and Museum
Reproduced courtesy of the artist

I would like to dedicate this book to my wife,
Margaret Mary

Contents

Section Five Two Scottish Art Colleges

Part 2 Individual Artists

Foreword
Alexander Moffat

BILL HARE'S FIRST collection of essays, *Scottish Artists in an Age of Radical Change* dealt primarily with the artists of post-war Scotland. The present collection looks in two directions, backwards to the 18th century and forwards into the present. That the essays range over such a period of time reflects Hare's standing as an art historian first and foremost and it is this historical perspective, permeating as it does all of his writings, which gives his new book such a unique authority.

Key themes and arguments emerge… a lack of serious collectors and patronage for the visual arts in Scotland is traced back to 1603 with the departure of the Scottish Court to London and sadly continues to this day resulting in the exodus of many of our most ambitious artists. The Enlightenment philosopher's contribution to aesthetic debate and ideas is examined with reference to the thoughts of Hutcheson, Hume and Reid. Hume's five key attributes for the good critic are discussed in detail, but ultimately Hare identifies with Reid's treatise *Beauty and Common Sense* and explains why. 'Like Reid, I am much more concerned to focus my visual attentions on the work of art itself and be aware of its effect on my sensibilities, rather than evaluating my critical judgements against those of others and the canon of taste.'

With 'Throwing Light on the Scottish Endarkenment', The Scottish Enlightenment is contrasted with the Scottish Endarkenment, both of which Hare argues are essential adjuncts to the story of Scottish art. For Hare, as opposed the values of the Enlightenment, The Endarkenment was involved with passion, mystery and the power of myth to connect us to our authentic selves.

Yet these two contrasting aspects of thought and feeling need not be seen as antipathetically opposed to each other. In nature, as in art they are there to combine and create the chiaroscuro by which we make visual sense of the world and our relationship to it.

The topics explored are wonderfully varied, from Raeburn's *Skating Minister* via Photography in Industrial Scotland, three essays each on contemporary abstraction and figuration and an illuminating take on the collection of antique casts belonging to Edinburgh College of Art which references both the birth of the European art academy and the subsequent beginnings of a similar institution in the Athens of the North in 1826. The arrival of Hare's new book is timely, given the current dearth of Scottish art historians. We are also experiencing the erosion of an informed public discourse surrounding the visual arts *vis-à-vis* national newspapers and magazines. One wonders how many of the artists Hare discusses are known to the general public or even art students? They all should be.

The Edinburgh Festival, launched in 1947 turned Edinburgh into an international centre for art and culture, whether it liked it or not, and the internationalisation of Scottish art is the main context for Hare's ideas and opinions. Does contemporary Scottish painting have a past? You'll find the answer in the first section of this book. In the second section Hare returns to familiar ground in a series of essays on individual artists beginning with Alan Davie and Eduardo Paolozzi and ending with Barbara Rae, Joyce Cairns, Steven Campbell and Douglas Gordon. In comparison with many who write about contemporary art, Hare is never self-indulgent or wilfully obscure – there is no bogus theorising to be found here. His reasoning is lucid and his masterly grasp of the long historical narrative is always placed at the service of the reader. Hare wears his learning, which is considerable, with a very light touch indeed.

INTRODUCTION

SOMETIMES AS A history of art tutor, to stimulate class discussion, I would ask my students who they thought made the most important contribution to the canonical status of Italian Renaissance art. Predictably, the usual suspects were rolled out – Michelangelo, Raphael and Leonardo. Sometimes a more enterprising individual in the group might consider patronage and suggest the Medici Family. After the dust of the debate had settled, and it was my turn, I would take a different tack and propose that that particular laurel crown should go to Giorgio Vasari. I would then argue that his *Lives of the Artists*, not only endowed sustained, researched, biographical celebrity on individual artists for the first time, but more importantly, created a progressive chronological lineage. Each of those Italian artists could be artistically and historically placed and critically assessed within a 'grand narrative'. In contrast, although Northern Europe had as many outstanding individual artists as Italy – such as van Eyck, van der Goes, van der Weyden, Bosch, Bruegel and Durer – they had no equivalent writer to Vasari to serve their individual reputation and put each of their artistic achievements into an integrated art historical story line.

Vasari's invaluable contribution to the creation of the enduring reputation of the art of the Italian Renaissance is outstanding, but it is not unique in the history of Western art. For instance, the critical, not to mention the commercial and popular aura, that now surrounds 19th century French painting, must owe a great deal to the championing of such supportive voices as those for example of Baudelaire and Zola. Also, much of the posthumous fame of Delacroix and van Gogh is certainly due to the later publication of their journals and diaries. Turning closer to home, the development of British modern art was very much directed by the critical guidance of Roger Fry and Clive Bell, and later David Sylvester and John Berger. Furthermore, in the mid-20th century the worldwide domination of American Abstract Expressionism was undoubtedly well served by the highly influential promotion of such literary figures as Clement Greenberg and Harold Rosenberg. More recently, the phenomenal impact of the British YBA artists on the international art scene in the 1990s, was greatly aided through the enthusiastic endorsement by the writer/critic Matthew Collins.

In Scotland there have undoubtedly been a notable number of outstanding individual artists, who through their distinctive art have created a national reputation, but rarely, an international one. Furthermore, within Scotland the visual arts has never enjoyed the same serious critical attention and promotion as, for example, Scottish literature. This has meant that no Scottish artist has gone on to gain the international renown of Scott or Stevenson – and in the 20th century does any Scottish artist have the global reputation of Muriel Spark?

Thus critical writing is unarguably vitally important, not only in the encouragement and support of the visual arts, but also in creating a serious respect and admiration for its role and importance within a nation's cultural identity. In contrast to other countries, in Scotland this has almost never been the case – and continues so to be.

No one would deny that there is a very active art scene in Scotland today, but the emphasis is almost exclusively placed on production. This is clearly demonstrated by the numerous art schools and colleges throughout the country, with the many young artists' support schemes, residencies and travelling scholarships. On the other hand, there is little or nothing in place to assess and promote the visual arts in Scotland through the publication of critical writings. This leads one to ask – what is the point in producing and encouraging a disproportionate number of young aspiring artists, if there is little opportunity for meaningful informed public discourse to discuss and encourage their creative efforts and abilities? Furthermore, if this critical dimension is lacking, then it is also certain that there will be little likelihood of a visually educated public – let alone adventurous collectors – to appreciate and support any new and innovative art of an experimental and ambitious nature. This situation inevitably has further dire implications on the art scene, resulting in the widespread domination of the self-congratulatory attitude of 'I don't know much about art, but I know what I like'. Then the conservative taste of 'I like what I know' becomes the prevalent self-satisfied order of the day; and Oscar Wilde's words will ring true in Scotland that they only know the price, not the value, of art.

Some might think the assessment above is over pessimistic and too one sided. If this is the case, then my scenario is still working for a good cause by presenting a necessary warning against cultural complacency. For I feel that this notable deficiency within the contemporary Scottish art world is to everyone's disadvantage – especially for ambitious artists and their keen supporters. As an art history lecturer, I was fortunate enough to teach an excellent Open University course entitled *Modern Art: Practice and Debate*. It was then that I fully realised how equally important *both* those components were – not only in themselves, but also, in their relationship to each other. Creative art practice is of course essential to the cultural wellbeing of any society. Critical debate however, is also absolutely necessary, if that art practice is to be encouraged and to maintain high aesthetic quality, along with social relevance. Furthermore, critical debate on artistic practice need not be the sole province of interested and concerned outsiders, but also, a necessary prerogative of the artists themselves. The history of modern art is full of such discursive artists' groupings – from the Impressionists to the Abstract Expressionists – where debate was the life blood of the modern art agenda. Hopefully, Scottish art colleges still are committed to encourage student debate and group solidarity. This should further develop a wider, more rewarding art scene – both for the artists involved and the Scottish art world as a whole.

I hope what I have presented is not just empty rhetoric, but is based on personal experience of working with, and writing about, Scottish art and artists over many years. Within my own experience, I have been extremely fortunate in having the opportunity to support Scottish art through my writings. The first inclination of having that ambition was when I was at Art College in the mid-'60s. There I realised I would never be the artist I aspired to be. Fortunately, through the advice of one of my tutors, I was encouraged to try to become an art historian. To my delight, at Edinburgh University I found that I did rather well as an art history student, winning an essay writing prize and going on to the prestigious Courtauld Institute for Art in London. After I returned to Scotland I was taken on by my former tutor, Duncan Macmillan at the Talbot Rice Gallery. There the exhibition policy was to promote Scottish art and artists – both historical and contemporary. This meant I was privileged to write for a number of important Scottish artists. There I was also involved with the setting up, and writing for, the first Scottish art magazine for decades, *Alba,* under the editorship of the indomitable Peter Hill. I also joined the university's art history department where they allowed me to develop my own courses on Scottish art history, a subject that proved surprisingly popular – especially with non-Scottish students.

Even with the demands of gallery work and art history teaching, I was always keen to publish my writings on Scottish art. Fortunately there were opportunities for me to do this. After *Alba* folded, I decided to approach London based publications. They were receptive, and keen to publish articles on contemporary Scottish art. I was appointed the Scottish art editor of *Galleries* magazine and remained in that post for a good number of years. I also regularly contributed *Contemporary Visual Art* with the encouraging support of the editor, Lynne Greene. Another fruitful collaboration in London was the Fleming Collection Gallery, where two of my ex-students worked and edited the magazine, *Scottish Art News.* North of the Border there were also periodicals who published my art copy – such as *Radical Scotland* and *Cencrastus,* edited by Raymond Ross. Furthermore, through my wide ranging contacts at the Talbot Rice Gallery I had, over the years, made a good number of acquaintances with Scottish artists and other gallery curators. This resulted in requests to write catalogue essays and to make contributions to artists' monographs.

Right up to the present, I have continued to find publishers interested enough to publish my writings. This is especially so with Luath Press, for whom, with the support of Gavin MacDougall, I have now produce three books.

So, on reaching my 80th year and still aspiring to be a published writer, my own good fortune seems to continue. However, I must admit I am concerned by the lack of opportunities for others. This seems especially so in the area of art periodicals – or the lack thereof. The era of the Scottish non-academic arts magazine seems to have passed and has been now superseded by the new age of online publishing. Of course some young authors might not mind the contemporary online outlets for their writings. I am sure however, that there are also many others who would still prefer to have their words made more permanent by being printed on the page.

Furthermore, from the evidence of the number of books that have continued to be published on Scottish art during the last few years, there is clearly a public who still prefer to read hard copy which they can hold in their hands. Books however, tend to be the domain of older established authors. Younger innovative voices still need periodicals and magazine outlets as a platform to air their challenging radical opinions about what they consider the most important issues facing contemporary art in Scotland. Undoubtedly, Scottish art – for the sake of its aspiring practitioners, its would-be commentators and its supportive public – would be much better served by stimulating and sustaining informed debate through the widespread aegis of the printed word.

Bill Hare
March 2024, Edinburgh

Section One

Essays on Scottish Art and Cultural History

SIGNS OF THE TIMES
Art and Industry in Scotland 1750–1985

*The clock, not the steam engine, is the key machine of the modern industrial
age. At the very beginning of modern technics (in the 13th century) appeared
prophetically the accurate automatic machine, which only after centuries of
further effort was also to prove the final consummation of these technics in every
department of industrial activity.*
Lewis Mumford, *Technics and Civilisation*, 1934

THE TITLE OF this exhibition is taken from an essay by Thomas Carlyle which
he published in the *Edinburgh Review* in June 1829. In it Carlyle forcefully
presented for the first time to his modern public the view that the ever-
increasing growth of industrialisation in this country was having a much more
profound effect than people realised. In the essay he writes:

> Were we required to characterise this age of ours by any single epithet
> we should be tempted to call it not an Heroical Devotional Philosophical
> or Moral age, but, above all others, the Mechanical Age. It is the Age of
> Machinery in every outward and inward sense of the word...

Mechanisation, the iron rule of the regulating time controller which was rapidly
taking over most aspects of 19th century daily experience ironically had its
origins in the Middle Ages. Ironically, because it was to Medieval society,
with its religious faith and traditional craftsmanship that Carlyle's followers
such as Ruskin, Morris and the Pre-Raphaelites, nostalgically looked at as an
alternative model to modern industrial Britain. In the monasteries of Europe,
mechanical time systems were developed to regulate the routine of the enclosed
Brethren. The life inside the monastries was, of course, highly artificial, and
the great majority of the people outside the cloistered walls lived off the land
and had to organise their work and leisure around the natural cycle of the
changing seasons. James Thomson, the great 18th century Scottish pastoral poet
celebrates this timeless rural existence by tracing it back to the Golden Dawn of
Mankind in his major poem, *The Seasons* (final revised version 1746):

> Then the glad Morning wak'd the gladden'd Race
> Of uncorrupted Men nor blush'd to see
> The Sluggard sleep beneath her sacred Beam.
> For their light Slumbers gently fum'd away,
> And up they rose as vigorous as the Sun,
> Or to the Culture of the willing Glebe,
> Or to the chearful Tendance of the Flock

However the men of the 18th century, observing the beginnings of what was to become the industrial revolution, were growing more and more conscious of a profound question. Was the history of society that of continual decline from the age of primitive perfection to contemporary corruption, or had society progressed by its development of moral, cultural and economic values to the summit of social excellence? If the latter was the case, particularly in democratic Britain, then what place did the concept of progress have in this 'best of all possible worlds'? In the end, Thomson and his contemporaries had to admit that even if, through Newton, they thought they had access to the physical laws of the Universe, they were unable to understand fully the workings of modern society.

> And lives the Man, whose universal Eye
> Has swept at once the unbounded Scheme of Things?

Man's view had to be limited and even contradictory. Thomson with all his 18th century optimism could believe, however, that timeless rural routine and the early urban industrial incursions could be harmoniously accommodated in picturesque tranquillity.

> Villages, embosom'd soft in Trees,
> And spiry Towns with surging columns mark'd
> Of household Smoak

Thomson's optimistic view is still echoed over a generation later by John Knox in his Claudian *The Clyde from Dalnottar Hill* (c1820). What Carlyle calls the 'grinding collision of the New with Old' is, as in Thomson, set in the distance, allowing the painting to convey all the celebratory qualities which the early 19th century inherited from the Age of Enlightenment. Yet, despite its relatively insignificant presence in the panoramic view of this stretch of the Clyde, Henry Bell's steamship *Comet* is the centre of attraction, because it is basically alien to the rest of the scene. Distanced as it may be, the 'collision' between the old and new way of 'doing things' is taking place. Not for this new mechanical being a dependence on the recurring, but unpredictable cycle of climatic changes as is the lot of the workers on the farms or the men in the sailing ships. The steamship defiantly takes on the forces of nature, knows exactly where it is by Newton's universal time system, and reaches its chosen destination by the power of mechanisation.

The sailing ship's days are numbered.

> The sailor furls his sail and lays down his oar, and bids a strong, unwearied servant, on vaporous wings bear him through the waters. Men have crossed oceans by steam; … There is no end to machinery.
> Thomas Carlyle, *Signs of the Times*

The spread of industrialisation was to replace the ancient way of life and bring a new experience of living to mankind. The old pattern of existence revolving with the continuous cycle of the seasons was being replaced by a new temporal system; a linear development of mechanical progress stretching out into the distance and the future. The regimented routine of medieval monastries was now enforced on the modern secular world. The clock or 'cloche' (French for bell) no longer called the faithful to prayer, but the urban proletariat to work. No more disturbing vision of the continuous mechanised work-time toil endured by the factory slaves of industrial Scotland is found in this exhibition than James Elder Christie's *Anchor Mills across the Hammils* (c1870). Christie's dark satanic painting is close to Charles Dicken's view of industrial Britain. The novelist knew and admired Carlyle. His portrait of Coketown in *Hard Times* (1854) is greatly influenced by the Scottish Sage, and could be a description of Christie's Paisley.

> It was a town of machinery and tall chimneys, out of which interminable serpents of smoke trailed themselves for ever and ever, and never got uncoiled. It has a black canal in it, and a river that ran purple with ill-smelling dye and vast piles of buildings full of windows where there was a rattling and trembling all day long and where the piston of a steam engine worked monotonously up and down like the head of an elephant in a state of melancholy madness.

Christie's painting of such a subject is a rare event in Scottish art. Relatively few artists wished to follow Carlyle's advice and 'look calmly around for a little on the perplexed scene where we stand'. In fact it was the photographers who were more inclined to concern themselves with recording the changing face of 19th century Scotland. With George Washington Wilson's *Forth Bridge under Construction* (c1887) the Victorian public were allowed to celebrate this great achievement of Scottish engineering, by a machine which apparently could stop the flow of time, and record in innumerable prints, a moment of experience in all its fascinating detail. Thus Wilson's photograph is a twin celebration of the Bridge and the Camera. Lady Eastlake, the Scottish wife of the President of the Royal Academy, observed in her early article, on *Photography (London Quarterly Review* 1857), that it was that particular medium which was the most in tune with the character of the new high-speed, industrial, democratic era.

> She [photography] is made for the present age, in which the desire for art resides in a small minority, but the craving or rather necessity for cheap, prompt and correct facts is in the public at large. Photography is the purveyor of such knowledge of the world. She is the sworn witness to everything presented to her view.

However, we have come to realise that the camera is not such a disinterested witness as Lady Eastlake suggests. The making of a photographic image does not finish with the instantaneous click of the shutter. There is also the selection and developing process where the photographer can impose his own interpretation on his subject; as does Thomas Easton with his highly dramatic, retouched silhouettes of *Carron Iron Works* (c1905).

Yet it was photography, 'sworn witness to everything presented to her view', along with the developments of modern physics which played an important part in questioning the accepted 'knowledge of the world' – knowledge based on Newtonian universally measurable linear time that was the foundation of the Industrial Revolution. The camera not only recorded the reassuring 'correct facts' such as individual likenesses and familiar objects and scenes, but also with increasing technical facility opened up areas of reality beyond human perception – high-speed, split-second action, microscopic activity, disjointed spatial and temporal relationships. For example, the multi-viewpoint photographic experiments of Muybridge, and Marey in the 1880s began to reveal that in the immediate free flow of experience there really was no such thing as a self-contained, detachable moment in time. Temporal reality was not necessarily objective and sequential, but fragmented, relative and ultimately simultaneous.

This alternative view of experience to the Renaissance and Newtonian one had a profound impact on 20th century visual art where 'meaning' is communicated instantaneously rather than by linear development as with literature or music. In the earlier part of this century not many Scottish artists responded to the challenge of these new ideas; modern art in Scottish terms has usually meant colourful decorative treatment of conventional strictly non-industrial subjects. Recently, however, there has been a growing number of artists who have avoided the pervasive influence of the Scottish colourist tradition and engaged the reality of our industrial, mechanised environment to search out what Eduardo Paolozzi has called the 'sublime of the everyday'. To be able to investigate and convey the complex shifting quality of modern experience the most successful artists in this field should be able, if necessary, to utilise the instruments and images of our technological world.

> Technical inventions such as the photographic enlarger, aerial photography and high speed flash have given us new tools with which to expand our field of vision beyond the limits imposed on previous generations.
> Eduardo Paolozzi, *From an unpublished manuscript*

Stephen Lawson's panoramic views literally 'expand our field of vision' not only spatially but temporally, defying the traditional notion that all visual art is restricted to relationships of space alone. The photo-collage technique employed by Lawson interconnects spatial and temporal changes as the camera records continuous spliced sections of the chosen scene through a regulated period of time. This complex relationship between time and space creates a dynamic experience which matches the dramatic grandeur of his industrial subjects.

In the same unpublished manuscript Paolozzi also writes:

Today the painter, for example, may find beneath the microscope a visual world that excites his senses far more than does the ordinary world of streets, trees and faces.

John Kirkwood's tinted etching *Discharge Crack II* (1976) is from the 'visual world beneath the microscope'. Using engineering drawing techniques, the artist grants us an imaginary glimpse into the microcosmic universe of electromagnetic energy, with atomic and subatomic simultaneous disintegration and regeneration. Here conventional notions of time and space no longer exist. The Miró-like vitality of this anthropomorphic electronic microworld is in contrast to the funereal tone of Kirkwood's bulkhead panel *Slit* (1980) and the apocalyptic destruction of the *Battle of Grangemouth* (1976). In the latter work, the photomontage technique allows the artist to project the present into a possible nightmare future. The warning is made: the continuous unholy bond between industrial/technological progress and military exploitation will lead mankind to the brink of destruction.

'Men are grown mechanical in head and in heart, as well as in hand' wrote Carlyle in *Signs of the Times*. Modern man surrounds himself with all kinds of machinery until these mechanical devices become his means of understanding and communicating with his man-made world. This mechanisation of life is a notable aspect of the work of Eduardo Paolozzi as can be seen in *Automobile Head* (1954). Still, Carlyle's message to his contemporaries was not totally pessimistic. If man and society could balance the mechanical with the 'dynamic' then there could be a radical beneficial change. Although a little vague, Carlyle defines the dynamic as

the primary; unmodified forces and energies of man, the mysterious springs of Love and Fear, and Wonder of Enthusiasm, Poetry, Religion, all which have a truly vital and infinite character.

The small childlike figure of Paolozzi's *Icarus* (1957) seems to be striving for this vital balance. This battered, but heroic figure is a survivor of 'the grinding collision of the New with Old'. In a pose that echoes Leonardo's Vitruvian Man he strides ancient myth and future potential; he is both father, Daedalus, the maker of things, and son, Icarus, the seeker of wonders.

It may appear ironic that the origins of our industrial society should be found in the spiritual, otherworldly environment of the 13th century monastery. Yet, if one thinks on it, the monastery, cut off from the natural world, with its timetabled routine of prayer and division of labour, is the micro-model on which the modern world based itself. Since then modern man has become increasingly aware that the more he progresses, the less sure he is about the workings of nature and society. What he has learned to do, through science and art, is to develop theories and models which approximate to the evolving historical experience. These aids do not fully explain, but help to make relative sense of that experience. They also however, condition our personal and social outlook for good or ill. Let us hope that the models we create for ourselves in the future are more humane than many we have imprisoned ourselves with in the past.

This catalogue essay was written for the exhibition *Signs of the Times – Art and Industry in Scotland, 1750–1985* shown at the Talbot Rice Gallery, The University of Edinburgh and the Collins Gallery, University of Strathclyde in 1986.

MADE FROM GIRDERS
Photography in Industrial Scotland

By our skill in Mechanism, it has come to pass, that in the management of external things we excel all other ages; while in whatever respects the pure moral nature, in true dignity of soul and character, we are perhaps inferior to most civilised ages.
Thomas Carlyle, *Signs of the Times*, 1829

THE INDUSTRIALISATION OF this country is inextricably linked with our illustrious predecessors, the Victorians. They did not begin that far-reaching revolution but it was their society which experienced its full impact and it was they who first had to try to understand and come to terms with the profound changes which were taking place. Even if there was a great deal of uncertainty about the social effects of industrialisation, most Victorians were supportive of it as the agent of progress.

The idea of progress, of course, involves the concept of superiority and there was little doubt in the minds of our 19th century ancestors that they were the most progressive nation of their age. However, when it came to comparisons with the achievements of previous civilisations, their sense of their own advanced position was less certain.

The Renaissance became the focus of this important 'Ancients versus Moderns' dispute amongst Victorian writers and artists. Those who were enthusiastic supporters of free economic and industrial development regarded the 16th century as the end of European feudalism and the beginning of the modern age founded on a commitment to rational thought and technological advancement. On the other hand, there were those such as Carlyle and his followers who felt that material gain had been bought at the cost of spiritual loss. Highly critical of their own times, they looked back past the Renaissance to what they perceived as the enviable 'organic' coherence of medieval society. This cohesiveness which seemed to reconcile successfully the mundane with the spiritual, was apparent in all aspects of medieval civilisation, especially in their art and architecture. The critics of the Modern Age could only agree with the architect AWN Pugin that 'a Parallel between the Noble Edifices of the Middle Ages and the Present Day, show[ed] the present Decay of Taste'. That was in 1836, and this feeling, especially through the influential voice of John Ruskin, became stronger and stronger throughout the 19th century.

Photography was born at almost the same moment as Carlyle wrote *Signs of the Times*, his highly critical assessment of contemporary society, which he christened 'the Mechanical Age'. It was not surprising, therefore, that the reception given to the camera by those who shared Carlyle's outlook, was less than cordial. Photographs, because of their mechanical origins, lacked any imaginative power or spiritual authority to elevate their subjects; they were as John Ruskin accused in 1870 'merely spoiled nature'. Yet there could still be found a dogsbody role for photography. Lady Eastlake, the wife of the President of the Royal Academy, in her essay *Photography* (1857) set the camera its allotted task 'for all that requires mere manual correctness, and mere manual slavery, without any employment of artistic feeling, she [photography] is the proper and therefore the perfect medium.' Thus the photographer was assigned the democratic mission to record and document the contemporary industrial scene, most of which was far below the notice of High Art.

Thankfully, many photographers in Scotland, through personal choice or professional requirements, met this challenge in the later 19th and 20th centuries. Without their efforts, much of the experiences and achievements of working people would have been as little known to us as those of earlier civilisations. Yet, like the anonymous craftsmen of the Middle Ages, they have made this important contribution without the need for individual self-expression but rising well above 'mere manual correctness'. With the appropriate subject, for example a shot of the construction of one of the great liners, a photograph can elevate our spirits as can a view of the soaring structure of a Gothic cathedral, or in other instances create a sense of reverence for a piece of machinery similar to that felt for a holy relic. Ultimately, there is the photograph which captures that communal bond of pride in industrial achievement which links the modern worker with his medieval counterpart.

If the 'scientists' of the Middle Ages had somehow invented photography, it surely would have been the triumph of alchemy. Like all craftsmen, the photographers would then have required a patron saint, who undoubtedly would have to be St Veronica. It was she who wiped the face of Jesus as he struggled under the cross on the road to Calvary. This compassionate saint would not only be appropriate because her veil, like the photographic negative, imprinted Christ's human suffering and transformed it into a revered image but also because she found truth, as the camera does, in areas of experience that are usually shunned or go unnoticed.

The great ambition of the medieval alchemist (as it is, in a manner of speaking, of the modern industrialist) was to turn base metal into gold. The achievement of photography is much greater. The camera does not 'merely' record reality. It redeems it. Photography has become our memory, our collective consciousness, retrieving from the past that which would have been forever lost and giving it a living presence again.

This catalogue essay was written for the exhibition, *Made from Girders – Photography in Industrial Scotland* shown at the Talbot Rice Gallery, The University of Edinburgh in 1987.

WHA'S LIKE US?
Scottish Art and Cultural Identity

TS Eliot – it's a Scottish name –
Afore he wrote 'The Waste Land' s'ud ha'e come
To Scotland here. Hie wad ha'e written
A better poem syne – like this, by gum.
Hugh MacDiarmid, *A Drunk Man Looks at the Thistle*, 1926

ENGLAND'S MOST INFLUENTIAL 20th century literary figure, the American exile
TS Eliot, traced the dislocation of sensibility in the English cultural tradition
to the beheading of England's most controversial 17th century political figure,
the Scottish exile, Charles I. After that, according to Eliot, it was downhill
all the way, leading inexorably to 'The Waste Land' and a handful of dust.
Of course, as Miss Rice-Davies would point out, being an Anglo-Catholic
Royalist, he would say that anyway. By contrast, however, there were many
who saw the development of English history in a very different manner. The
18th century Whigs, for example, celebrated a new dawn breaking with the
Glorious Revolution of 1688, which led to optimistic democratic liberalism,
the Victorian free market triumphs of the 19th century and the crowning glory
of Western Civilisation – the British Empire.

This was accomplished by the English cleverly palming off their civil war
to their immediate neighbours, so that they could quickly put the religious–
political upheavals of the 17th century behind them. So effective has this move
been that the Irish are still fighting the English sectarian war on the streets of
Ulster. Not having the bottle of their fellow Celts, the 'knavish' Scots (to quote
the British National Anthem) quickly threw in the towel and their lot with
their Southern masters. Firstly at the Union in 1707 and finally when the last
of the Northern Scots had the stuffing knocked out of them at the last major
land battle to take place on British soil in 1746.

As if by coincidence, at about the time the English army, ably aided by
the newly anglicised Lowlands and turncoat Clan chiefs, was laying waste
to the Highlands after Culloden, the then little-known Irish exile, Edmund
Burke, was publishing his theories about the origins of that most influential
cultural phenomenon, the Sublime. It was his writings that first created the
18th century taste for a bit of rough. So if the age of elegance desired a dash
of barbaric wildness to give it a buzz, then the decimated hillsides of northern
Britain had more than enough to spare. The Scottish Enlightenment circles
duly felt that this newly discovered ancient Caledonia should have a history
which went back to at least the dawn of time. So, as if to order, out of the
misty glens emerged Ossian, whose great sagas of heroic deeds, 'discovered' by

James Macpherson, had just the right primitive appeal for the jaded palates of cultivated circles in Edinburgh, London, Napoleon and further afield.

This need to invent a Scottish identity out of a romantic historical landscape ('every field sings a battle') and from what was left of a rapidly disappearing rural society, was most successfully accomplished by the much honoured duo of Sir Walter Scott and Sir David Wilkie and their Victorian followers. Ultimately it was their view of Scottish life which soon became grotesquely distorted and fixed in the collective consciousness of their fellow Scots, which was used to avoid confrontation with the social effects of the impact of the modern urban and industrial experience. In other countries, those new experiences created the conditions in which a national consciousness could develop. Yet Scotland, by contrast, with its economic and cultural subservience to its mighty partner, involvement with the forces of contemporary history was generally evaded, especially by artists and their patrons. On the whole, the received image of Victorian Scotland was a toss-up between Highland Tartanry and Lowland kailyard.

When the taste for sentimental realism finally began to wane, towards the turn of the 20th century, it was not surprising that Scottish artists and their patrons turned to the least intellectually demanding and socially contentious aspects of Post-Impressionism. In fact all the vacuous critical talk about the *belle peinture* of Scottish modern art was in reality just another form of pictorial escapism. Horatio MacCulloch's gloomy *Glencoe* was merely replaced by SJ Peploe's sunlit Iona beaches, while unnoticed by Scottish art, Scotland's heavy industry lurched into a terminal downward spiral.

With its value to the British economy in decline, Scotland, not surprisingly, became less and less relevant to the changing political and cultural framework of the United Kingdom. The marginalisation of Scotland throughout the 20th century has meant that the Scots have hardly been required to fashion a new image of themselves for outsiders, except to shift the emphasis from the pathetic to the comic – a la Sir Harry Lauder and Rab C Nesbit. In the more serious area of fine arts, Scottish artists were released, if they wished, to take up the challenge of international Modernism. However, with a few notable exceptions (most of whom quickly left Scotland), this challenge was never met. With no economic infrastructure for sustained cultural activities and patronage, there was little support for radical artists who chose to work outside the conservative Royal Scottish Academy/art college establishment. Nor was there much critical encouragement or informed public support for the visual arts because of the near total lack of independent galleries and art publications.

Thus by the early 1980s, when the Scottish Arts Council naively organised the doomed *Scottish Art Now*, as the first (and the last) in a proposed series of Edinburgh Festival exhibitions of contemporary art produced in Scotland, the direction and status of the visual arts north of the border was in complete disarray. Pleasing no one, the exhibition's 'dull international aesthetics' (*Guardian*) were castigated by the local press: 'This is Art – But is it Rubbish?'

(*Edinburgh Evening News*) and dismissed by the national critics as both 'derivative and dull' (*Sunday Times*).

Yet all was not lost, for those in the west of Scotland saw this as a golden opportunity to steal the limelight from Edinburgh's artistic mafia. In a blinding flash, a puff of smoke, as the art critic of the *Glasgow Herald* so vividly put it, *Scottish Art Now* became overnight *New Image Glasgow*. The *Guardian* critic was whisked away and had a St Paul-style conversion on the train to Queen Street station. Then with evangelical zeal he set about drawing his English readers' attention to *The Glow that Came from Glasgow*. With such recognition from the South and subsequent international acclaim for the works of Steven Campbell and the rest of the 'Glasgow Pups', it is hardly surprising that within certain sections of the Scottish art scene a mutual admiration (here's tae us, wha's like us?) attitude had to rear its head. This outbreak of self-congratulations reached its climax when the Scottish National Gallery of Modern Art at last felt obliged to get in on the act and give official recognition by presenting the 'triumphant' *Vigorous Imagination – New Scottish Art* exhibition.

With such a turnabout in its fortunes, it is difficult to assess objectively the state of the arts in Scotland. This lack of critical perspective is not only to be found amongst Scottish commentators, but those outside, as instanced by Brandon Taylor's review (*Art Monthly*, 107) of Steven Campbell's last London show. There the critic seemed to be taking Campbell to task mainly for having been so successful within the capitalist art market. (Here in Scotland we are less inclined to begrudge Campbell his financial success when the Scottish National Gallery of Modern Art is prepared to pay Lucian Freud £300,000 for the privilege of owning one of his now fashionable paintings.) A much more crucial accusation of the recent Scottish art phenomenon, however, was raised by Stuart Morgan's assessment that the *Vigorous Imagination* was 'a study in provincial values' (*Alba* 7).

Exactly what 'provincial values' are, I am not sure. Provincialism itself is usually seen as a lack of confidence in being able to perceive a sense of cultural locality from within, leading to a dependency mentality where all really important events happen outside and have to be imported – in a word, Scottish Inferiorism. This cap in hand attitude is the 'auld, auld story' which MacDiarmid raged against in his poem, *The Parrot Cry*: England frae whom a' blessings flow / What could we dae without ye?

Despite all the recent trumpet blowing, there is still more than enough of that sycophantic Anglophilia going around the Scottish Art establishment, where the continuing lack of self-confidence is reflected in the number of top administrative positions held by non-Scots placemen. More than any, it is with 'these peepul' (to echo Billy Connolly) that real provincialism lies. For example, it could only have been such an attitude of patronising provincialism within the Scottish Arts Council which led to the organisation of the quarter-of-a-million-pound disaster *The Edinburgh International – Reason and Emotion in Contemporary Art*. Its aura of pedagogical superiority in bringing classical values of civilisation to the primitive barbarians north of the border created such outcry amongst the natives that they have hardly been so united in resistance since the occupation of Edward the Confessor.

Yet the strong resentment which was directed towards *The Edinburgh International* is indicative of a growing self-assurance in non-establishment quarters where the demand is for a national/international outlook on a more equitable exchange basis. This newfound confidence has been built on the lively (nae, vigorous) expanding art scene within the various regions throughout Scotland. This is reflected in the ever-increasing demand for entry into the four Scottish art colleges, the setting up of a number of semi-independent studio and workshop complexes across the country, the numerous exhibition spaces now available (a number of which are run by the artists themselves) and at long last a Scottish art magazine (*Alba*) which seriously discusses the visual arts within a national and international dimension. It would seem that all we need now is Scottish collectors (public and private) to support new Scottish art, whether it is in or out of favour with the changing taste of the international art market!

Thanks to the Scottish Arts Council's policy of decentralisation, these various facilities and activities have been established and developed, with selective emphasis, within different centres. For example, Aberdeen's Peacock Printmakers Workshop is the most successful in the country, while Duncan of Jordanstone College of Art in Dundee has become a leading exponent of media studies. All that being said, the main focus of recognition for the renaissance in Scottish arts has undoubtedly been on Glasgow. This has not come about by accident; the forces of history have helped to bring about the 'Glasgow Phenomenon'. The search for new direction which has affected art since the discrediting of the progressive chronological orientation of Modernism has coincided with the acute crisis of identity which has fallen on this once great city of the former Empire. It is in Glasgow more than anywhere that a community has had to reassess its own cultural values and public image in a post-industrial society. There the best Scottish writers and artists have made valuable contributions to this process of reassessment within Glasgow. Through sociopolitical debate, they have observed and adapted to these new circumstances in order to rework stereotypes and media clichés in an imaginative dialogue with postmodern eclecticism. The New Glasgow belongs to them.

The quest for a real cultural identity differs from that of a Holy Cause or Just War, where the enemy is clearly defined and can be clearly targeted. The struggle is more like that of a civil war, where the enemy is just as much within as without, where fact and fiction are inseparably interconnected, where myth and reality merge, and finally where victory belongs to those who best understand the historical process working through contemporary events.

This article was published in *Art Monthly*, May 1989.

Past and Present

Does Scottish Contemporary Painting Have a Past?

FOR MOST POLITICALLY aware people in Scotland the 1980s was, to say the least, a frustrating period. This stems from what is now referred to in Scotland as the 'Referendum Fiasco' of 1979. In that year the nearly defunct Labour Government, introduced a referendum on devolved political and economic power to the Scottish people in an attempt to stave off the Scottish Nationalist threat to their electoral power in Scotland. However, although the majority of Scots who voted plumped for devolution, a group of frightened Labour members of Parliament managed to deny the will of the Scottish people through introducing the requirement of a 40% minimum vote on the total electorate – in other words an unused vote was counted as a no vote! Since then the Labour party, whom the Scottish electorate continue to support, have been defeated at four consecutive general elections by a Conservative Government strenuously committed to the union of Scotland and England ruled from Westminster. Thus, to all intents and purposes, the majority of the Scottish people have been politically disenfranchised.

This situation has created a political vacuum in Scotland which has been most spectacularly filled by the creative achievements of Scottish artists and writers. They, unlike the politicians, have addressed the cultural and social issues which are directly relevant to most people in Scotland. It is those artists and writers who have been the true heroes and heroines of the 1980s. However, they work within a Scottish art scene which is a complicated one. For example, both right- and left-wing cultural institutions have been keen to claim the success story of Scottish art for themselves; there is also the never-ending rivalry between Glasgow and Edinburgh and between national and local arts organisations; and from certain quarters the predictable accusation of a 'sell-out' when critical and commercial success is recognised, especially if that recognition comes from south of the border. Success, as with failure, is a complex business in Scotland.

To the outside world, Scotland no doubt appears to be a small and remote place. Thus, it must come as a surprise that such a country should have contributed so much to human thought and endeavour. This is especially true in the areas of philosophy, science and engineering. In the arts however, the international respect for the great triumphs of Scottish literature has not unfortunately been equally enjoyed by Scottish painting. While the rest of the world reads and admires the writings of Scott, Burns, Carlyle, Stevenson and MacDiarmid, the history and achievement of Scottish painting is only now beginning to be appreciated by the wider public, both in Britain and abroad. In particular, this growing acknowledgement of the importance and distinctive character of Scottish contemporary painting has been recognised mainly because of the tremendous energy and serious commitment that has marked the art scene in Scotland throughout the 1980s. The aim of this article, therefore is to survey the breadth and vitality of recent Scottish painting, and to place it within a wider historical and international context.

Both within and outside Scotland, the 1980s have been hailed as a remarkable success story for Scottish art in general and painting in particular. The international reputation of the Scots, both those of the older generation such as Alan Davie, John Bellany, Bruce McLean and Elizabeth Blackadder, and also the new emerging painters such as Steven Campbell, Ken Currie, Peter Howson, Adrian Wiszniewski, Gwen Hardie and Kate Whiteford speaks for itself. While there have been the usual accusations in some quarters of over-hype, the 80s has arguably been the most exciting and rewarding for Scottish art this century.

As we moved into the 1990s, however, and began to experience the harsh effects of the international economic recession, the art scene in Scotland, as is the case worldwide, began to contract and exude much less confidence than before. Yet it should be said that this loss of nerve is more an attitude to be found in the art market and institutions than amongst the artists themselves. Still it does allow some sceptical commentators to dismiss the 1980s as a freak, 'flash in the pan' phenomenon. I take a different view, and will attempt to show that the achievements of the artists included in this article have not appeared 'out of the blue', but are built on a long tradition within the history of the visual arts in Scotland. To gain a fuller understanding of contemporary Scottish painting it is necessary then to be aware of the historical and social forces which Scottish artists have inherited from the history of Scottish art.

My reference, a moment ago, to the present restrictions, bring me to the first and possibly the most important factor in any discussion of Scottish art – the question of support and patronage. The fact that over the centuries many of Scotland's most successful artists have found it necessary to leave their country to develop their careers is indicative of the financial and cultural difficulties a small country like Scotland faces. This is especially so when it has such close economic links with its larger nextdoor neighbour, England. This continuing problem of sustaining a vibrant, indigenous visual art community against an unsympathetic economic background goes back at least to the early 17th century. With the Union of the Crowns in 1603 and the departure of the Scottish court to London, court patronage of the arts also moved south. Along with the loss of royal and aristocratic support there was the additional burden of a national church, whose extreme protestant attitudes were hardly conducive to large ecclesiastical commissions. Therefore, it is little wonder that until the Enlightenment era of the 18th century, there was only limited and local activity in the visual arts in Scotland. However, from the mid-18th century, progressive Scottish society turned its back on the religious conflicts of the previous era, and set to transform itself into a dynamic modern community. In all areas of social, economic and cultural endeavour, the Scots of the Enlightenment strove after fuller intellectual understanding and material progress. This progressive outlook was also reflected in the spectacular developments in painting and some of the major names of Scottish art; Allan Ramsay. (1713–84), Henry Raeburn (1756–1823) and David Wilkie (1785–1841) are the products of this period, sometimes known as 'The Golden Age of Scottish Painting'. It may seem that there may be little connection between the painting of the Scottish Enlightenment and the work of the contemporary artists under discussion here. However, behind the superficial appearances of differing period fashions and styles there are fundamental connections and shared concerns between Scottish painting, past and present.

Firstly, although the Scottish Enlightenment was on the whole a secular phenomenon, it shared with Scottish protestant theology a strong commitment to the profound importance of individual personal experience. The moral philosophers of the period sought for a deeper understanding of the inner life of the human mind and senses, but within a social, rather than a spiritual framework. Turning now to contemporary Scottish painting, with its strong emphasis on the figure and later landscape for instance, one can also see a broadly similar involvement with particular human and social experiences, rather than universal abstract speculations. The second important ideal which contemporary painting has inherited from the Scottish Enlightenment is the conviction that art, like all important human activities, is ultimately an intellectual discipline. This, I believe, can be discerned both in the paintings and in the statements of intent made by contemporary artists. The work of these painters can be seen as an ongoing dialogue between the workings of the human eye/mind and the natural and social order of the world around them. For these artists the basis of this empirical confrontation with reality is the intellectual development of trained perception through close observation and long practiced skills of drawing and painting. This brings us to the position of the Academy and the central importance of the four art schools in Scotland.

The concept of the Academy came into being during the 16th century in Italy. The learned and rational aspects of art were emphasised along with design and drawing as the basis of academic training. However, it was the French, in the 17th century under Louis XIV and his first minister Colbert, who devised the definitive model for the modern art academy. Over the next two centuries art academies were established in every country which had aspirations to be part of the international civilised community. The influence of such institutions reached its zenith during the 19th century with, for example, the virtual cultural dictatorship of the French Salon in Paris and, to a slightly lesser degree, the Royal Academy in London. Since the rise of Modernism in this century, the academies have lost their former authority and influence.

In Scotland, however, they do things differently, and the Royal Scottish Academy has remained powerful enough even today to engender both respect and resentment in the native artistic community. To understand this is to be aware of a strong sense of tradition that characterises the outlook of many Scottish artists. Although most of the painters included in this article would regard themselves as radical, in that they wish to change people's attitudes to a wide range of different concerns, they are not iconoclastic avant-gardeists who desire to obliterate the past and solely concentrate on being fashionably new for novelty's sake. This frantic pursuit of trendy novelty, which has much dominated cosmopolitan art centres throughout the 1980s, and which many, like the leading critic Robert Hughes, vehemently denounce, has fortunately found little encouragement in Scotland.

Why Scottish artists, right up to the present, should have such a strong sense of tradition, probably goes back to the establishment of the Royal Scottish Academy in Edinburgh at the beginning of the 19th century. Firstly, the RSA was a fairly late arrival, compared to its continental and southern counterparts, and, as such because of its long and difficult birth, was particularly highly valued in Scotland. Secondly, because the country had lost its political sovereignty with the Union of the Parliaments in 1707, any institution which gave focus to national identity was, and in many cases still is, greatly honoured. Thirdly, the Academy gave its members, as a body of professional citizens, not only a sense of social status, but also a voice in the nation's cultural affairs. Whether it has exercised that voice enough, and in the right manner, depends for each artist on which side of the social and artistic barricade they choose to belong. Fourthly, another vitally important function of the Academy was as an educational institution for the training of students. In the Academy studios, the handing on and exchanging of ideas about the execution and purpose of art could be facilitated from one generation to the next. Since the late 19th century the RSA has shed this educational responsibility to the four regional art schools in Edinburgh, Glasgow, Dundee and Aberdeen. Yet such is the moderate size of the artistic community in Scotland that there are still close links between the Academy and the art schools, as many of the teaching staff there are also leading members of the RSA. Therefore, up until now at least, there is a decided academic character to much Scottish painting, particularly with its emphasis on draughtsmanship and painterly technique. The influence of an academic outlook in Scottish painting is further reflected in the conventional subject matter which most artists tend to choose for their work. I will return to this a little later.

Again to take up this question of patronage in Scotland. An important function of the RSA has been to exhibit annually the work of its members and selected practising artists from all over the country. In many cases, this was the only opportunity that some painters had to present their wares to the general public, and, as such, was an important event in the Scottish art calendar. However, throughout the 19th century resentment towards the RSA began to grow, as it was felt by many, that it merely catered for the art establishment in Edinburgh. Other towns and cities, especially Glasgow, therefore, began to set up their own independent exhibiting societies. This burgeoning sense of local identity and civic pride was a sign that the wealth generated by commerce and industry was widely spread throughout Scotland during the Victorian era. The trend towards greater decentralisation encouraged patronage on a local scale, as well as establishing numerous civic art galleries which are still important exhibition venues and public purchasers of Scottish art. The location of artistic centres throughout Scotland, with local art galleries, art schools, workshops and studio spaces, gives Scottish art a wide spread of regional variety.

Fortunately public patronage still continues to be an important source of support for Scottish artists. Not only does the work purchased by a local authority, a university, the Scottish Arts Council or the Scottish National Gallery of Modern Art, give artists some well-earned financial reward and impetus to their career, but further encourages them to risk producing more challenging and experimental work which would be unlikely to find a buyer in the private market. In Scotland, quite a high proportion of art produced in the 1980s was geared to address, both in scale and subject, a public audience rather than a private patron.

On the other hand, it has to be admitted that Scottish art has never been loyally supported by the private collector, who has preferred to buy historical rather than contemporary work. This lack of support has contributed, until recently at least, to the steady exodus of many of Scotland's best artists. However, on the positive side, this has meant that the art of those exiled Scots has been enriched by contact with the leading international art movements. This of course is not a recent experience for Scottish painters. The importance of direct contact with the work of other artists outside Scotland has always been seen as a vital requirement for widening a young painter's horizons. In the 18th century most serious-minded Scottish painters made their pilgrimage to Rome, while Paris became the artistic Mecca for the Scots during the modern period up to the immediate post-war years. Now, with the aid of postgraduate travelling scholarships, many younger artists have made prolonged study visits to the more recent art capitals, such as New York and Berlin. Therefore, artists in Scotland do not rely solely on their experience of international art by passively browsing through art magazines and looking at slides. They try to make direct contact with the historical and contemporary art of other countries which they feel can help them to enrich their own work. One of the most gratifying aspects of recent Scottish painting is the way it reflects an equally balanced dialogue between the international art scene and its own indigenous native culture. Unlike earlier periods in the 20th century when much Scottish art was a mere pastiche of imported styles, the best painting being produced now has its own distinctive individual character. To realise how this has been achieved, it is necessary to have a brief look at Scottish painting in the modern period.

Apart from the heroic efforts of isolated figures such as James Cowie (1886–1956) and William Johnstone (1897–1981), who remained out with the mainstream of the art establishment, modern painting produced in Scotland until the last war was fairly undistinguished. To be fair, in some ways this was not solely the fault of the artists themselves – many of whom had immense pictorial facility. Rather they were the inheritors of an accumulating problem that had bedevilled Scottish art since the early 19th century. This perennial dilemma involved the crucial issue concerning the choice and treatment of subjects which were appropriate to the authentic Scottish experience.

The debate on the whole question of Scottish identity goes right back to the Union of 1707. Then Scotland gave up its political independence to become a junior partner in the rapidly expanding imperial enterprise of Great Britain and the British Empire. This left Scotland financially better off, but a nation without a civic government; so creating a schizophrenic situation for the Scots whose hearts might be in the Highlands, but the rest of their bodies were controlled from London. Initially, however, the intellectual excitement and optimistic outlook of the 18th century Enlightenment, with its committed belief in universal order both in the human and natural world seemed to transcend and so largely deflect attention from Scotland's own particular identity problems. One only has to look at the great portraits of Allan Ramsay or Henry Raeburn to sense that the artists also shared the confidence of their patrons. And although an air of uncertainty began to appear in the later work of Raeburn and David Wilkie, it was not really until the Victorian era that the belief in painting as a vital part of the intellectual climate of Scottish society began to be lost in a cloud of Highland mist and kailyard sentiment.

For most of the later 19th century much of Scottish art, as with Scottish industry, moved into the export business. Thus instead of working for the direct demands of a Scottish public, painters now supplied manufactured images of Scotland for an outside market and a nostalgic-minded home public. This fed also into the home demand for painting, where private patronage was mainly taken over by industrialists who, wishing to forget the polluted source and human cost of their wealth, preferred an image of Scotland which was steeped in rural nostalgia. Such was the wholescale involvement of Scottish Victorian art, in presenting a one-sided, distorted view of life in Scotland – with endless pictures of desolate cottages and ruined castles swathed in swirling mists; or sanitised farm labourers and their families praying round the family bible – that one would hardly know from the painting produced in the 19th century, that Scotland was one of the most advanced industrial countries in the world. The received image of Victorian Scotland has been a toss-up between soaring mountain tartanry and humble cottage kailyard. It was little wonder then, that by the beginning of this century many of the young progressive Scottish artists were strongly reacting against the dark brown Victorian paintings of sentimental narratives and romanticised Highland landscapes. These 'modern' artists, such as the Scottish Colourists like FCB Cadell (1883–1937), Leslie Hunter (1871–1931), and SJ Peploe (1871–1935), eagerly made contact with the most avant-garde ideas in painting, especially those being developed in Paris in the first decade of this century. They were determined to eschew all the anecdotal subject matter and slick illustrative style which had clogged 19th century Scottish painting. Following the example of the Fauves (the Cubists were too radical and far too dark), these early 20th century Scottish modernists began to move the focus of subject matter in Scottish painting away from the human figure within a particular identifiable social context, to concentrate on 'pure', non-literary motifs such as the humble still-lifes and incidental glimpses of the natural world. Thus they could fix all their creative energies solely on the pictorial problems of compositional arrangements and colour harmonies. Unfortunately, the content of such paintings was so nondescript that stylistic quotation became its main *raison d'etre*, resulting in mere pastiches of modern art: with a tint of French Fauvism, a stroke of German Expressionism and a later dash of Abstract Expressionism. Much 20th century Scottish painting was therefore, all style and little substance.

This *belle peinture* school of Scottish modern painting, as it became known, has dominated the art scene in this country for most of the last century, and against which many of the current artists have strongly reacted. Yet these *belle peinture* artists were merely the latest victims of the continuing crisis of identity within Scottish society and culture. In their determination to avoid the accusation of being parochial and reactionary, they rushed to embrace the cosmopolitan values of Modernism and shed most of the distinctive characteristics of Scottish art. Unlike their French, German or Spanish counterparts, who could adopt the language of modern painting to reflect their own indigenous cultural and social experiences, earlier 20th century Scottish painters mostly turned their eyes away from the past, or from what was going on in the streets and workplaces throughout Scotland. Thus the bland, modernistic pictures they produced were not only 'politically correct', but also completely safe to be placed on the walls of any middle-class drawing room. Even if such paintings were a little over-sensuous for the Scottish Puritan temperament, these expressions of decorative delights were produced with so much refined taste that they would never offend anyone with any degree of genteel sensibility. In contrast to much Scottish painting today, little of the work of The Scottish Colourists or the later Edinburgh School of WG Gillies (1898–1973), William McTaggart (1903–81) and John Maxwell (1903–62), took up the challenge of modern art as a radical vehicle for critical engagement with contemporary Scottish experience.

Isolated outraged voices, such as that of Hugh MacDiarmid, hammered against such vacuous, unrepresentative examples of modern art; but to little avail. The *belle peinture* school of Scottish painting, with its stranglehold on the RSA, the Scottish art schools and the very limited commercial gallery system, continued to dominate and stultify the art scene in Scotland for most of this century until the 1960s. Before then Scottish painters who had serious ambitions to further their art within a wider international context – William Johnstone, Robert Colquhoun (1914–62), Robert MacBryde (1916–72) or Alan Davie, for example – felt it incumbent on themselves to move elsewhere.

Yet few of these emigre artists lost their deep sense of their native roots. They may have left their country, but as the exiled Czech musician Rafael Kubelik described his own feelings, they kept their nation in their hearts. These artists continued to draw creative strength from their Scottish origins, while acting as an inspirational example to younger artists. This was certainly the case with both Johnstone and Davie and later, John Bellany.

By the 1960s, however, the liberating euphoria that was generated by that decade began to take effect on the creative arts in Scotland. On the visual art scene, the situation began to change immeasurably for the better and it can now be seen that much of the groundwork which led to the success story Scottish painting in the 1980s was laid two decades earlier.

Firstly, some of what happened in the 1960s had beneficial effects which were more psychological than practical. For instance, the opening in Edinburgh of the Scottish Gallery of Modern Art in 1960, unfortunately did not create a great new source of state patronage for Scottish artists, but it did, however, grant a degree of status to modern art which the Scottish general public had previously refused to recognise. Another event in the mid-1960s was staged to alter people's attitude towards contemporary art. Following the example of the great French Realist painter, Gustave Courbet, and also inspired by the critical views of Hugh MacDiarmid, the young art students, John Bellany and Sandy Moffat, defiantly hung their uncompromisingly realist paintings on the railings outside the sanctified portals of the RSA during the Edinburgh International Festival. Such a gesture sought to emphasise that art, if it has any real justification for serious critical attention, should be both relevant to a whole range of human experiences and accessible to all who wish to widen their social, intellectual and emotional awareness. These pictures hanging out on the street, demanded attention and consideration at a time when there was a growing feeling that painting was a dying art form. Furthermore, following in the great tradition of northern European art, these two young artists returned the figure and pictorial narrative to a position of central importance in their work; not in any anecdotal sense, but with monumental significance. Bellany's and Moffat's example and later teaching have been extremely influential on the art of the 1980s.

On a more directly practical level, the most important development on the Scottish art scene in the 1960s was the creation of The Scottish Arts Council in 1967. Unlike other public art institutions, its brief was to support directly artists in advancing their careers, and widening the availability of contemporary art to the general public. The manner in which this has been achieved has been through financial help to individual artists in the form of awards and bursaries, and at the same time by funding semi- and non-commercial galleries to exhibit a wide range of different types of contemporary art from Scotland and abroad. Thus, not only were opportunities increased for artists to present their work through one-person and group exhibitions, but also a new seriously interested public was created for the visual arts. Such was the case, for example, when Richard Demarco invited, the then little-known Joseph Beuys to show and perform in Edinburgh in the early 1970s. The great German artist's ideal of art and life being an integral part of each other, and his strong metaphysical emphasis on the living force of the spirit in the material world struck a deep sympathetic chord with many people in Scotland. Beuys' artistic philosophy has proved a lasting inspiration to a number of Scottish artists, especially those whose art deals with social and environmental issues. Through his art and example, Beuys invited artists to broaden the whole basis and approach of their work, and look for new ways to address crucial questions, both in human society and the natural world. With the spread of non-commercial galleries, Scottish artists could now be much more ambitious and challenging in their art.

Over the last two decades, not only has the network of galleries expanded, but the sheer number of artists practising throughout Scotland has increased dramatically. The whole atmosphere of change and expansion has been most noticeable in the Scottish art schools, where the majority of students now train to become professional artists, rather than just art teachers, which tended to be the case in the past. Furthermore, there is a much stronger sense of solidarity and supportive community amongst artists working in Scotland, especially with the younger generation, who look to each other for mutual support. This is reflected in the establishment of the many artist-run workshops and galleries throughout the country. For example, there are at present five Scottish printmakers workshops and many Scottish painters are also extremely fine printmakers in their own right.

Yet for all the creativity which has been engendered in the Scottish art scene since the 1960s, there are still certain deficiencies, apart from the continual government underfunding which is the perennial curse of the arts in this country. For instance, there is little serious art criticism published in Scotland, and this deficiency has at least two detrimental effects. Firstly, without the critical support, it is difficult to create a more informed public who are seriously interested in the visual arts. Secondly, the wider international status of Scottish art in general and individual artists in particular, is dependent on the attention that is given by non-Scottish critics. Not surprisingly, such outside occasional visitors cannot be expected to have the same degree of understanding and sympathy as that of home-based writers. Therefore without solid critical backup, artists are even more vulnerable to the shifting moods of taste and fashion on the international art scene.

In addition to this lack of sustained critical support, there is no consistent private buying and collecting of contemporary art in Scotland. As a result, although many of the more successful Scottish artists now choose to stay and work in Scotland, they tend to have dealers from outside. While it should be stressed that most painters feel their galleries are understanding and supportive of their art, in a commercial world, certain pressures can be exerted on individual artists to meet outsiders' views of what is the appropriate image for Scottish art. Yet all that being said, it is exhilarating and gratifying that Scottish painting should be creating such critical and commercial impact abroad.

I would now like to look at some of the reasons for this upsurge in interest that has been generated by contemporary Scottish painting. It was pointed out at the opening, that, on the international scale of recognition, the visual arts, until recently, have been much less conspicuous than other areas of Scottish achievement such as science or literature. That is not to say that Scotland has not produced major figures in painting, such as Allan Ramsay and Henry Raeburn in the 18th century, David Wilkie and William McTaggart (1835–1911) in the next, and during this century, William Johnstone, JD Ferguson (1871–1961), Joan Eardley (1921–63), Alan Davie and John Bellany. However, it has to be conceded that in most general books on the history of art, Scotland's contribution tends to be overlooked. I would suggest that this lack of recognition has less to do with the quality of serious work produced by Scottish artists over the last three centuries, and more to do with the fact that historians and critics tend to be of the shared opinion that art can only be created in the great cosmopolitan centres of the art world such as Rome, Paris or New York. Scottish art, as with that of many other neglected countries, has suffered greatly from this blinkered outlook. However, one of the most important changes that took place during the 1980s was the undermining of the modernist ideal of universal conformity to general principles of aesthetic credibility. As the monopolistic authority of institutionalised Modernism finally began to disintegrate from the 1960s onwards, alternative interpretations of the development of modern art began to emerge. Therefore, with the influence of centres of cultural authority starting to be challenged from all points of the compass, Scotland, as with other previously marginalised countries, was well-placed to flourish in the new critically democratic climate. Now, many people were beginning to realise that there were possible alternative readings of the history of the 20th century officially sanctioned canon of French Impressionism to American Abstract Expressionism. For example, critics began to recognise that just as important was the great northern European tradition of modern art from van Gogh, Munch, the German Expressionists, through to the COBRA group and up to Beuys, Baselitz and Kiefer. Within that history of realist expressionist painting, Scottish art clearly had a secure place and long distinctive tradition. This has given contemporary Scottish painting much more confidence, and a keener sense of its own identity, in its relationship to the outside art world. At last that long native tradition of Scottish art with its emphasis on direct observation, psychological analysis, metaphysical speculation and moral and social criticism can be clearly placed within the much wider context of international 20th century art.

Furthermore when we turn to the current art scene, many of the common stylistic characteristics which critics have discerned in the 'New Painting' of the 1980s: bold figuration, evocative narrative, emphatic technique and poetic atmosphere for instance, have been distinguishing qualities in much of the best of Scottish painting. Unlike previous periods when Scottish artists felt it beholden on themselves to disguise the authentic character of their natural artistic inclinations with modernistic fancy dress, contemporary painters can express themselves in their inherited pictorial tradition and be appreciated by the rest of the world. In the 1980s Scottish painting rediscovered its own voice.

In the 1980s 'subject' as opposed to motif returned to centre stage in contemporary Scottish art. The best artists however, cannot be seen as merely illustrators. They are concerned to allow their personal vision to be not only expressed through their choice of subject, but also by their stylistic method of interpretation and presentation. This concern with developing a personal style is vitally important. For style is the distinctive, some may even say the uniquely individual voice of the artist; the means by which the artist gives a recognisable presence to a painting and so allows the spectator to engage in a dialogue of ideas and feelings with the work itself.

Looking at recent publications and contemporary exhibitions over the last year, one is struck by the sheer range and variety of work being produced in the area of new Scottish painting. Unlike previous eras in Scottish art, it would be very difficult, if not impossible, to formulate any unifying characteristics based on stylistic similarities. So is there a critical approach that might present these artists as a more coherent school of painting? I think that might be possible, if we move our attention away from the question of stylistic expression and concentrate on choice and interpretation of content. Then internal connections between various artists begin to emerge.

The most immediately recognisable group within these Scottish artists is the abstract painters. Although Scottish figurative painting received much of the critical attention during the 1980s, high quality abstract painting continued to be produced throughout the decade. The Scots, in fact, were pioneers in the development of 20th century British abstraction, especially through the painting of William Johnstone, William Gear and the early work of Alan Davie. Not surprisingly, because of the Scots' long-established concern with the metaphysical dimension of experience, the work of these earlier Scottish abstract painters was closely connected with Surrealism. Thus, in their paintings they used the power of intuitive gesture, the force of expressive colour, and the associative meanings of shapes and symbols, to release primordial aspects of the human psyche and make links with the primitive and natural world. This surrealist dimension to early abstraction, however, is not so noticeable in contemporary Scottish painting. On the whole, the current abstract painters seem to have less concern for the psychological release of spontaneous expression than for the more formal demands of pictorial composition and colour relationships. Gesture and application of paint is still of crucial importance, but now more for its own sake, and less for any symbolic or metaphysical expression. The sources of inspiration for many of the abstract painters seem to vary from initial connections with specific aspects of the outside world, as, for example, in the work of Denis Buchan, Alexander Fraser (when he was an abstract painter), Jim Pattison and Russell Colombo, to those other abstractionists such as John McLean, Fred Pollock, Iain Robertson, Callum Innes and Alan Johnston, whose pictures are much more independent and rigorously 'pared down' to the essential language of drawing and painting.

While it is clearly easier to recognise and group the abstract artists, I think it is also possible to make meaningful connections between figurative painters. Thus, by doing so, the variety of work can be viewed within a more structured framework which makes connections and inter-relationships more likely to be perceived.

The common factor which links most of these Scottish painters is their art education. Most of them studied at one of the four art schools, and a good number teach or have taught there. These institutions pride themselves on their longstanding commitment to traditional academic values, based on drawing, respect for materials and a knowledge of the great art of the past. Looking through their work this becomes very evident: quality draughtsmanship, technical facility and intelligent, witty reinterpretation of artistic conventions and genres are the hallmarks of much contemporary Scottish painting. It is with the broad concept of the different genres, that is, the academic classification of painting into different types of subject matter, that it is possible to group the non-abstract painters.

Briefly, a short explanation of the genre system might be required here. Originally this method of classification was formulated in the academies to help to differentiate between a great painting and a merely good one. At the top were the great history paintings as they concerned themselves with universal, high moral themes taken from the Bible and the Classics. Then came portrait painting, because, as was usually the case in the past, it dealt with the most important people in society. Next were the pictures that presented the everyday life of ordinary people. This type of painting was known – and thus can cause a little confusion – as genre. Finally, at the bottom end of the academic league table of excellence, was landscape and lowly still life, where human subject matter was less likely to be included or was excluded altogether. This hierarchy of artistic judgement based on the humanist notion of man being the measure of all things, was overturned in the modern era, with the collapse in the belief that the academies were the sole arbitrators of aesthetic standards. For instance, most of the innovative art of the 19th and 20th centuries was in the area of the lower genres – landscape and still life. However, although the value judgements connected with the genre system have been abandoned, the broad division of painting into these different types of subjects still exists both for the artists and their public. Furthermore, the choice and treatment of subject is in many ways still the most important basis of understanding between the work of art and the spectator.

Firstly, which group of artists could be regarded as history painters? It may seem contradictory but the artists who I would classify as history painters, have little interest in resurrecting visions of the past. Scottish art, particularly in the 19th century, has had more than its share of that! Today the painters working within this particular genre are drawn towards history painting for its moral and intellectual authority, not for its retrospective tradition. The best history painting in Scotland concerns itself with modern, not past times, engaging in a critical dialogue with its public, on such crucial issues facing human society, as the nuclear threat, chronic environmental pollution, social and economic injustice. The history painters in contemporary Scottish art are those who most overtly use the rhetorical power of painting to make critical observations about social and political issues. This would cover the work of, for example, Ken Currie, John Kirkwood, Glen Onwin, Fred Crayk, Sandy Moffat and Tom Lawson. I would also classify Kate Whiteford as a history painter, as her work, through its use of ancient signs and symbols, deals with the origins of social and cultural identity.

The recurring question of identity brings us to the second genre, portraiture. Here the individual's sense of his or her own personal and social identity is focused upon. Portraiture was the dominant subject in 18th century Scottish Enlightenment painting when the study of human nature and society was the main concern in philosophical social thinking. However, during the 19th century, portraiture was superseded by the rise of landscape painting and there are few conventional portrait painters in contemporary Scottish art; although David Donaldson, Sandy Moffat, John Bellany, Fred Crayk and Alison Watt have produced some excellent work in this area. Yet, if we widen our view of the aims of portrait painting to encompass the broad notion of it as a close analysis of experience and identity, expressed by the powerful presence of the human figure, then a whole group of artists comes together. I refer to those painters such as Gwen Hardie, June Redfern, Lys Hansen and Margaret Hunter. These women artists present for our scrutiny the figure, usually nude and female, in order to raise disturbing questions concerning gender and sexuality, liberty and conformity, and the shifting relationship between inner and outer reality in the psychology of human experience. It is also possible to see similar concerns in the work of Adrian Wiszniewski.

When art moves from examining the individual human experience to the wider social one, we are usually dealing with genre painting. Within the Northern European tradition, Scottish art has a long association with this kind of painting going back to David Allan (1744–96) and of course David Wilkie, who established genre painting as a serious artistic concern. This type of subject matter, the everyday life of ordinary people, however, became debased and discredited when Victorian artists and their public used it as a vehicle for sentimental elegies to a mythical lost world of rustic arcadia. Not surprisingly, there has been little genre painting of significance in Scotland during this century. Now however, since John Bellany expanded the potential for this type of subject matter on to a heroic scale with his monumental pictures of the Scottish fishing community, there has been a great revival in genre painting. Joyce Cairns and Keith McIntyre are artists who have most readily responded to Bellany's example. Others, such as Peter Howson, Stephen Conroy, Henry Kondracki and Peter Thomson, have dealt with the alienation, and the ritualistic harshness and humour that characterises much of everyday modern life, this time within an urban context.

Since the 19th century Scottish landscape painting has become by far the most popular subject in art, both with artists and their public. This is hardly surprising since Scotland, although a small geographical entity, is blessed with a vast range of different types of scenery. Yet it was not only its scenic qualities which made the landscape so alluring to the Scots. With the lack of nationhood, the people of Scotland desperately needed a symbolic substitute for such a loss, and the landscape, with all its historical and tragic associations, fitted the role perfectly. Contemporary Scottish landscape painters do not necessarily avoid the historical associative dimension of the subject, but they are also closely attentive to the specific qualities of the natural world as something to be respected in their own right. The approach to landscape painting can be broadly divided into two. On the one hand, there is the expressive gestural response which links with such figures from the past as William McTaggart and Joan Eardley, and here includes John Houston, Barbara Rae, Duncan Shanks and Kate Downie, who treat the urban scene very much as a landscape. On the other side, in the tradition of William Dyce (1806–64) and James Cowie, there is the meditative, analytical method, with its emphatic graphic character which is practiced by Frances Walker, Liz Ogilvie and Reinhard Behrens.

Finally, we come to the still life painters. From what would appear to be the least inspiring type of subject, these artists produce a wide range of high quality painting, which can hold its own against any of the other genres. Again the explanation for this phenomenon may go back to the influence of art school training in Scotland and its emphasis on close and prolonged study from the model/object. Yet what transforms the work of these artists from what could be a fairly dry academic exercise, is the different techniques employed, and the concentrated intensity of their vision. To appreciate the wide range of technical approaches, one only has to compare the meticulous analytical work of David Evans, Eileen Lawrence, or John Mooney with the robust painterliness of Jack Knox, or the elusive visual poetry of Elizabeth Blackadder and Ian Howard.

The ultimate strength of still life painting lies in the fact that essentially, it is the most characteristic of Scottish art. By this, I mean, it involves the very foundation of the practice of the visual arts in Scotland. It is the direct confrontation between the artist and his subject, where study can be at its most analytically concentrated. The best of all Scottish art, both past and present, has had this empirical basis; where close observation and hard-won technical facility have allowed the artist to examine and translate into the painterly language of marks, signs and images the world of appearances. Furthermore, through the intensity of the artist's interrogation, this world of appearances begins to open up to all kinds of material, social and metaphysical speculations on the nature of things and their relationship to each other.

I am conscious that the 'genre' groupings that I have just applied could be accused of being fairly arbitrary. There are some artists who cannot be pinned down to one type of subject, and, for instance, move freely, for example, between landscape and still life. I have only placed such artists within a certain grouping because I feel that they produce their best work when painting that particular type of subject. What is more important is how each artist uses, in a positive or critical manner, the conventions associated with each of the genres. For instance, the history painters exploit the traditional scale and moral authority associated with that type of painting to question and attack a whole range of contemporary political and social attitudes. While, on the other hand, the still life painters take a genre which is usually not regarded as having a serious intellectual status, and, through their sustained observations, raise all kinds of thoughtful questions about the connections between ourselves and the world of natural and material objects with which we surround ourselves.

Lastly, there are those artists whose work cannot be readily placed within the broad spectrum of the academic genres at all; for example, Matthew Inglis, Alexander Fraser, Calum Colvin, Steven Campbell, Bruce McLean, or Alan Davie. That is as it should be. All art which wishes to remain vital needs to question and extend existing conventions, as well as having a healthy respect for the great traditions of the past. In addition, artists must also have a keen sense of their own personal, social and cultural identity, while at the same time be receptive to ideas and influences from outside. After a lengthy and generally disappointing period in 20th century art, the contemporary painters seem to have got the balance about right again. Hence their remarkable successes over the last decade both in Britain and abroad. Furthermore, Scottish art in the 1990s, despite the unfavourable economic conditions and the great uncertainty about Scotland's political future within the United Kingdom, can continue from strength to strength.

This essay was published in *Contemporary Painting in Scotland* (Craftsman House, Australia, 1992) and *Cencrastus* (issue 44, 1992).

MERCURE D'ÉCOSSE

Henry Raeburn's 'Skating Minister'

*It is the exhibition of mind, that has given Italian Art its pre-eminence and
no art that is not intellectual can be worthy of Scotland.*
David Wilkie, Rome, 1827

THE CANONISATION OF a work of art can be just as long and complex a
process as that of a Catholic saint. The painting of the Reverend Robert
Walker (the dates of its execution are still open to dispute), by Edinburgh's
great Enlightenment portraitist, Henry Raeburn, is a good case in point. After
the picture left the artist's studio it remained in obscurity within the Walker
family throughout the 19th century and even failed to reach its bidding price
at Christie's when it came up for auction in 1914. The work was purchased
privately in 1926, but only came to public attention in 1949, when it was
acquired by the National Gallery of Scotland (NGS). Since then however, it has
gradually gained renown. And over the last decade or so, under the skilful
management of the present extremely publicity conscious, NGS Director,
Timothy Clifford, 'The Skating Minister' has rapidly become a Scottish
cultural icon – its silhouetted image being marketed, not only as the NGS's own
logo, but also being applied to a whole range of various products from bars of
chocolates to jigsaw puzzles. Furthermore, the great popularity of the picture
is not only confined to Scotland, for example it was the star attraction of the
important survey exhibition, *British Painting from Hogarth to Turner,* shown
at the Prado, Madrid in 1988–1989, and its high cult status was further
confirmed when its image was used as the cover illustration by the major art
publishers, Thames and Hudson, in *British Painting, The Golden Age.*

Yet even as such adulation, doubt and mystery continue to dog this
picture's reputation, as witnessed for example by the Thames and Hudson's
own commentary, 'The painting is not typical of Raeburn, and doubts have
been expressed about the tradition attribution' (Vaughan, p97). Disputes
over the dating and authorship of the *Revd Robert Walker* are not recent,
as Duncan Thomson, the most respected expert on the work of Raeburn,
acknowledged in the NGS's catalogue for their major retrospective of the
artist's work, '... a belief gained currency that, despite the traditional
attribution and the picture's reliable provenance, it was not the work of
Raeburn at all, because its scale, handling and canvas were completely
untypical (p88). Thomson however, goes on to point out, 'This belief
however, failed to supply any remotely reasonable suggestion as to who the
alternative artist might be' (p88). Thus leaving the ball firmly in the court of
the anti-Raeburn camp, Thomson finishes on a note of justifiable triumph

by describing the work as 'archetypal Raeburn' and 'one of the most famous paintings in the world' (p90).

I have no dispute with Duncan Thomson's assessment of the painting's canonic status. However, in this essay I do wish to suggest an alternative attitude to his statement that, 'There is no obvious source for Raeburn's image' (p90). Here I will argue that there is a crucially important 'source' for the form of this portrait, and that access to this opens up such a range of alternative readings that this painting is transformed from being 'a curiosity in the history of taste' (p90) to use Thomson's words, into a work of immense intellectual, aesthetic and moral depth.

Apart from the evidence of his diploma *Self Portrait* (1815) for his election to the Royal Academy in London which from the pose clearly indicates his intellectual approach to painting, like many men of genius, Raeburn is a rather shadowy figure who rarely put pen to paper either to write or even draw. As such we do not know too much about the smaller details of his life. A case in point is his visit to Italy and Rome sometime in 1784–1785, which undoubtedly would have been an extremely important experience for an 18th century artist trying to establish his professional credentials. Questions arise – what would he have done there? Who would he have contacted? What works would he have studied and have been of use to him in his career as a professional portrait painter?

These are all important questions and relevant to this enquiry is a statement made in his obituary of 1823, 'Sculpture was also an object of his peculiar study; and so great was his taste for it, that at Rome, he at one time entertained the idea of devoting himself to that noble art as a profession in preference to painting' (NGS catalogue p82). If such was the case, then Raeburn would certainly be familiar with the works of the great Italian sculptors, including that of Giambologna; and there is one particular work by him that is crucially relevant to a full appreciation of the *Revd Robert Walker* portrait.

Before I move on to the Giambologna connection however, I would also like to refer to another important occurrence which took place during this brief period of travels in Raeburn's career. It is generally accepted that Raeburn made a special effort to visit the studio of Sir Joshua Reynolds (PRA) in London either 'before or after his stay in Rome' (NGS catalogue p40). If Raeburn was in any way influenced by Reynolds it is usually suggested that this can be seen in the loosening up of his painterly technique after his return to Edinburgh. (It could be argued for instance that the dramatic, romantic background to the Walker picture does have a 'Reynoldesque touch'). However, I would like to suggest a much more important link with Reynolds in this Raeburn portrait. That connection actually comes through another work – Zoffany's famous group portrait of *The Academicians of the Royal Academy* (1771–72). At the centre of this august artistic company is Sir Joshua Reynolds, first President of the Royal Academy and directly above him there is appropriately placed a plaster cast of Giambologna's *Mercury* (1575–79). I say appropriately because the god, Mercury, personified eloquence and reason, the qualities of a teacher. Reynolds as head of the institutionalised British art establishment, was committed to his self-appointed role as the great educator of the visual culture of his age. This he laid out in his annual lectures to the Royal Academy and in his *Discourses on Art,* where he guides painters with the idea that a lower branch of art like portraiture, 'may be improved by borrowing from the grand' *(Discourses,* IV).

Today there is much critical hostility and academic reluctance within some Scottish art history circles to link too closely 18th century Scottish painting with Reynolds' aesthetic philosophy of eclecticism and quotation. The contemporary attitude is that Scottish art is characterised by a strong naturalistic approach that is at odds with Reynolds' academic idealism. Still it has to be remembered that throughout the century after the Union between Scotland and England in 1707, most ambitious enterprising Scots wished to ingratiate themselves with wider British society and so felt the need to anglify their modes and manners – a good example of this would be the likes of Hume and Boswell exorcising all 'Scotticisms' from their writings. Thus it is not surprising that an 18th century Scottish painter such as Raeburn, should also wish to ape some of the features of what was regarded as a more elevated manner of portraiture. If that is so then his *Revd Robert Walker* may be, amongst many other things, a subtle homage to Reynolds, as was for example his portrait of *George Chambers* of about same period, which owes much in its composition to Reynolds' image of the physician *Dr John Ash* (1788) (NGS catalogue p15).

Yet even without Reynolds' example, the use of pictorial quotation could be found in earlier Scottish portraiture. In fact it could be argued that Allan Ramsay, Raeburn's illustrious predecessor, established this kind of learned practice within British art, even before Reynolds; for example when he gave his image of *MacLeod of MacLeod* (1747–48) the pose of the *Apollo Belvedere.* Raeburn himself would also have noted the frequent use of quotations in the work of the great Italian painters, such as Tintoretto and Titian, both of whom had adopted poses from Michelangelo. This is something which Raeburn himself does when he adapts a Sistine Chapel 'Creation' reference into the pointing gesture of *Sir John Clerk* of *Penicuik and his Wife* (1791–92).

All that I have presented will, I hope, clearly indicate that Raeburn was not a 'mere face-painter' but a highly intelligent and educated artist even by the time he returned from Rome in the mid-1780s. By then his ambition was clearly to see off any portraitist rivals in Edinburgh and establish himself as the unchallenged court painter to the luminaries of the later Scottish Enlightenment. In order to show that he was worthy of this position he had to illustrate in his work the qualities which were so admired by his learned contemporaries and potential customers intellect, wit, balance, moderation and inventiveness (see N Phillipson's essay in NGS catalogue p29–38). Raeburn's small, but absorbing portrait of the *Revd Robert Walker* does demonstrate all these qualities, and the painting may have remained in the artist's studio for some considerable period for that very purpose.

Beginning with the quality of wit, something that was keenly admired in polite 18th century European society, this is more than what we find merely amusing today. Certainly the *Revd Robert Walker* is there to amuse, and much of its popular appeal relies on the rather incongruous spectacle of a sombrely attired Scottish Presbyterian minister intently enjoying himself in this unexpected manner (see Gladstone-Millar). Most people should also quickly pick up on the textual–visual pun of Walker/skating. However, that pun dimension of this picture only really begins to open up to meaningful connection once the Giambologna *Mercury* quotation is revealed. Then, for instance, this would encourage the viewer to see Walker's splendid hat (to which Raeburn clearly paid a great deal of attention) as an allusion to the god's famous helmet, and even more strikingly, the Reverend's fancy red-ribboned ice skates are his equivalent to the wings on the feet of Mercury. Furthermore, there is also an ingenious literary pun embedded in the complex text of the painting; in that whilst Mercury is the messenger of the gods, our Reverend Walker is a minister of God!

One of the great achievements of the Renaissance which the later Enlightenment most admired was how it managed to accommodate and balance the seemingly unbridgeable gulf between Christian theology and classical paganism. Raeburn would have seen for himself how the Renaissance masters such as Michelangelo and Giambologna had skilfully managed to reconcile these apparently conflicting ideologies and out of it produce art of immense visual and philosophical power. In his humble, but highly inventive manner, Raeburn, with this painting demonstrates that he is following their illustrious example.

It is however to the more particular concerns of the Scottish Enlightenment which I now wish to turn and show that Raeburn's painting is also very much engaged with the intellectual issues of his time. One of the distinguishing aspects of the concerns of those engaged with the Enlightenment in Scotland, was to investigate and trace the origins of a whole range of different phenomena – from the geological structure of the Earth (James Hutton) to the formation of human society (Adam Ferguson). When it came to the visual arts, artists were fascinated by Pliny's apocryphal account of the birth of painting, when a Corinth maid, fearing that her lover, going off to war, would never return, traces his silhouetted shadow on the wall of her room. There are at least two important versions of this myth by Raeburn's contemporaries, David Allan and Alexander Runciman. Furthermore the practice of the silhouetted portrait had become very fashionable in Raeburn's day and the most celebrated practitioner of this mode of portraiture was the Scottish artist, James Tassie. Raeburn must have been well aware of these different versions of the silhouetted form when he devised his own medallion relief self-portrait in 1792. Interestingly Thomson points out, 'Raeburn had a particular interest in the expressive properties of pure profile: for example the *Revd Robert Walker* which it (Raeburn's own relief self-portrait) resembles to a remarkable degree'. Thus the striking use of the silhouetted form to be found in Raeburn's work clearly relates not only to the elevated high cultural notion of classical art (Greek vase painting, Roman cameos, etc) and mythology but also to the academic belief that line and drawing are the true foundation of the intellectual nature of painting.

If Raeburn was well aware of the art of James Tassie, who was based in faraway London, he must have been even more familiar with the work of another, but different kind of portraitist, living in the same city as himself. I refer to the barber-cum-artist, John Kay. Kay was a self-taught satirical caricaturist, who took it upon himself to become the pictorial recorder of the manners and idiosyncrasies of the various personalities of his day. Kay's simple, but incisive and perceptive etchings were produced in a broadsheet form and rapidly circulated around the town, showing his subjects in a more comic, down-to-earth manner, such as in a sporting pose: much to the amusement of his fellow citizens.

Thus from what I have just discussed concerning Raeburn's awareness of the work of both Tassie and Kay, I would suggest in the *Revd Robert Walker* the artist again strikes an important balance. This time between, on the one hand, the high ideals of the noble art of painting, tracing its origins back to classical mythology; and on the other, the world of popular print dealing with the contemporary everyday social life of the city. In Raeburn's painting high art and popular culture meet and both held equal interest for Scottish Enlightenment thought as a whole.

I would now like to turn to another important issue of debate within 18th century Scottish society and point to a further possible reading of Raeburn's picture. Here again the artist takes an amusing, light-hearted slant on an extremely controversial topic for his contemporaries – that concerning the biblical miracles. It was in the area of faith and belief concerning the miraculous that the secular, scientific rationalism of the Enlightenment came directly into conflict with the teachings of the scriptures and the church. The major figure most associated with this debate was David Hume, who in his *Of Miracles* (1748) set out to demonstrate that no eyewitness report of any miracle could be reasonably trusted. It is also clear from his argument that he personally did not believe in the occurrence of any miraculous event because that would offend the laws of nature.

In our painting, Raeburn, again with imaginative wit, addresses this contentious issue. Here we are presented with an appropriately named Scottish cleric, inspiringly following in the footsteps of his Master. Furthermore, unlike the founder of the Roman Catholic church, again appropriately named Peter, Walker does not sink like a stone. The simple reason for this seemingly miraculous difference is that, unlike the over-eager disciple who does offend the laws of nature, by trying to walk on the Sea of Galilee, our Scottish minister glides across a wintry frozen Edinburgh loch and is still in complete harmony with his natural environment.

Turning from the Christian aspect, I would like to return once more to the mercurial theme of the *Revd Robert Walker*. In his early career, before becoming a painter, Raeburn trained as a goldsmith/engraver, and from this apprenticeship he would be well aware of the mutability of substances. Mercury, of course, is the deity who, both in pagan and alchemistic terms, is most associated with this fluctuating, transmutating condition. This is alluded to throughout Raeburn's painting. For example, within the picture itself we have the transformation of the waters of Duddingston Loch from liquid into solid ice form. Furthermore every painter is well acquainted with the changing properties of his oil medium, which is initially worked in a semi-liquid form and when the image is finally secured, is allowed to dry into a solid, durable material. In fact in our picture the mercurial nature of painting is clearly underlined by the marked contrast between the landscape background in which the loose, scumble character of the paint reveals its original liquidity; and the tight rendering of the figure and foreground, where the paint has dried to such a solid impenetrable mass, that Walker's skates can only scrape the surface.

Finally, I want to turn again to discuss briefly the relationship between Reynolds' aesthetic philosophy and Raeburn's own practice. I have already pointed out some similarities of approach and attitude between the two painters but I would like now to focus on a crucial difference. Reynolds was well aware of the pitfalls of quotation in portraiture, as he pointed out, 'The simplicity of the antique air and attitude, however much to be admired, is ridiculous when joined to a figure in modern dress' *(Discourses,* v). To avoid such bathetic disasters, Reynolds employed quotation as a means to gain full pictorial allegory. Hence he was always much more successful in this area with his female subjects. For example *Mrs Siddons* (1784) becomes the personification of the Tragic Muse, with the aid of heavy-handed allusions to Michelangelo's Sistine sybils. Reynolds is always striving after the abstract and 'the general idea'. On the contrary, Raeburn, like Ramsay before him, avoids such intent in his portraits. For the Scottish artists, 'the minute breaks and peculiarities', which Reynolds so despises are as crucially important as any allegorical abstractions.

I will again demonstrate what I mean by taking the *Revd Robert Walker* as a perfect example of balance between the particular and general. No one seems to have taken much notice that our skating figure fits neatly into a circle. Now if Reynolds had employed such a compositional device we would have been encouraged to make connections with such as Leonardo's *Vitruvius Man* and the platonic concept of human, physical and intellectual, beauty. Now there may be a slight degree of this in Raeburn's picture. He had just returned from Italy where the interdependence between idealised art and geometric rules was almost a dogma. (Interestingly this is demonstrated by a portrait of Giambologna, which is owned by the NGS showing the sculptor at his desk with a pair of dividers in his hand). However, unlike an idealising classicist, Raeburn does not use the circle device to take us away from the particular individuality of his subject, but in fact to relate it more significantly to him. For the Reverend Walker was a member of the Edinburgh Skating Club, and one of the exercises which he was required to perform was to be able 'to skate in a perfect circle on each foot consecutively' (Gladstone-Millar, p40).

Although Raeburn is obviously too early chronologically to be considered seriously as a modern artist, he, like Hals, Velasquez and Goya, anticipates distinctive features which are closely associated with modern Realism in 19th century French art. This is especially so in the manner in which Raeburn, like the later Manet or Seurat, balances and plays off the abstract against the particular; the intellectual against the sensual (note the shivering cold atmosphere of the slate-grey ice set against the glowing pink ember of the dying evening sky); and the mythological and eternal against the contemporary and the mundane. In fact Baudelaire's definition of the *Painter of Modern Life*, as 'the painter of the fleeting moment and of all that it suggests of the eternal' so readily applies to Raeburn's the *Revd Robert Walker* that if Seurat's *Sunday Afternoon on the Island of La Grande Jatte* (1884–86) was transferred to the frozen scene of Duddingston Loch, the silhouetted figure of our 'Skating Minister' would not look that out of place – except of course, that being a good Scottish Presbyterian he could not be seen to be enjoying himself on the Sabbath!

References

Gladstone-Millar, L, *The Reverend Robert Walker, Skating on Duddingston Lock by Sir Henry Raeburn*, Edinburgh, Saint Andrew Press, 1997
The Trustees of the National Gallery of Scotland, *Raeburn: The Art of Sir Henry Raeburn 1756–1823*, Edinburgh, 1997.
Vaughan, William, *British Painting: The Golden Age*, Thames and Hudson, London, 1999.

This essay was published in *Études Écossaises* (issue 6, 1999).

DESPERATELY SEEKING SELF
A History of Scottish Self-Portraiture

*Then I endeavour to examine my own conduct, when I endeavour to pass
sentence upon it, and either to approve or condemn it, it is evident that in all
such cases, I divide myself, as it were, into two persons; and that I, the exam-
iner and judge, represent a different character from the other I, the person
whose conduct is examined into and judged of.*
Adam Smith, *The Theory of Moral Sentiments*, 1759

Man is not truly one, but truly two.
Robert Louis Stevenson, *The Strange Case of Dr Jekyll and Mr Hyde*, 1886

*Self-consciousness, as the term is ordinarily used, implies two things: an
awareness of oneself by oneself, and an awareness of one self as an object of
someone else's observation.*
RD Laing, *The Divided Self*, 1960

THE SOCIO-PSYCHOLOGICAL EXPERIENCE present in RD Laing's *The Divided
Self*, from which this exhibition takes its title, seems to have always been a
consequence of modern life and, for whatever complex reasons, the Scots
in particular, have been acutely aware and deeply affected by this divisive,
alienated condition. In the never-ending rehearsal of revealing and veiling
at the heart of self-portraiture this optical dialogue of observed self and
observing other is turned into a social ritual and cultural artefact. Thus, this
most fascinating of genres in the visual arts is not simply a realisation of self,
but equally important, an assessment of identity within an ever-changing
historical and ideological environment. Revealing oneself to the other's gaze
is a dangerous business at any level – from the biological to the psychological.
As Laing points out in *The Divided Self*:

> The very fact of being visible exposes an animal to the risk of attack from
> its enemies, and no animal is without enemies. Being visible is therefore
> a basic biological risk; being invisible is a basic biological defence. We all
> employ some form of camouflage.

Laing's observations can readily be applied to the study of self-portraiture. We,
the viewers, are not merely expected to recognise, but also to assess the delicate
balance the artist has struck between exposure and camouflage within this
particular cultural representation and presentation of biological, sociological
and psychological self. With this in mind let us now turn to Scottish self-
portraiture and examine how it has developed since the 17th century.

As a result of a range of restricting factors, involving both politics and patronage, the self-portrait came relatively late to Scottish art. On the Continent, with the spread of Renaissance humanism and the development of new technological aids to mimetic representation, such as oil paint and more efficient mirrors, self-portraiture gradually became a recognisable artistic phenomenon throughout the 15th and 16th centuries. In Scotland however, this did not occur until the 17th century and was then pioneered by the 'father of Scottish painting', George Jamesone, when he produced at least four known self-portraits during the late 1630s and early 1640s.

In *Self-portrait* (c.1642), Jamesone proudly presents himself very much as the successful artist/business gentleman. His rich, but sombre dress, along with his engaging look strike a Rubens-like air of self-confidence, but on a much more modest scale, with the tools of his trade still at the ready in his hand. He proudly offers his artistic skills and commercial wares to his potential customer/patron, yet mixed with this business promotion are also allusions to his classical learning. For instance, the thematic play-off between the rows of contemporary portraits on the back wall and the heavily symbolic memento mori still life beside the artist, demonstrates pragmatically the undeniable implications of Horace's dictum – as life is short so art is long. Thus, Jamesone, the painter of portraits, is offering to his public a kind of iconic immortality on the basis that if they refuse to have their individuality recorded by him they will inevitably end up posthumously looking like everyone else – as the image of the dreadful skull on the shield clearly indicates.

If Jamesone's painting is an early example of Scottish self-portraiture in which the painter presents his particular services to his fellow citizens, it is also a complex discourse on the personal and professional identity, and the social and cultural standing, of the artist. The visual iconography not only deals with the theme of Thanatos (death) but also Eros in the form of the large mythological painting, *The Chastisement of Cupid* in the top right corner. To find this display of erotic sexuality (even in its subdued state) may seem surprising within the strongly religious society of 17th-century Scotland, but it reappears again in much more blatant form, around a hundred years later in the self-portrait of Richard Waitt. As this picture indicates, Waitt was self-taught and may have studied Jamesone's work. His painting skills clearly suffer from certain technical inadequacies, particularly in the area of linear perspective and anatomical understanding. However, he more than makes up for this through the robust vigour of his approach and the confidence of his artistic personality. Here the artist plays a slightly different role to his predecessor – for now what is on offer is the power of the painter to reveal prohibited forms of sensual delight. Such erotic areas were normally out-of-bounds, yet they were made acceptable to the cultivated classes by such classical tropes as *The Toilet of Venus* theme. Even in staunch Presbyterian Scotland we find the artist (admittedly not very convincingly to modern eyes) facilitating and guiding the male gaze towards the sexually alluring object of his repressed desires.

Scotland in the early 18th century, after the traumatic upheavals of the recent religious and civil wars and the highly controversial Union of the Scottish and English Parliaments in 1707, was an uncertain society going through a period of profound readjustment to its new political and cultural situation. In this emerging civic society, change and progress were already replacing longstanding traditions. Amongst many other things affected by these changes were the role and status of the Scottish artist. This new and radical situation is clearly spelt out in Roderick Chalmers' group self-portrait, *The Incorporation of Wrights and Masons at Holyrood* (1720), where his own readily identified gentleman-artist is seated at his easel and stands out in marked contrast from the rest of the artisan company he is still forced to keep. The now upwardly mobile artist with his ambition to join the professional classes confidently looks out at us while his former fellow craftsmen deferentially still concentrate all their attention on their manual skills. Thus, belatedly, but with eager anticipation, the Scottish artist of post-Union Scotland now looked to climb the social ladder from artisan to gentleman class – and maybe even higher. In the 18th century this ambition could only be achieved realistically through portrait painting. In this the aspiring Scottish artist would have been encouraged by foreign imported figures such as Sir John de Medina, who not only ran a very lucrative portrait practice, but was also knighted for his services to the arts in Scotland. Furthermore, it must have been additionally encouraging that a member of the Scottish nobility like William Aikman should decide to follow the career of a professional portrait painter. In marked contrast to the Scottish works previously discussed Aikman's self-portrait gives no indication that he is the painter of his own image. The entire focus of attention is on the finely tuned balance between his elusive personality and his individual appearance, which clearly indicates his social standing and high culture through his full wig, lace cravat and silken cloak.

The delicate restraint of Aikman's highly refined self-image is very much in contrast to the aggressive commercial self-promotion found in the picture of James Norie. Yet even though these two painters were from markedly different social classes, all Scottish artists in the first half of the 18th century had to face a crucial choice for their careers – whether to remain in Scotland or seek larger, but more uncertain opportunities, elsewhere. Those that chose to remain, like Waitt, Norie or John Alexander (seen in his self-portrait with his patron the Duke of Hamilton), could advance their careers from individual support from sympathetic members of the nobility and the increasing wealth of the expanding middle classes. Yet these stay-at-home artists, until Raeburn at least, would only remain at best, large fish in a relatively small Caledonian pond.

In the early 18th century Aikman set the trend for generations of subsequent Scottish artists by attempting to break into the London art scene. Maybe his acutely sensitive self-portrait, in contrast to de Medina's robust baroque style, with its innovative manipulation of soft focus light and atmosphere was created to appeal to the more sophisticated cosmopolitan taste. If so it failed, for, despite having support from the powerful Scottish aristocratic presence in London, especially in the form of the Duke of Argyll, Aikman's professional ambitions were never realised. It was left to his much more artistically talented and socially adroit follower, Allan Ramsay, to achieve all the rewards and position, including Painter Royal, that Aikman aspired to gain. Not surprisingly, Ramsay produced a number of self-portraits throughout his illustrious career and by the time he created this modest pastel for his own pleasure he had acquired an international reputation. In fact this work was probably executed during one of Ramsay's visits to Rome, but it also reveals his first-hand acquaintance with the contemporary pastel technique of French rococo portraiture from his frequent trips to Paris. In this particular work, through the unmediated scrutiny of his individual personality and distinctive appearance, Ramsay's intensely analytical drawing places the artist at the heart of the European Enlightenment enterprise, where the direct empirical approach was the basis of all human enquiry.

If Scotland had bartered away its political independence to the new British state in 1707, many Scots were also eager to broaden their horizons and see themselves within a wider European context. With the establishment of the Grand Tour in the mid-18th century these cultural and professional ambitions could be realised. Following the earlier example of Aikman and Ramsay, Rome became such an artistic Mecca for so many young Scottish artists that they formed a remarkable presence in the Eternal City. The Scottish artists' colony in Italy was presided over by the great neoclassicist, Gavin Hamilton in Rome; and the renowned Greek vase collector, Sir William Hamilton, British ambassador in Naples. Both these men's advice and support was of great benefit to the studies and subsequent careers of visiting artists. David Allan was one such artist when he painted his nonchalantly self-confident portrait for his patrons, the Cathcart Family. Here he can reassure his benefactors that he is taking full advantage of what Rome has to offer him in the pursuit of his, and his patrons', aim to become an artist of European status. This ambition was confirmed when Allan won the *Concorso Balestra* at the Academy San Luca as the most promising young artist in the whole of Europe in the mid-1770s.

If David Allan's experience of Italy demonstrated what a young Scottish artist of the time could achieve on the European art scene, others were not so fortunate. The tragically short career of John Runciman ended at the age of 24 in Naples. His few surviving works reveal him to have been a highly imaginative and innovative artist, who anticipated many features in his painting that would become the hallmark of the later full Romantic style. Some of these can be seen in his brooding self-portrait which appears to conceal as much as it reveals about the personality of the artist. With such a work a new type of Scottish self-portrait began to emerge. Now, along with the delineation and presentation of social and professional self, the much more elusive inner psychological personality is alluded to by the artist's face being half in and half out of shadow. Furthermore, the divided self of the artist seems to be as much the scrutiniser of the person standing in front of the picture as an object of their gaze. This emphasis on the optical two-way dialogue of examining looks between artist and viewer can also be found in the later double self-portrait of Runciman's elder brother, Alexander, and his friend from their days in Rome, John Brown. Here the tools of the painter's trade take on much more significance than a mere indication of his profession. They have now become symbols of his artistic genius. The power of the artist's source of inspiration, Shakespeare's *The Tempest,* energises the whole being of the painter and that creatively invigorating force seems to surge through to his contorted hands to find release in the creative act of painting itself. These self-portraits of the Runcimans are early manifestations of the divided self where the romantic artist wishes as much to stand apart from conventional society as his predecessor desired to integrate into it.

By the later 18th century the self-image of Scottish artists had become much more complex and variable. This may have been their own particular response to the multifaceted and contradictory nature of Scottish society, in which oppositions abounded – between Lowland and Highland societies, declining rural communities and expanding urban masses, auld licht and new light Presbyterians, and between the Enlightenment emphasis on progressive development within a British imperial dimension and a deep longing to reconnect with the fading vitality of Scottish history and its mythic past. All these dialectical tensions were so expressively presented in Sir Walter Scott's writings that this period of late 18th/early 19th century became known as the Age of Scott.

The art scene of this period was dominated by Henry Raeburn, and later by David Wilkie (both of whom knew and painted portraits of Walter Scott), but lesser figures also deserve attention. For instance the cult of Romantic Primitivism, as found in the writings of Robert Burns and the later work of David Allan, can also be traced to the prints and paintings of John Kay and Alexander Carse. Where previously artists like Jamesone and Waitt wished to divert attention away from their lack of academic skill, now the naivety of an artist's style and unsophisticated technique could be taken as a stamp of their moral integrity and artistic authenticity. In the self-portrait of Carse for example, the very lack of finesse only adds to the particular attraction of his no-nonsense, straightforward manner of self-presentation. Similarly John Kay's print of himself in his studio has the accumulative quality which is usually the hallmark of much naïve folk art. A barber by trade, but artist by inclination, Kay took on the self-appointed task of portraying the galaxy of 'hotbed of genius' characters that inhabited the Enlightened Edinburgh of his day. In Kay's prints his subjects still live their daily lives out on the streets of the Old Town, whereas in Raeburn's portraits, the same figures of the *literati* are to be found in the elegant setting of their Robert Adam-designed New Town apartments. By skilfully giving his subjects the image of themselves they so eagerly desired, Raeburn became one of the most successful portrait painters of his era. His famous thoughtful self-portrait of 1815 for instance, was intended as his reception piece for his membership to the Royal Academy in London clearly demonstrating his British reputation. Raeburn also produced another self-image, surprisingly this time in the form of a paste medallion, probably cast for him by James Tassie, the renowned cameo portraitist. Unlike the rather mechanically produced work of Tassie, Raeburn's innate and intuitive skills as a painter allowed him to breathe vitality into this very formal medium and express the plastic, tactile qualities of his flowing hair, unruly cravat and splendid high-collar coat. Even within the constrictions of miniature relief sculpture, Raeburn demonstrates his amazing ability to give his diminutive self-image an extremely lively and striking presence.

Because Raeburn chose to remain in Scotland throughout his distinguished career, he became such a towering figure of admiration for the generation of Scottish portraitists coming to the fore at the turn of the 19th century that his influence was almost ubiquitous. The 'Raeburn look' can clearly be discerned, not only in the self-portraits of Andrew Geddes and William Yellowlees, but even in the miniature of Andrew Robertson. They all present themselves in dramatically lit isolation with that romantic look of intense concentration which goes back through Raeburn to Runciman. Out of that pack of young hopefuls emerged the next major figure who would not only dominate the Scottish, but also the London art scene, until his death in the 1840s. In this early self-portrait, David Wilkie presents himself to the world as the youthful romantic artist *par excellence*. Like his other contemporaries he draws upon all the same Raeburnesque conventions, but whereas the older master's profoundly painterly approach suggests presence, Wilkie, through close analytical delineation, gives much greater material factuality to his image. Whereas Raeburn's empiricism is always touched with a poetic abstracting quality, Wilkie's work has a much more physical, tangible imminence. In his potent image of bristling, but wary, expectation, Wilkie does not only anticipate his own future development, but also, through his dazzlingly successful London career, the emergence of British art from its earlier Romantic era into the Victorian age. After the protracted Napoleonic Wars the lure of the revolution-torn Continent had little attraction for mid-19th century artists. As British society radically modernised, Scottish artists, under the immensely pervasive influence of Walter Scott's writings, looked, along with their patrons and public, to the landscape and history of Scotland as their main sources for a sense of a distinctive Scottish identity. The cult of antiquarianism for instance can be found in Robert Scott Lauder's fancy dress tableau which harks back to an earlier, nobler age. Another keenly sought refuge from industrial, urban modernity was the rural cottage narrative picture which Wilkie had successfully introduced to his enthralled public and was further exploited by the Faed Brothers. This couthy kailyard world seems to be the setting for William Kidd's jolly depiction of himself and his doting wife.

In contrast to all this theatrical role-playing, other Scottish artists, however, took a very different approach by presenting themselves as the epitome of the respectable Victorian gentleman. This restrained, non-demonstrative approach to self-portraiture can be found in the work of Alexander Roche, William Orchardson and the post-'Glasgow Boy' James Guthrie for example. The most interesting of this group is the self-image of William McTaggart (National Gallery of Scotland). He at least still retains traces of the late romantic artist/genius persona as he intensifies the vigorous brushwork technique of Raeburn and Wilkie to an even higher degree of expressive energy.

By the last quarter of the 19th century there was a strong reaction by the younger generation of Scottish artists to Victorian 'glue pot' painting and the stereotypical picturesque image of Scotland as only a place of desolate misty mountains and quaint wholesome peasantry. From this dissatisfaction emerged the first coherent group of modern British artists in the form of the Glasgow Boys. They reconnected with art on the Continent and adapted French Realism to their *plein air* depictions of rural farming subjects. They closely identified with their subject matter and the image of the artist/worker in the landscape is powerfully expressed in Guthrie's surrogate self-portrait, *Hard At It,* 1883 (Kelvingrove Art Gallery). On the other hand, William Darling McKay takes a more relaxed and leisurely approach to painting himself out-of-doors.

The emphasis on the theme and practice of work in modern realist art, as expressed not only in subject matter, but also through the heavily worked surfaces of the Glasgow Boys' pictures, is also to be found in the self-portraits of the Scottish printmakers of the early modern era. They were all remarkable individuals – Muirhead Bone, William Strang, James McBey and later Ian Fleming, refused to be seduced by the lure of radical innovative Modernism. Their uncompromising commitment to the authentic power of directly observed realism gives their work a striking immediacy. Going against the trend they demonstrate in their self-portraits their superb graphic skills and seem to glory in the artisan origins of their highly demanding printing craft.

The controversial issue of the complex relationship between art and craft dominated the critical discussion of visual culture in the late Victorian period up until 1914. An important aspect of this debate was the conspicuous emergence of women artists onto the Scottish art scene. More and more female artists were now going to art schools and eagerly availing themselves of new opportunities, such as the life class and the design studio which had previously been denied them. At the forefront of this artistic gender revolution was Glasgow School of Art under the enlightened leadership of Fra and Jessie Newbery. In Edinburgh Patrick Geddes was also an exponent of similar innovative ideas on art and craft and was a keen supporter of the redoubtable Phoebe Traquair. Her very restrained self-portrait, which has the same close tonal quality found in Gwen John, gives little indication, except for the piercing gaze, of the immense creative energy of Traquair, who, singlehandedly, carried out a wide range of epic decorative schemes for the spiritual enlightenment of her adopted city, Edinburgh.

In the West of Scotland the modern movement was very much dominated by Charles Rennie Mackintosh and the other members of the 'Glasgow Four'. However there were other figures who made important contributions, including some young women painters who are now critically grouped together as the Glasgow Girls. Two of their self-portraits make a striking contrast. Bessie MacNicol for instance, like Traquair, gives herself a three-quarters turned head and shoulder presentation and also uses a very restrained palette. Whereas the Traquair is bathed in an aura of spiritual light, MacNicol is full of mysterious, sensual allure through her dramatic use of *chiaroscuro*. Dorothy Carleton Smyth on the other hand presents herself, palette and brushes in hand, working in her studio. Her composition subversively usurps all the conventional props of the successful professional male artist and this may be the reason why Smyth has such a wry, defiant look on her cheeky face. However the most richly challenging female self-portrait produced in the early 20th century was undoubtedly that of Cecile Walton's *Romance* (1920). This densely iconographic image raises a number of pertinent questions about art and gender. All these issues concerning the protean identity of the woman artist here overlap in the painter's self-imagery – from creative artist, compliant model, dutiful wife, loving mother, cultural and religious icon to sexual object. In this densely layered work the multi-role female masquerade is represented through the modern experience of fragmentation and alienation – with a decidedly feminist dimension.

Walton's deeply autobiographical self-portrait should also be considered within the historical context of the aftermath of World War 1. The devastating effect the post-war trauma had on Scottish artists can be seen if a comparison is made between JD Fergusson's self-portrait from 1909 and Stanley Cursiter's self-portrait with his family, executed in 1925. Fergusson's archmodernist picture was painted in Paris and is redolent with all the allure of modernity, as he adapts the conventions of earlier Scottish self-portraiture – head and shoulders, three-quarters turned head, broad-rimmed hat, face half in shadow etc – to present himself as the epitome of the Baudelairian *flaneur* of the modern city. Before 1914, Cursiter was also bedazzled by the glittering allure of modern painting as he sought to capture the dynamic excitement of the urban scene in the pictorial language of Cubo-Futurism. After the outbreak of war however, like most of his generation of British artists, he quickly eschewed any more dalliance with visual radicalism and sought refuge in the safe conventions of bourgeois naturalism as found in his wistful family group self-portrait. Thus after 1914, direct contact with the cutting edge of European Modernism that marked the best of the Scottish Colourists' work before the war temporarily came to an end.

Throughout the inter-war period Scottish modern art tended to stagnate, although it did produce individual artists with exciting, distinctive qualities.

Undoubtedly the dominant figure in Scotland during this time was William Gillies. A very private man, his strikingly different version of self-portrait with family appears to be an ingenious modern reworking of Velazquez's *Las Meninas* 1656, in the way it elaborates on revealing and concealing at the same time. Furthermore, the artist divides up the domestic space and securely locks each member of the family into their own private compartmentalised world, as though to keep any outside threat safely at bay.

During this period a few independent spirits stood apart from the dominance of Gillies and the Edinburgh School's pervasive influence on the inter-war Scottish art scene. William McCance in his self-portrait takes up the image of the modern artist inherited from JD Fergusson. As with Fergusson there is little emphasis on individual appearance as the figure is subjected to a cubistic treatment of form. Like a scene from TS Eliot's *Prufrock,* the nondescript setting is deliberately ordinary and mundane.

McCance was yet another Scot working south of the Border for most of his career as was the case with his fellow Scot, William Johnstone. Through his lifelong friendship with Hugh MacDiarmid, Johnstone was at the centre of British Modernism, pioneering the development of abstract painting in this country. The self-portrait of an abstract artist may seem a contradiction in terms, but there is a link and consistency between abstraction and figuration in all of Johnstone's work. His art constantly seeks to reveal the underlying structures and innate forces behind shifting surface appearances, whether it be in nature or with his own face. In this darkly brooding self-image the modern divided self is reconnected and reintegrated with its deep, primordial origins.

Lastly, the third outsider of this phase in Scottish art was James Cowie, who, although he remained in Scotland, was always regarded as a maverick figure. Yet, whereas McCance and Johnstone were treated with suspicion because they were committed modernists, Cowie, by contrast, was out of step in the other direction, as he was seen by his *belle peinture* contemporaries as an academic reactionary. In fact he was much more complex than this; for example, he was one of the few pre-war Scottish artists who took Surrealism seriously. On the other hand, he also had a deep respect for the European tradition of great painting and this is clearly evident in his late self-portrait, *The Blue Shirt* (1950). The composition is based on Poussin's renowned self-portrait of 1650 in the Louvre. Cowie even has the French master's *The Inspiration of the Epic Poet* c1636–39 so placed in the background that it is his own bald head that seems to receive the laurel crown of artistic achievement. There is, however, one crucial difference between Poussin's and Cowie's self-presentation. Whereas the 17th century classicist is seen as a man of immense learning, confidently engaging the viewer with the profound intelligence of his gaze, Cowie is revealed as a modern artist who is desperately attempting, but with much uncertainty as indicated by the unfinished rendering of his hands, to work out his own relationship with all the cultural objects with which he has surrounded himself. Alas it seems, modernity in general and two world wars in particular have now inevitably brought about an irreconcilable break with that cultural tradition to which Cowie yearns to reconnect.

Not surprisingly under the circumstances there are few Scottish self-portraits directly inspired by modern warfare. A rare exception is that by Robert Henderson Blyth from World War II. Whether this stoical, chirpy self-image tells us much about the deeper traumatic effects of such experiences, despite some indications as to the physical destruction and day-to-day hardships endured by the combatants, is open to question.

After 1945 the young Scottish artists who emerged on the art scene of the new welfare Britain were very different in attitude and outlook compared to their counterparts from 1918. They did not want to avoid the radical challenges of contemporary Modernism, but to embrace them in order to seek out and effectively express their particular relationship with the new world order that was being forged after the long period of devastation throughout the earlier 20th century. The immediate post-war and pre-Cold War Europe of the mid to later 1940s was very much open house to ambitious young artists and many enterprising Scottish artists eagerly took advantage of this situation. All these youngsters went on study trips to the Continent and even had sustained periods working abroad, especially in newly liberated Paris.

William Gear is an example of this international outlook, who, after his contact with the COBRA group in Paris, returned to become the leading British abstract artist, controversially winning the first prize for painting at the Festival of Britain in 1951. As with William Johnstone, Gear's intriguing self-portrait echoes a central concern in his non-figurative work. Here the artist graphically stimulates a pictorial equivalent to the way the human eye tends to look through, rather than directly at, the object of its attention. This the artist expresses by the bold manner in which he plays off surface and depth, proximity and distance. In contrast, Eduardo Paolozzi's self-portrait drawing is all pictorial surface and no perspectival depth, as the facial features and hands overlap and intertwine to make up a fragmented mosaic of the artist's collage-like image. In this work Paolozzi is already anticipating the new realities of the postmodern world of mass media, where everything takes place on a constantly changing electronic screen and the concept of a fixed, immutable self seems to be gone forever.

Paolozzi famously regarded himself not as the 'father of pop art, but the son of Surrealism'. Alan Davie's art also has a strong surrealist edge to it. Both artists were fascinated with the Surrealists' use of metamorphosis, but whereas Paolozzi draws his protean imagery from popular culture and technological graphics, Davies delves into the rich reservoir of signs and symbols to be found in what Jung termed the collective unconscious. For the artist to make contact with such cosmic iconography he must, like the shaman, lose himself and his individuality and become a receptive medium in order to body forth these subterranean forces. Thus Davie's self-portrait is of the artist's hands intuitively pouring forth the symbolic language of our innate spiritual being. For Davie the conventional self-portrait is yet another symptom of our dominating ego which has to be overthrown to allow the authentic collective subconscious to reconnect us with our mythic origins. Then there will be no self to be divided, for our spiritual being will be reunited with the whole of the cosmic universe.

There were of course more conventional approaches to self-portraiture by post-war artists, especially the ones painted in Scotland itself. Those by the young Joan Eardley and Robert Colquhoun both capture the psychological tension of uncertainty and anticipation that these two Glasgow art school students must have felt at the end of the war. Ironically the English-born Eardley chose to follow her career in Scotland, while Colquhoun, like most of his male contemporaries, felt he needed the challenges of the London art scene to stimulate his career. The older Anne Redpath by contrast moved in the other direction. She was of Gillies' generation, but had put her career on hold to bring up her family abroad. By the mid-1930s she had returned to Scotland to take up painting again and her wartime self-portrait conveys the sensitive but resolute determination that marked Redpath, along with Eardley, as one of the most successful artists working in post-war Scotland.

In the 1950s and '60s the Scottish art colleges were still the main centres of creativity and influence north of the Border. Figures like David Donaldson, Jack Knox and Robin Philipson, all heads of painting departments, used the self-portrait not only to present their self-images, but also to express their attitudes to the practice and role of painting. Not surprisingly this was usually conveyed in the modern academic fashion by allusions to the work of the old masters. Knox for instance, in his sparse, but densely referential work manages to make subtle connections with a range of sources – from Velazquez, through David to Munch. This deep concern to place Scottish art within a European tradition is also at the heart of the work of one of the renowned modern self-portraitists, John Bellany. From the outset of his career, when he made such a powerful impression with his epic paintings at Edinburgh College of Art in the early '60s, Bellany's art has always been deeply autobiographical. At the same time, however, the highly personalised content in his pictures is also layered with associations, connecting his childhood fishing community subject matter with the great tradition of northern European and modern expressionist art. The theme of human mortality is at the heart of Bellany's work and in this particular self-portrait, as we also found in that of Jamesone's for example, there is another *momento mori* presence. In Bellany's case, however, the reminder of death is not a general concept involving the mortality of all mankind, but rather it is a terrifying anticipation of the artist's own individual death – *timor mortis conturbat nie* – as the medieval poet William Dunbar wrote.

Bellany moved to London in the late '60s. This was the era of the counterculture revolution and London was the centre of political and artistic radicalism. Many Scottish artists and writers were at the forefront of this movement. Bruce McLean for instance came out of St Martin's College along with Richard Long, Barry Flanagan and Gilbert and George. These young sculptors were experimenting with a range of new mediums, including performance art in which the artist turns himself into a piece of living sculpture. McLean's *Pose Work for Plinth* (1971) is a seminal example of this, where he satirically parodies the elitist conventions of subject matter, style and presentation of such high modernist sculpture as that of Henry Moore. McLean's generation of rebellious artists were committed to the necessity of bringing art and life closer and closer together. This demand for all-inclusiveness was central to the aims of Boyle Family. Most famous for their truly sublime *World Series* in which they reproduce exact facsimiles of random areas of the Earth's surface, Boyle Family also subjected the body of Mark Boyle to a similar kind of treatment in their *Body Works* (1979). In this case randomly selected pieces of skin were removed and photographed with an electron microscope. Out of this enterprise grew the *Skin Series* and *DEATH PROCESSion* where, on the first day of each year, one square inch of skin was removed and recorded. In Boyle Family's work we have the *DEATH PROCESSion* self-portrait of Mark Boyle from 1979 in which the conventional sign of identity – the photographed face – is juxtaposed with a blown-up detail of his own skin surface. Now the Cartesian dualism between mind and body is challenged through the equal, non-hierarchical presentation of two very different indicators of individual identity – and all within the ultimate levelling context of universal human mortality as suggested by the title.

In the 1980s, for a range of reasons, painting briefly came back as a fashionable medium of representation and expression. At this time a group of young Scottish painters made reputations for themselves, some with an international dimension. The four most successful male representatives of this phenomenon were all students of Glasgow School of Art. For instance, Steven Campbell, following on from Bruce McLean, used parody to deconstruct the pictorial language of narrative painting. The same quirky, subversive approach can also be found in his enigmatic self-portrait *Natural Follies at Bee Junction* (1985). Ken Currie by contrast, turned to the style of modern social realism in his early epic canvases which dealt, for the first time in Scottish art, with historical and contemporary urban working-class experiences. Currie's doughty self-portrait shows the presence of the artist as a resolute and unflinching witness to the turbulent, and in many cases, inhuman times in which we live. Again, Adrian Wisniewski has a very different approach to his art. Much more of a romantic, his paintings do not have either the raucousness of Campbell or the rancour of Currie, but emit a quiet, laid-back, lyrical quality. Wisniewski portrays himself, like the young men in his other pictures, as a rather wistful dreamer who may use the painterly technique of van Gogh but without all the concomitant angst. On the other hand, with the fourth member of these 'New Glasgow Boys', angst has always been the order of the day. Peter Howson's self-portrait, *Acheron*

(2004), is a golden opportunity to include himself in a pagan horror story, involving death and a terrifying journey through the afterlife. Interestingly, John Kirkwood, in his photomontage *State of the Nation* (1990) also places himself within an apocalyptic vision. This time, like a latter-day St John the Divine, the artist seems to be witnessing the final destruction of mankind through nuclear annihilation. With these last two artists self-portraiture aspires to the epic dimensions of grand history painting through visionary imagination of the artist.

There have been an increasing number of notable women artists in the post-war and recent period of Scottish art. Eardley and Redpath have already been mentioned, but the self-portraits of Pat Douthwaite and Elizabeth Blackadder also give an indication of the rich variety of work by women artists. Strikingly, almost all the Scottish women artists who came to the fore in the 1980s and '90s concentrated on the female bodily presence which usually had a strong autobiographical dimension. In Gwen Hardie's *I Am* the artist uses a raw, almost graffiti-like graphic style to turn her body inside out in a grotesque act of contorted self-revelation. Here the containing line of the classically constructed ideal of female beauty is broken asunder. On the other hand Lys Hansen's *It Happened by the Wall – I Spy* (1992) has her outer presence withdrawing into her self-contained protective shell with only one eye to engage with the outside world. The female eye is again prominent in Joyce Cairn's jaunty nautical self-portrait. The intriguing conjunction of artist and seagull may be a witty allusion to the trope that conventionally links the female with the world of nature. Lastly, Helen Flockhart's obsessively detailed self-portrait has a distinctively folksy aura to it. Yet once again the artist is challenging the conventions concerning the role of women in Western culture. Craft, especially involving the highly detailed textile patterning found in this picture was usually seen as the work of anonymous women, whose individuality was never permitted to express itself in what they so skilfully made. Flockhart's own implacable presence mutely challenges this imposed hierarchy of values concerning art, craft and gender.

Another victim of this postmodern re-examination of social and cultural standards has been painting itself. Undoubtedly since the 1960s this once dominant medium of expression has been on the defensive. That is not in any way to say that it has become irrelevant or redundant. Not only the paintings just discussed, but also the works of William Crozier, Alberto Morrocco, John Johnstone, John Byrne, Craig Mulholland, David McClure, John McLean, Jock McFadyen, Leonard McComb and Saul Robertson, runner-up in this year's prestigious BP portrait competition, all clearly indicate that painting is still a highly favoured and inventively utilised medium amongst contemporary female and male Scottish artists.

On the other hand it has to be conceded that for many of the younger generation coming out of the Scottish art colleges in the 1990s, painting no longer seems the adequate or appropriate medium to engage with contemporary society and its postmodern culture. In 1988 Eduardo Paolozzi

seemed to endorse this new attitude towards self-portraiture when he stated:
> Perhaps what might describe the modern condition is that in making a self-portrait the artist (unlike Rembrandt or van Gogh), may not stare at himself in a mirror but try and obtain the result by other means.

Many of the younger Scottish artists took up this challenge and preferred to pursue their own artistic agendas using alternative modes, such as performance and installation for example. Even when they did turn to traditional art forms, they were usually treated in a radical and usually subversive manner. For instance, taking a leaf out of Bruce McLean's book, Kenny Hunter's *Non-Progress* (2006) undermines the conventions of the traditional portrait bust on plinth format by literally turning it on its head. As can be detected in the work by Hunter there is a strong neo-dadaist, anarchistic streak at play in much contemporary Scottish art. This can also be found in Beagles and Ramsay's *Black Pudding Self-Portrait* (2004)which is accompanied by cooking instructions. Taken to an even more extreme degree this mischievous duo undercut the normal *raison d'etre* of portraiture. Here individuality has been boiled down to a couple of identical 'puddens', each of which contains a pint of the artists' blood. Yet which pudding 'represents' which artist is anyone's guess in this ironic meditation on the popular notion that we are what we eat *à la Écossaise*.

Photography and video (as seen in the work of Clive Thomson) have probably been the major challenge to painting over the last decade. What has made this development so interesting is the wide range of ways the photographic medium has been used, including the portrayal of self. For instance Angela Palmer again employs the bust on a plinth format, but by transferring Magnetic Resonance Imagery scans of herself onto etched layers of Perspex she can build up a three-dimensional X-ray of herself in a very hallucinatory manner. Calum Colvin's work combines installation and photography in an extremely sophisticated and inventive fashion. Through the construction of elaborate painted tableaux, which are then photographed, the artist produces fascinating images that are both intriguing and baffling. In his surrogate self-portrait, *Narcissus* (1987), he proudly displays – only to mock – the self-obsessed, doomed male artist in all his reflected kitsch-infested glory.

Lastly, two of the most provocative and intriguing recent Scottish self-portraits also employ the medium of photography. Douglas Gordon, the first Scot to win the Turner prize, used for a publicity image the passport mugshot, *Self-Portrait as Kurt Cobain, as Andy Warhol, as Myra Hindley, as Marilyn Monroe* (1996). As the throwaway and seemingly open-ended title appears to suggest the artist will constantly camouflage his identity behind an endless repertoire of ready-made personalities. Following the lead of his main inspiration, Marcel Duchamp, and his female alter ego, Rrose Sélavy, Gordon has turned his own self-image into an anti-portrait in which nothing can be securely identified in this quick-change theatre dressing room of self-reflecting mirrors.

In striking contrast, John Mullen and Lee O'Connor in their morphed triple self-portrait have gone in the entirely opposite direction to Gordon. Whereas Gordon has instigated the complete disintegration of a unified self, they have created a new, but entirely nonexistent being from photographic elements of their own facial images. Confronted by this uncanny computer-generated face, are we permitted to ask what are we looking at? Is it really a self-portrait or merely a straight portrait of another person? And if so, of whom? Who is this Frankenstein-like creation? Is he merely a phantom or in fact the face of the Baudrillardian hyper-reality which hypnotically beckons us all towards a not-too-distant 'Brave New World' where image has completely taken over from reality.

Finally we might now ask what have we discovered and learnt from this journey through the history of Scottish self-portrait? Of course there is no clear and unified answer to this. If nothing else the wide variety of different types of Scottish self-portraits demonstrate that the concept and depiction of self is an extremely elusive and protean phenomenon. It is constantly changing and variable in its nature and form – from one historical period to another, from one social circumstance to another, and ultimately from one individual artist to another. If that is the case, then is the seeking after self within this particular artistic generic format a fool's errand? Is the visual representation of self merely a will-o'-the wisp attempt at capturing passing impressions, a mirage of our unfulfilled desires and unsatisfied longings for a certainty of being? David Hume, for instance, would appear to think so, as seen from his own particular views on the nature of self as expressed in his *A Treatise of Human Nature:*

> For my part, when I enter most intimately into what I call myself, I always stumble on some particular perception or other, of heat or cold, light or shade, love or hatred, pain or pleasure. I never can catch myself at any time without a perception, and never can observe anything but the perception...
> If anyone, upon serious and unprejudiced reflection, thinks he has a different notion of himself, I must confess that I can reason no longer with him.

Thus for Hume self certainly has no metaphysical dimensions, and is merely the intellectual and social process by which we make some kind of unifying order out of the plethora of sensations which constantly bombard our senses. Following on from this, Robert Louis Stevenson, in *Dr Jekyll and Mr Hyde,* presents an even bleaker view on the hopelessness of pinning down a fixed notion of self. For Stevenson's Jekyll any unity of self is just a convention which socially camouflages the myriad of concealed repressed personas which are bubbling under the surface of our polite personality but which in the end will burst asunder. Then as the good doctor predicts:

I hazard the guess that man will be ultimately known for a mere polity of multifarious, incongruous and independent denizens.

Many present day cultural theorists and critical commentators on the 'multifarious' nature of our contemporary postmodern age would readily endorse Dr Jekyll's prophetic words. On the other hand, however, despite all the different egotistical personas we all rehearse in the negotiations of our daily lives, there still remains for most of us a belief in a core identity of self behind our mask of social camouflage. This view is lucidly expressed by the poet Norman McCaig in 'Summer Farm' while musing on his relationship with the farmyard environment in which he finds himself:

> Self under self, a pile of selves I stand
> Threaded on time, and with a metaphysical hand
> Lift the farm like a lid and see
> Farm within farm, and in the centre me.

Yet even if we are inclined to side with the visionary poet over the sceptical philosopher, and agree that there is such an innate thing as 'me' within myself; we are also forced to admit, however, that it is as elusive and challenging to seek it out as the 'self' in self-portraiture.

This catalogue essay was written for the exhibition *Divided Selves: The Scottish Self-Portrait from the 17th Century to the Present*, shown at the Talbot Rice Gallery, The University of Edinburgh and The Fleming Collection, London, in 2006.

ATHENA IN THE BOEOTIA OF THE NORTH
The Newly Restored Cast Collection of Edinburgh College of Art

Frown not on England: England owns him not:
Athena, ŋo! thy plunderer was a Scot.
Ask'st thou the difference? From fair Phyles' towers
Survey Boeotia;–Caledonia's ours.
And well I know within that bastard land
Hath Wisdom's goddess never held command.
Lord Byron, 'The Curse of Minerva', 1812

Shamanism could be described as the deepest root of the idea of spiritual life,
deeper even than the mythological level of the later stages of Greek culture,
for example. But even the Greeks retained their link with shamanistic or
magical behaviour. The mythological view of the world, the designation of
particular places as sacred, and the building of temples on the Acropolis all
belongs to a later stage.
Joseph Beuys

There is nothing as invisible as a monument. They are impregnated with
something that repels attention, causing the glance to roll right off, like water
droplets off an oilcloth, without even pausing for a moment.
Robert Musil, *The Posthumous Papers of a Living Author*, 1936

MANY WOULD AGREE with Freud that, despite all its alluring attractions, civilisation is a mixed blessing in which there are always both contented winners and discontented losers. According to Freud in his *Civilisation and its Discontents*, the psychological origins of civilisation grew out of the dominating desire of our super ego to repress and control the unruly id in all of us. Furthermore, in geographical terms, this has meant that for civilisation to thrive and flourish peripheral backward regions – Byron's 'bastard lands'– Boeotia in ancient Greece, or the Scottish Highlands in modern Britain for example, have always had to be contained and controlled by the progressive forces of the metropolitan civilising centre. This historical process for instance, can clearly and strikingly be seen to have taken place in Scotland immediately after the calamitous failure of the last Jacobite uprising in the middle of the 18th century. Following Culloden and the subsequent ruthless repression of the northern Celtic hordes – the emerging enlightened Scots would embrace and be embraced by the comfort blanket of economic and cultural security offered by their highly civilised southern neighbours. These northern Britons – as they now liked to think of themselves – could safely shed their previous rude habits and cover their hairy Hibernian bodies with the sartorial trappings of civilisation – thus turning their former brutishness into Britishness.

Yet as that great Victorian sage, Thomas Carlyle, laboriously argued in *Sartor Resatus* such crossdressing can have a disturbing effect on the subject's sense of identity. Especially if you are a 'historical people', as David Hume described the Scots. Then you are also fearful of jettisoning your past in case you might lose your distinctive national and cultural identity (the baby/bathwater syndrome). This mixing up of past and present can, for instance, be discerned in two illuminating post-Culloden portraits of the Scottish cultural and social elite. For example Pompeo Batoni – court painter to the British Grand Tourists in Rome – presents in his portrait of Colonel William Gordon of Fyvie a figure symbolically layered with sartorial allegiances. Striking a swaggering, swashbuckling pose, Gordon, standing in the ruins of the Coliseum and being offered the orb of victory from a statue of Roma herself, confidently takes on the mantle of the new imperial hero. Yet as can be seen from his curiously eclectic costume – a combination of toga-like tartan plaid laid over the crimson and gold braided jacket of his British officer jacket – Gordon's real triumph is the manner in which he has been able to negotiate and combine an array of conflicting loyalties and identities from ancient Celt, through modern Briton, to European man of taste.

If Colonel Gordon wished to display his credentials as a loyal Hanoverian at the centre of the civilised world; by contrast, his fellow Scot, Norman Macleod, 22nd Clan Chief of the Macleods of Skye, preferred Allan Ramsay to set his portrait in his ancestral domain on the outer periphery of Western civilisation. Like Gordon, Macleod also reneged on his former Jacobite feudal sympathies and shrewdly threw in his lot with the modern forces of British military might. Thus, although at the time when the portrait was painted in the later 1740s the wearing of Highland dress was proscribed, because Macleod, after much dithering, supplied his clansmen to the British army's victory at Culloden, he could safely have his image swayed in a cascade of tartan wrapping. To offset this outburst of Caledonian commitment however, Macleod cunningly strikes a classical pose in order to demonstrate his cultural credentials to his London audience – where the portrait was painted– even if it does produce the rather incongruous sight of the *Apollo Belvedere* striding through the bracken in tartan trews.

This choice of the *Apollo Belvedere* by a Scottish painter and noble sitter is significant for two reasons – one concerning the subject, the other the status of this particular Greco-Roman statue. Firstly, the *Apollo Belvedere* is a representation of the Pythian Apollo. In this particular guise, Apollo – 'Lord of the Silver Bow' as Homer called him – is about to release his arrow and slay the monstrous she-dragon, Python at Delphi, which would then become Apollo's sacred sanctuary. For the ancient Greeks this myth symbolised the triumph of divine and subsequently human reason, over the dark chthonic forces of Nature, which not only lurked in the bowels of the Earth, but also within the savage regions of human society and the human mind. With such

a momentous event we return to the violent origins of Western civilisation
through the crushing of the barbaric 'Other' by the ordering forces of
civilisation: or to put it another way, within Freudian terms, the intellectual
Super Ego of Dr Jekyll taking over control from the instinctive Id of Mr
Hyde. Secondly, turning to the cultural status of the *Apollo Belvedere,*
this statue – from the time of its discovery during the Renaissance to the
Enlightenment period – rapidly became the artistic and fashionable icon of
classical ideal beauty. This judgement was internationally agreed, especially
after the publication of the writings on ancient Greek art by the German
scholar JJ Winckelmann in the middle of the 18th century, where he eulogised
on the beautiful male nude figure which for him embodied the perfect
balance between 'noble simplicity and quiet grandeur'. Winckelmann's ideas
and writings, emanating from Rome, soon dominated the aesthetic taste of
the Grand Tourists – many of whom were Scots. This Hellenisation of the
Northern imagination and cultural aspirations quickly spread throughout
Enlightenment Europe and subsequently became the holy writ for all
ambitious art academies.

The neoclassical art academy was undoubtedly the Enlightenment's
most notable and influential contribution to the history of Western art and
became the powerhouse of artistic teaching and practice throughout the
18th and 19th centuries. Needless to say no civilised country or city could
be taken seriously without such an important national or civic institution
for itself. Not surprisingly peripheral and stateless Scotland was severely
disadvantaged for its own ambitions for such cultural recognition and was
markedly late in acquiring its own Royal Scottish Academy in 1826. The
preparatory groundwork for this keenly sought symbol of cultural recognition
was however, laid much earlier. Various smaller independent art training
establishments – such as the St Luke's, the Foulis' and the Trustees' academies
operated in Edinburgh and Glasgow throughout the 18th century. A mixture
of industrial design and fine art courses were provided, and for the latter,
a few sculptural casts after the antique were provided. Yet with the rapid
spread of Scotland's own particular brand of Philhellenism, the amassing of
casts – taken from numerous works within celebrated European and British
collections – soon grew into an addictive obsession for the Scottish art
establishment. This was especially the case with Edinburgh, as it was obliged
to turn to culture, rather than politics, to assert its position as a European
metropolitan capital of distinction.

If individual Scots – seeking to flaunt their fashionable taste and classical
education – could dress themselves up as Greco-Roman gods and ancient
heroes for their *à la Grec* portraits; why not also apply the same stylistic fancy
dress to civic buildings – or even a whole city such as Edinburgh? Thus, the
Scottish capital turned away from the dark Gothic savagery of 'Auld Reekie'
and turned towards the enlightened classical civility of the 'Athens of the
North'. Furthermore, by the early 19th century Scotland could also claim that

its capital's academy had now acquired 'one of the largest and best collections of casts from the antique in the United Kingdom.' Throughout the century the Royal Scottish Academy continued to acquire more and more pieces for its cast collection. This collecting mania continued to such an extent that the especially designed Statue Gallery in William Playfair's neo-Greek Temple to the visual arts at the foot of the Mound, eventually could no longer cope with the sheer volume of plaster models which now outnumbered the students they were intended to instruct. Needless to say, as contemporary Victorian photographs show, overcrowding became a pressing problem.

The solution to the consequences of this particular example of Scottish compulsive behaviour was to remove the teaching of art students from the Royal Scottish Academy and transfer that role over to a new educational body who would be provided with a specially designed building to house Scotland's treasured cast collection. Even though this was carried out during the first decade of the 20th century – by which time for instance, Picasso had already painted *Les Demoiselles d'Avignon* (1907) – the newly commissioned Edinburgh College of Art was still committed to an academic neoclassical programme of art education with its cast collection being integral to the architectural and pedagogical ethos of its domain. Furthermore, if a century earlier 'The Athens of the North' had failed miserably to create on its own acropolis a replica temple to its adopted protective deity; then it was now up to the new Edinburgh College of Art to provide a fitting interior sanctuary for Athena, her Olympian family and her ancient Athenian subjects. Although this relationship between Athena and the new Edinburgh College of Art seemed to be a perfect union, unfortunately it was stillborn right from the outset. This can be witnessed in the commissioned photographs of Edinburgh's newly opened Art College which shows Athena's designate domain as a moribund mausoleum populated by petrified presences.

It is difficult to assess how much, or more appropriately, how little, the Athenian casts were actually used for teaching purposes in the drawing classes of Edinburgh College of Art. There is certainly little evidence however, from the work of students and ex-students that they gained much guidance or creative inspiration from that particular source during their art education. In fact there are good reasons to explain this apparent lack of interest in the casts as an art teaching aid. Just after the opening of the Edinburgh College of Art the First World War broke out. During its four-year conflict European civilisation waged a relentless and horrific assault on the human body. It is therefore little surprise then that after 1918 the classical ideal of the body beautiful carried little conviction – until the Nazis took it up again and used it for their own perverted propagandist purposes. During the inter-war years the cast collection at Edinburgh was mainly ignored; only to be used occasionally as props for the College's annual Dionysian students' *Revels*. During this period the whole tenor of the teaching at Edinburgh of Art had moved away from an Athenian approach– with its emphasis on Apollonian rules and conventions – to one much more in the emotional and subjective spirit of Dionysus. Within the Edinburgh School the making of art was now seen as more to do with personal taste than objective reason; less concerned with sense and more involved with sensibility. As a consequence the decorative landscape and the delicate still life supplanted the classical conquering hero, the fallen warrior and the reclining goddess.

After the 20th century's second cataclysmic disaster however there was one major Scottish artist – with a brief connection to Edinburgh College of Art in his early career – who returned, both to the figure and ancient themes, for the subject content of his art. Eduardo Paolozzi's savagely brutal and severely brutalised sculptures of the post-war period were his own cathartic response to living in a traumatised age which was trying to come to terms with the aftermath of the Holocaust, and also attempting to learn how to cope with the imminent possibility of the total nuclear annihilation of human civilisation. Being under such an apocalyptic threat Paolozzi felt it necessary to turn to ancient art and myth for his creative inspiration. Unfortunately, because of its undesirable association with fascist and Stalinist preference for Classicism, Paolozzi was obliged to turn his back on the sophisticated achievements of the academic tradition and return to an earlier and less historically contaminated type of sculpture. To achieve this Paolozzi had to formulate his own sculptural method. This was based on his adaptation of the primitive practice of *bricolage*. In this way found ready-made objects – culled from the detritus of modern consumer society – were collaged together and cast into new forms to become the raw matter for the construction of his art brut statues. Although bearing ancient Greek names – such as *Jason, Icarus* and *Elektra* – these monstrous deformed creations of Paolozzi would have certainly horrified Athena, for they represented the very forces of darkness which her father, Zeus, and the rest of the Olympian gods, had struggled to contain and defeat during the primordial stages of Creation. In Freudian terms these hybrid mutants and cyborgs – part human, part beast, part robot – were a frightening manifestation of what he called 'the return of the repressed'. For Athena they must have been a disturbing omen, heralding the approaching barbarians soon to be heard hammering at the gates of her citadel.

Athena's forebodings soon proved correct. In 1970 a small group of Teutonic terrorists from Dusseldorf Kunst Akademie – led by their charismatic Celtic chief, Joseph Beuys – captured and set up camp in Athena's northern statuary during their exhibition for the Edinburgh Festival of that year. Under the enigmatic and palindromic banner of *Strategy: Get Arts* these Gothic invaders performed a range of esoteric rituals – from Klaus Rinke's deluge of the building's main portal, through Stefen Wewerke's scattering of broken chairs across the grand staircase, to Guther Uecker's constantly banging studio door which at the time must have given Athena a splitting headache. It was Beuys however, who left the most indelible mark and lasting impression during this occupation of the Edinburgh College of Art building. Unlike Athena, who always remained close to the Scottish capital, Beuys was captivated by his pilgrimage to Caledonia's rugged northern landscape which he called 'the last great wilderness of Europe'. After his preparatory reconnoitre to the 'land of Macbeth and Ossian' on Rannoch Moor, he returned to Edinburgh College of Art to carry out his *Celtic (Kinloch Rannoch) Scottish Symphony*. This four-hour, twice daily 'action', as Beuys termed it, was loosely structured and improvised round a complex set of interconnecting holistic rituals – involving music, film, blackboard instruction, a silent grand piano, base materials, such as felt and a shamanistic performance which exorcised the spirit of the place and returned it to 'world of the Celts'. Immediately after these acts of desecration ceased and order was restored, the horrified Edinburgh College of Art's authorities took steps to placate the outraged anger of Athena for this violation of her domain, by removing all traces of this alien intrusion – including painting over the piece of vandalism *Blue/yellow/white/red* perpetrated by Blinky Palermo on the classical architectural frieze around the main staircase.

Unfortunately, as far as Athena was concerned this soon proved an empty gesture as her custodians subsequently reneged on their earlier iconoclasm and had Palermo's wall painting 'reinstated as a work of art'. Furthermore, the profound influence of Joseph Beuys' artistic thought ('thinking forms'), cultural debate ('spoken forms') and creative practice ('social sculpture') on the student body at Edinburgh College of Art and other Scottish art colleges, has only increased from decade to decade since *Strategy: Get Arts*. Yet Athena has not been ignored completely. Thanks to the efforts of a small band of dedicated disciples the surviving collection of cast sculptures – after decades of neglect and mistreatment – have recently been conscientiously restored to their former respectable condition again. Yet, whether this will make them more 'visible' to staff and students within Edinburgh College of Art is still to be seen. This may prove to be a difficult challenge. As Robert Musil pointed out in his essay *Monuments,* 'Anything that endures over time sacrifices its ability to make an impression. Anything that constitutes the walls of our life, the backdrop of our consciousness forfeits its capacity to play a role in that consciousness.' Maybe however, *Cast Contemporaries* will prove Musil wrong in the end.

Athena, for all her vaunted wisdom, must wonder how and why she ever allowed herself to have anything to do with this Northern 'bastard land'. As with the similar fate of Medea at the hands of a fickle lover, Athena must now feel like a scorned spouse abandoned in an alien country. To add to her sense of bitter loss Athena will sadly look back to much happier times when she was worshipped and adored by her Hibernian lover. Then her enlightened admirer, aspiring to be worthy of such a paradigm of perfection, was completely enthralled to her every wish: everything he touched in stone or plaster was an open declaration of everlasting devotion to her very name. Yet ironically just at the point when this self-styled modern Athenian declared his commitment to their eternal union by building a temple to house her divine presence, the rift between them appeared, and his former passion began rapidly to wane and wither away. From then on this cold-hearted Scot turned his back on her and all that reminded him of his former feelings.

So much for love in a cold climate – from Athena's chilly perspective, the Athens of the North must now seem more like the Reykjavik of the South. And finally, to add present injury to past insult, her arch enemy, Sparta has built a horticultural outpost poised for attack, less than 30 miles west of her less than secure *Castellum est urbs*.

This catalogue essay was written for the exhibition, *Cast Contemporaries* shown at Edinburgh College of Art in 2012.

SECTION TWO
Essays on Scottish Modern Art

A MODERN BESTIARY
Scottish Artists and the Animal World

IN GLASGOW'S POLLOCK House collection there are two tempera paintings
by William Blake. One depicts *Adam Naming the Beasts of the Field* (1810)
and its companion *Eve naming the Birds of the Air* (1810). We are shown
Adam and Eve, entrusted with the cataloguing and safekeeping of all God's
vast earthly creation. After the Fall humanity no longer occupied such a lofty
position and our relationship with the animal kingdom, especially in modern
times, has become more and more complicated.

Blake and his contemporaries, working in what is now known as the
Romantic era, were the first generation of artists, as opposed to individuals
like Leonardo, to take a profound interest in the unbounding variety of the
natural world. It was there that artists and poets looked to find inspiring
subjects that mirrored their thoughts and feelings. Since the early 19th
century, the Romantic outlook has become, to a greater or lesser extent, an
integral part of most people's attitudes to the human experience of life and art.

The success and vitality of the current Scottish art scene has many
characteristics in common with the Romantic period. Maybe the most
conspicuous being the sheer variety of approaches and attitudes towards
choice of subject matter, stylistic interpretation and technical improvisation
employed by Scottish artists today. Therefore, it is opportune that the first
Scottish Bestiary should be attempted at this time when there are so many
talented, but different types of artists equipped and ready to tackle such an
exciting project.

Furthermore, George Mackay Brown's writings in poetry and prose provide
the wide range of subjects for *The Scottish Bestiary* – 19 animals, both real
and mythical, plus man himself. Mackay Brown's rich descriptive text provides
a great stimulus to the interpretative powers of the seven artists involved. Each
of them: John Bellany, Steven Campbell, Peter Howson, Jack Knox, Bruce
McLean, June Redfern and Adrian Wisniewski, were allowed to approach
the challenge in their own distinctive manner, both stylistically, and with the
ever-available expertise of the Peacock workshop, graphically as well. This
successful collaboration, made possible by the characteristically ambitious
initiative of Charles Booth-Clibborn between poet, artist and printer, is yet
another example of the spirit of confidence and achievement that exemplifies
much of the artistic activity in Scotland at present.

Although *Aesop's Fables* is the most celebrated collection of animal stories,
the great majority of European fables in this genre were produced in medieval
times. The finest in Scotland is undoubtedly Robert Henryson's *Moral Fables*
which even if, like George Mackay Brown's, is deeply serious in its critical,

moral and social intent, it does not neglect the necessary infusion of humour: 'Amangis ernist to ming ane merie sport' as expressed by Henryson. *The Scottish Bestiary* also strikes a flexible balance between 'ernist' and 'merie sport'. Each artist tends by personal inclination towards either seriousness or amusement, but overall the different approaches complement each other well.

John Bellany, for example, with his newfound *joi de vivre,* expresses a light-hearted, some may say 'cavalier' attitude to his role as illustrator. He prefers to populate his etchings mostly with slight adaptations of his own creations, who convey not animal grotesque, but rather a delightful sense of exotic fancy dress. Taking a similar independent approach, Steven Campbell's distinctive artistic personality dominates the treatment of the human element in *The Scottish Bestiary.* Modern man is no longer the measure of all things, and Campbell's rough-hewn wood cuts reflect the uncertainty of his confused relationship with the natural. Campbell however, finds this a cause more for wry humour rather than deep angst. Man can no longer just dance to the music of time, he has to join in the Lewis Carrol's Lobster Quadrille. Adrian Wiszniewski also takes a light, if less comic approach. The creatures, such as the fearsome dragon and the unicorn, which he portrays in his prints, have had their mythical powers drained. They are reduced to the role of playful pets who can now only safely exist in the protective environment of an art nouveau drawing room. If Wiszniewski's beasts have become domesticated and even humanised as with his unicorn, the ebb and flow relationship between animal and human nature in June Redfern's work is strikingly different. She appears to hold with Henryson's view that: '…mony men in opertaoun, ar llike to beistisin conditioun'. The emphasis is on the human psyche, whether with unconstrained freedom in *The Seal,* or the predatory revenge in *The Wolf.* Furthermore, because Redfern's creations are half-beast/half-woman, this seems to intensify the emotional potency of the image which is further heightened by a splash of raw colour in the background.

The artists discussed have on the whole, inclined to illustrate their subjects in a relatively independent and personal manner. This also applies to Bruce McLean whose screenprints of *The Salmon* and *The Stoor-Worm* are virtuoso performances of acrobatic and balletic movement. Peter Howson and Jack Knox by contrast, in two very different, but equally successful interpretations of their subjects, choose to keep more strictly to their literary sources. Howson's multicoloured screenprint for Mackay Brown's Robert Burns-inspired story of the field mouse stimulates all the cosy, domestic aura of the text's theme. Here for a brief moment at least, man and beast feel no threat from each other. Appropriately, the artist grafts a Disney-like graphic style to his own in order to create the warm atmosphere of the scene and also conveys the contrasting sense of scale between the studious farm-boy, Rab, and his wee furry companion.

In the art of illustrative narrative one of the most crucial decisions the artist has to make is the choice of scene which he selects to focus upon. Howson chooses to present a rare interlude of harmony between the human and the non-human world. Jack Knox's lithograph illustration for *The Whale*, on the other hand, is the numbing finale to the saga, where only total alienation exists between man and the animal protagonist. The harpooned body of the great whale is in its final death throes, the fading silhouette of the killer ship is disappearing over the horizon – this is romantic tragedy at its most acute. Yet this is not played out on a grand operatic level à la Delacroix. In fact the power of Knox's image lies in its directness and apparent simplicity of his approach. The artist sheds all traces of graphic sophistication. Here what we are presented with is an imagined eyewitness account by someone – a sailor perhaps – who has only the rudiments of drawing skills, yet is compelled to record the last moments of this titanic struggle between man and the most monumental of nature's creations.

The Scottish Bestiary is, arguably, one of the most important printmaking ventures to be undertaken in Scotland this century. Everyone who has worked on it should be congratulated, with particular praise to Arthur Watson and Peacock Printmakers who have managed to produce, in a limited period of time, a set of high quality prints by seven of Scotland's most stimulating contemporary artists.

This essay was published by Peacock Printmakers, Aberdeen and *Alba* (issue 2, 1986).

GLASGOW BELONGS TO WHOM?
Civic Identity and the Visual Arts in Scotland

THE ONGOING AND seemingly irreconcilable antagonism between high art and low culture (aka art and kitsch) has been a running sore in the body politic of modern British social debate since the days of Matthew Arnold. This critical civil war between those who doggedly support aesthetic quality and lofty cultural standards on the one hand, and those who fiercely champion accessible contemporary art forms and popular entertainment on the other, is probably most exemplified by the critical writings of TS Eliot and George Orwell. In the visual arts of this country this sociopolitical struggle has been: no less vigorously fought – from the Ruskin versus Whistler court case to Lord Clark's *Civilization* set against John Berger's *Ways of Seeing,* the battle lines have been clearly etched on the public's consciousness. Coming right up to the present this division between cultural elitism and mass populism is still a topic of great contention as witnessed by the recent editorial in *Art Review* (October 1999). There David Lee robustly airs all the old issues yet again, with the usual dire warnings of barbarians hammering at the city gates.

> The Culture Minister should not force museums to become amusement arcades in order that he can announce triumphantly to the dinosaur Left that those who previously ignored museums are now coming round. He should encourage hardline elitism and concern himself with making museums free while further extending opening hours. The rest is up to the individual. To try to appeal to the uneducated by spoiling the experience of the museum for the rest, with the inevitable result of demeaning the art itself, is unhinged.
>
> The Culture Minister ought to think hard before forcing museums down the populist avenue antipathetic to their real purpose and which trivialises knowledge and learning and discourages scrutiny. The potential for irreparable damage is enormous, the first results already visible.

Such cultural Jeremiahs have been with us for an awfully long time. For this essay I would like to focus on this apparently never-ending debate but within the particular context of the role played by the visual arts in the civic politics of Glasgow over the last two decades.

From the outset we should remember that because of its particular circumstances and development the overall history and character of the visual arts in Scotland is decidedly different from that pertaining to England. The most striking contrast is that within the Scottish context there is little or no public art in any real national or sovereign sense – that may explain, for instance, why there is no discernible sculptural tradition in Scotland. The causes for this are long and complex but a few salient factors need to be noted here. More than in any other area, public art requires an infrastructure of extended patronage, and this the visual arts has decidedly lacked north of the border. From the Reformation onwards the Church for example, has been hostile to images, preferring the Word, over which it could have much more control within the social as well as the spiritual life of the Scottish people. Furthermore, in the area of secular patronage the visual arts were also poorly served. When the Stuart royal dynasty moved to London and on to the British throne in 1603 they, and their Scottish nobility, quickly Anglified their image and turned to non-Scottish artists to glorify their self-regarding importance.

Thus the dominant characteristic of art in Scotland is primarily of a private nature, with informal naturalistic portraiture predominating during the Scottish Enlightenment and this then being replaced in the Victorian period by a preference for deserted romantic landscape or nostalgic genre scenes from a lost rural idyll. It may be because of this predominantly private and subjective strain in Scottish art that it was here that there was a much more positive response to modern art, compared to the suspicion and hostility that it encountered from most of the public art institutions in England.

With this Scottish enthusiasm for modern art, Glasgow led the way – with dealers like Alexander Reid, whose portrait by van Gogh now hangs in the Kelvingrove Gallery; with collectors such as William Burrell, who skilfully acquired some of the finest examples of modern French painting in the country; and with the internationally acclaimed group of progressive young painters, The Glasgow Boys. Right at the heart of the town, as the jewel in the crown of Glasgow's reputation as one of the leading modern cities, there was Charles Rennie Mackintosh's celebrated building for the Glasgow School of Art. Mackintosh's masterpiece was opened at the turn of the century, just as Glasgow's role as the second city of the Empire was beginning to wane with the decline of Britain's imperial and commercial power. From then on the cultural reputation of the city increasingly lost out to its popularly conceived image as a culturally inhospitable urban wasteland, where only artists of exceptional social and artistic commitment, such as Joan Eardley, could produce modern painting of the highest quality.

By the time Joan Eardley died in the early 1960s, Glasgow was spinning into a spiral of chronic urban decay. Only drastic measures seemed the solution to the city's plight, and so the civic fathers eagerly turned to the utopian culture of modern architecture and town planning for their salvation. Mass population deportation, the likes of which had not been witnessed since the Highland clearances, was imposed on Glasgow's urban working population, who were lured and transported to the Brave New World of the highrise housing scheme ghettos dotted around the city perimeter. This then allowed the historic town centre to be gutted and turned into an eight-lane motorway. Thus the heart of this great metropolis was ripped out in the name of progress, or as the cynics thought, political and economic expediency; and one cannot help thinking that Eduardo Paolozzi might have had Glasgow in mind when he wrote in black despair, 'Modernism is the acceptance of the concrete landscape and the destruction of the human soul.'

Very rapidly the modernist dream solution was shown to be a mirage, which quickly turned into a terrifying nightmare with many parts of the sprawling urban mass becoming crime-infested no-go areas. Thus yet again the city fathers were urgently required to find a new way of reinventing the image of Glasgow but which did not involve further discredited social engineering, or too much cost. To this end the Labour-controlled council reversed its traditional anti-art and culture stance and now looked to support the usually neglected area of cultural amenities by heavily promoting the museums and art galleries of the city.

Throughout the 1980s and early 1990s there were a number of crucial players in the miraculous project of transforming Glasgow from 'No Mean City' into UK Garden City and then triumphantly European City of Culture 1990. Undoubtedly a central figure in all this was the powerful leader of the council later to become Lord Provost, Pat Lally. It was he who gave full backing to the various ambitious schemes of the English-imported Director of Glasgow Museums, Julian Spalding, by setting aside a separate art purchasing budget of £3,000,000 at the Director's discretion, and supporting Spalding's pet idea to establish a Glasgow Gallery of Modern Art (GOMA). One of the reasons why such high profile civic enterprises could be achieved in the 1980s and early 1990s was that under successive Tory Governments Scotland remained loyal to Labour, thus becoming disenfranchised and unable to represent itself politically as a nation. Thus it fell to the Scottish cities, and especially Glasgow, to fill this sociopolitical vacuum by attempting (not always successfully) to identify with the creative forces within the civic community and encourage a strong sense of distinctive cultural identity.

These creative forces were most spectacularly represented by the young artists emerging from the Glasgow School of Art in the 1980s. The reasons which brought about this phenomenal success are complex, but their achievement in relation to their native city is more easy to discern. The New Glasgow Boys – Steven Campbell, Peter Howson, Ken Currie Adrian Wiszniewski *et al* – were part of a worldwide art fashion which returned contemporary art to figurative painting and pictorial narrative. Thus these new boys on the block were uncontaminated by discredited Modernism and appeared to speak in a visual language that was immediately accessible to the ordinary citizens of Glasgow.

This was particularly true of Howson and Currie who drew their subjects and inspiration from the street life and political histories of the working-class community. Furthermore both used a raw aggressive pictorial idiom which seemed to echo west-coast Scottish urban patois. This particularly applied to Howson, who soon became court painter to the New Image Glasgow, his work being eagerly sought out and promoted by Lally and his museum director. Spalding, identifying himself as a man of the people, but with distinctive Thatcherite overtones, enthusiastically praised Howson on the way his 'paintings and drawing celebrated the struggle of *individual* lives' (my italics) and how 'he often depicted the struggle as heroic'. All these eulogies were a clear reference to Howson's most celebrated work *The Heroic Dosser* (1987), which presents a Glasgow hardman tramp straining to rise out of the gutter of his ruined life and slum environment. Not surprisingly this macho image became the unofficial icon of the newly regenerated Glasgow and complemented the ad-men's soft, cuddly Mister Blob of the *Glasgow's Smiles Better* campaign.

While Howson quickly became the city fathers' favourite artistic son, Currie's art was much more problematic and difficult to accommodate into Glasgow's official publicity image-making schemes. Unlike Howson, Currie was a politically committed artist and in the 1980s was a member of the Communist Party. Thus he was identified and supported by those who were deeply suspicious, if not downright antithetical to the populist art policies of the Labour-controlled city council. At this time Currie's most important patron was Elspeth King, the curator of the People's Palace, which is Glasgow's own local history museum and which was relatively neglected compared to the money being lavished on the Burrell and Kelvingrove Galleries in the more suburban parts of the city. King commissioned Currie to produce an epic mural history of the Scottish Labour movement in the same year as Howson's *Noble Dosser*. Currie's magnum opus was the first major public art work in Scotland to treat seriously such a central aspect of the nation's modern social and historical experience. Needless to say, it created a great deal of controversy, clearly marking the deep divisions between the various left and right-wing forces attempting to capture the heart of the city and promote the authentic voice of the people of Glasgow. The civic war eventually led to a showdown between King and Spalding who, with the might of Lally's backing, enforced, like something out of a Greek tragedy, the banishment of the People's Palace champion from the city altogether.

The highly politicised artistic policy of Lally and Spalding achieved its full, if hollow, triumph in 1996 with the much fanfared opening of GOMA. Art critics from all over were bussed, all expenses paid, to witness this important occasion. Spalding's accompanying self-congratulatory publication *Gallery of Modern Art Glasgow* laid out his approach and attitude to art and civic society in an unequivocal manner. He dismissed 'the vacuousness of so much modern art' and triumphantly announced 'Modern art is, I think, over.' For Spalding contemporary art, or at least the stuff he bought for Glasgow, was 'made by people for people'. Unfortunately such unabashed populist sentiments cut little ice with the hard-nosed London critics who were scathing in their attacks on the mediocre quality and undistinguished presentation of Glasgow's contemporary art collection. Furthermore, not being a very popular figure himself with the art community of Glasgow, few rushed to Spalding's defence, and adding further insult to injury the city's own paper, *The Herald*, allowed their critic, Claire Henry, to write a damning piece entitled 'A Sour Taste', which ended by pointing out the seeming falseness of his egalitarian posturing:

Some gallery directors put the artist first. Inspired directors involve their staff and welcome dealers, middle men, anyone and everyone – but especially the local art community. Spalding has already made sure that GOMA is 'his' museum; and the book 'his' book. Thus the blame for an inappropriate display and exceedingly poor book can be laid at his door too.

Yet in many ways by the time GOMA opened in the mid-1990s it had already become irrelevant to the pressing issues of how contemporary art serves the civic community. Relevant public art was certainly not what was bought on the personal whim of individual publicly funded patronage and stuck in a local museum. Now if art wished to serve the community it had to find a way to allow artists to engage directly with the lives and urban environment of the city's diverse populous.

As was the norm with most declining post-industrial urban areas, Glasgow had been severely subjected to the most conspicuous aspects of the public art projects in the 1970s and 1980s, with the ubiquitous gable-end mural appearing to be slapped on every run-down housing block in the city. This attempted aestheticising intervention was however usually resented by many in the local community, as famously exemplified by the graffiti defiantly scrawled across a public mural in the Partick area: 'The artist's work is all in vain, The Tiny Partick strike again.' Such artistic missionary work was clearly failing, equally for the residents and the artists involved. This sense of failure was one of the reasons for the setting up of the Environmental Art department at Glasgow School of Art in 1986, which took as its guiding principle that 'the context is half the work'. Now young artists keen to practise their work outside the traditional gallery space and in the social civic domain were trained to engage in a long period of preparatory field research. Thus the development and final formation of their site-specific work had to grow out of a sustained dialogue between their own creative intentions and the requirements of the local environment and community which they were to serve.

Over the last two decades young artists in Glasgow have become increasingly independent of controlling institutional support and more involved with collective, self-sustaining action. In fact they have become their own local community within the city, running their own galleries, studio spaces and generating and developing their own public art projects in collaboration with facilitating, consultative agencies such as Glasgow Visual Art Projects. Now those seriously involved in public art projects fully realise that neither Modernism, in the guise of a generalised, utopian formalist art, nor populism, with its bland folksy insincerity, can be allowed to intervene and impose an all-embracing aesthetic solution to the particular pressing problems of contemporary urban life. Each public space is resistant to certain approaches and accommodating to others. Nothing should be easily taken for granted, and everything involved is 'the contested process of place-making', as Joanna Spark points out in her *Artists as Researchers*.

In that essay Spark also raised the contentious question on which to end; 'Does it matter if people in the community do not understand the "language" used by artists to articulate place?' This, in the area of public art, brings us back to the debate on which we opened – that between the language and status of contemporary art and popular local culture. However, this apparent gulf in artistic and communal communication can be bridged by responsive artists, especially those working in the area of text-based art. Two excellent examples of this practice are the work of Jackie Donachie, a graduate of Glasgow School of Art's Environmental Art Department, and the internationally acclaimed Turner Prize Winner Douglas Gordon. For instance Donachie, in her *Great Western Road* project (1990), sensitively adapted and targeted her work for those working people in the city who are reliant on public transport, by installing texts on the roofs of bus shelters so that they could only be read from the upper decks. Her cryptic slogans, although in familiar ad-speak, addressed local issues; the concerns, dreams and desires of those living, working and regularly passing through that particular urban environment.

To date the most successful piece of public art produced for Glasgow is Douglas Gordon's *Empire* (1999). Although sited in the heart of the city's thronging shopping precinct this enigmatic work is again, like that of Donachie, off the beaten track, tucked away in a narrow alley off Argyle Street. The work itself is disturbingly yet also intriguingly simple – merely a piece of neon signage forming the word EMPIRE, but presented in its mirror-image form and attached to reflective plates on a bare brick wall. It is placed fairly high up and, having to compete with a cluster of pub signs on the other side of the lane, one can easily miss it altogether. However, once discerned *Empire* opens up layers of collective and personal associations – from the universal culture of Hollywood cinema, à la Hitchcock's *Vertigo,* to the avant-garde films of Andy Warhol, to the imperial history of Glasgow's role as second city of the Empire, through to the local popular culture of the famous *Glasgow Empire* music hall. In this very successful contemporary world of public art Gordon subtly negotiates a space and form in which the city can express the multifarious nature of its histories and people.

The official and popular ownership of a city is a complex and highly contested, ongoing process. Each political movement, each community and each citizen needs to find a language, a voice, a set of images and texts to represent their place and role within their ever-changing urban environment. No British city has involved itself more in this daunting quest for a revised and relatively contemporary civic identity than Glasgow. The struggle may have been a long and highly contested one, yet it does clearly demonstrate the passion and commitment that Glaswegians have for their beloved city.

This essay was published in *Dumbing Down: Culture: Politics and the Mass Media* (ed. Ivo Mosley, Imprint Academic, UK, USA) in 2000.

BEYOND APPEARANCES

Painting and Picturing in Scottish Modern and Contemporary Art

Beyond Appearances is a broad wideranging exhibition which will present and visually examine some of the different ways Scottish art has reacted and contributed to international Modernism. This major thematic exhibition of around 50 works will focus on the distinctive relationship Scottish painting developed with such important movements in modern and contemporary art as Realism, Expressionism, Symbolism, Abstraction, Surrealism and Conceptionalism. In particular *Beyond Appearances* will seek to look at the complex ways in which Scottish artists and their public responded to the perceived nature and purpose of figuration and abstraction in the overall development of modern and contemporary art. These various artistic attitudes and creative strategies involved 'painting' on the one hand – where increasingly the medium took on a much more significant role – and 'picturing' on the other – where new ways of critical interpretation were required – to grasp the significance of the innovative practices of the avant-garde. Thus *Beyond Appearances* is as equally concerned with the conditions and processes of making modern and contemporary Scottish art, as with appreciating and aesthetically evaluating the finished art object.

The wide array of works in *Beyond Appearances* will span over a century of Scottish art, beginning with the early developments of Modernism in painting at the end of the 19th century. The exhibition will open with the art of the first Scottish modern master, William McTaggart and his elemental, near-abstract seascapes; then will move on to the use of decorative symbolism, found in the work of some of the Glasgow Boys and in the Edinburgh and Glasgow arts and crafts movement. Before the First World War a few Scottish artists also became seriously involved in continental Modernism. These included JD Fergusson, based in Paris at the time, SJ and WW Peploe; the Cubo-Futurist, Stanley Cursiter; and Duncan Grant, who may have painted the first truly abstract picture in Britain. After the traumatic horrors of World War 1 Scottish artists in the inter-war years tended to distance themselves from radical Modernism. The two notable exceptions to this evasive trend, both of whom worked outside Scotland, were William McCance and William Johnstone. The latter was the major pioneer of surrealist biomorphic abstraction in British painting and was equally significant as the English sculptors Henry Moore and Barbara Hepworth.

After 1945 a remarkable number of Scottish artists were at the forefront of the post-war British avant-garde movement and *Beyond Appearances* will feature the innovative work of this important generation of radical artists, including William Gear, Alan Davie, Eduardo Paolozzi, William Turnbull, Joan Eardley, Wilhelmina Barns-Graham, Margaret Mellis and the later paintings of William Johnstone. The exhibition will then move on to the artists who emerged during the revolutionary upheavals of the 1960s and '70s. These will involve for example, the London Scots abstractionists – John McLean, Fred Pollock, Alan Gouk and Colin Cina – as well as the arch champion of figurative Expressionism during this period, John Bellany. In this section there will also be included the challenging 'painting' of Boyle Family, a 'performance' piece by Bruce McLean, one of John Kirkwood's Bulkheads, a Saltmarsh study by Glen Owin and a sea piece by Liz Ogilvie.

The last section of *Beyond Appearances* will visually examine how painting has strategically managed to survive and prosper in a period of alternative mediums, when many thought that it was dead and buried. For instance Scottish abstraction is very much a feature of the contemporary art scene, and this can be broadly divided by painterly technique. On the one side, there are the gestural practitioners like Iain Robertson, Russell Colombo and Hock-Aun; and, on the other, there are the exponents of hard-edge practice, such as Alan Johnson, Ken Dingwell and Calum Innes. By contrast there have also been recent painters (this time mainly female) who have still retained strong links with figuration, but have felt obliged to utilise the pictorial language of abstraction for expressive effect. This final group of artists will include Barbara Rae, Eileen Lawrence, Joyce Cairns, Gwen Hardie, Alison Watt as well as a recent work by Ken Currie.

Hugh MacDiarmid, the most fervent advocate of international Modernism in 20th century Scottish literature, championed the challenging phrase 'Caledonian Antisyzygy' to describe the fractured and contradictory nature and history of Scottish culture. This critical perception could equally be applied to Scottish modern and contemporary art. *Beyond Appearances* aims to bring together a rich array of contrasting responses from Scottish artists to the various demands on the practice and art of painting during the age of modernity. Out of these contrasting antitheses – figuration and abstraction, realism and symbolism, the serious and the absurd, the sacred and the profane, the beautiful and the grotesque – there emerges some kind of synthesis which transcends beyond historical appearances and puts us in receptive contact with a deeper universal experience where we all can…

> see the Infinite,
> And Scotland in true scale to it
> Hugh MacDiarmid, *A Drunk Man Looks at the Thistle* (1926)

This essay was written for the catalogue to the exhibition, *Beyond Appearances: Painting and Picturing in Scottish Modern and Contemporary Art*, shown at the City Art Centre, Edinburgh in 2007.

Throwing Light on the Scottish Endarkenment
Art and Unreason 1945 to Present

WHEN MY CO-CURATOR, and long-time colleague at The University of Edinburgh, Andrew Patrizio and I came up with this title of *The Scottish Endarkenment* for our Dovecot Gallery exhibition at this year's Edinburgh Festival, we imagined that we had created a provocative and intriguing neologism for our own specific purpose. It turns out however, that the concept – 'to endarken' – goes way back to an archaic semantic source. With such ancient psychological origins it is not so surprising then that we have had such a widespread enthusiastic response to our plans for this exhibition. As soon as we mentioned the proposed title of our exhibition everyone, for whatever reason, seemed to 'get it'. It is as though we have unconsciously tapped into those shared – yet still vague and amorphous – desires and fears at the core of the Scottish psyche. Even now after putting this exhibition together *The Scottish Endarkenment* is still very much open to a variety of tentative and speculative suggestions and interpretations as to what it might mean. It may help however, if we begin by examining – and making some critical comparisons with its assumed antithesis – the firmly established and universally acknowledged Scottish Enlightenment.

Most have heard of The Scottish Enlightenment and have some idea what that stands for within Scottish social history. Historically it is usually placed sometime after the Union of 1707 when Scotland became an integral part of the newly established British state. This was a period of radical and irreversible change when Scotland rapidly moved from being a predominately rural and religious community into becoming a modern secular society. This was most clearly demonstrated as the power of education moved away from Church parish school control to that of the universities where humanist philosophic debate and empirical scientific experimentation began to challenge theological authority and ecclesiastical tradition. In philosophical terms this revolution was inspired and guided by the writings of David Hume, yet it was the economic theories of Adam Smith in his *An Enquiry into the Nature and Causes of the Wealth of Nations* (1776) which had a much greater direct impact on the everyday lives of most Scots. Smith's ideas, when subsequently turned into practical reality, would soon lead to the seismic impact of the Industrial Revolution on an expanding and mobile Scottish society of fast-growing large cities and towns where wealth was now generated by a vast interconnected system of mechanised production. As a result the Scottish nation found itself at the forefront of the impact of innovative technology and commercial practice, rapidly becoming a major contributor to the industrial, trading and economic triumph of Great Britain and the imperial power of its vast global empire.

While the intellectual ideas, the scientific rigour and technological achievements of the Scottish Enlightenment have always been held in high esteem, there have also been those who have taken a much more sceptical – even hostile – view of its rationalistic ideology and materialistic achievements. Since the 18th century there has been a growing feeling amongst a number of important and influential Scots that many of our inherited moral and social values – and even our common humanity – have been irredeemably damaged and possibly lost in the pursuit of the Enlightenment's more mundane aim of the pursuit after material progress and monitory profit. These warning voices which have echoed right down to the present can be found both in the sciences and the arts.

In the area of sociology for instance, Thomas Carlyle, from his early polemical essay *Signs of the Times* (1829), was deeply concerned with the deteriorating effect that mass mechanisation ('we have grown mechanical in hand and heart') – and the ruthless pursuit of profit – was having on the ethical and spiritual character of his fellow Victorians and their newly industrialised and urbanised society. Carlyle likened his view of this newly emerging bourgeois capitalist world – where vast wealth for the few came at the expense of vast misery for the many – to 'spreading a nightmare'. At the same time James Hogg, in his profoundly disturbing novel *The Private Memoirs and Confessions of a Justified Sinner* (1824) conjured up another, more psychological 'nightmare' in religious terms. There he revealed and examined a festering layer of the perverted Calvinist psyche which had not been touched, let alone altered, by Enlightenment rationality. Rather, 'the return of the repressed' was still ominously lying in wait to burst out with all its fanatically destructive vengeance. This dark romantic gothic tale had a profound effect on John Bellany for instance, as seen in his highly disturbing imaginative portrait of Hogg as *The Ettrick Shepherd* (1967) which vividly conjures up the unsettling nature of psychological duality between the good and the bad shepherd. Towards the end of the 19th century Robert Louis Stevenson in his universally acclaimed *The Strange Case of Doctor Jekyll and Mr Hyde* (1886) picked up on both Carlyle and Hogg. His Manichean horror fable satirises enlightened Victorian society's cringing submission to the omnipotent authority of reason and science, and its blindness to the inner dangers which stalk and threaten its misplaced sense of security. Furthermore, the pioneering anthropologist James Frazer in his immensely influential *The Golden Bough* (1890) further revealed that primordial non-rational forces of primitive superstition and magic were still lurking just behind the fragile mask of civilisation in Western society. This is most succinctly visualised in Douglas Gordon's photographic double self-portrait *Monster* (1995/6), where with only a few pieces of sticky tape his appearance can be changed from the seemingly normal to the abjectly grotesque. Yet, appearances aside, one is still obliged to ask, which is the actual monster and where is the monstrous to be found?

More recently another Scot, the radical psychiatrist RD Laing in his celebrated cult classic study of schizophrenia in modern society *The Divided Self* (1960) gives a factually researched endorsement to RL Stevenson's fictionalised account of the disastrous effects that the suppressive tyranny of Enlightenment scientific dogma can have on the individual human mind in particular and institutionalised society in general. The highly visceral work of Lys Hansen in her *Divided Self Trilogy* (1985) powerfully expresses the impact that psychological schism and social suppression – especially on women – can have in a most violent manner.

Many Scottish scientists and writers have continued to use their knowledge and imagination to question and rile against what they see as the dangerous ideals and aims of much of the Enlightenment project which, for them, has pushed the world towards one near-apocalyptic disaster after another. On the other hand however, Scottish visual artists have until recently mainly avoided such a questioning and critical position in their work. The reasons for this are complex, but if we return to the Scottish Enlightenment, David Hume might be of some assistance in speculating why this might be. Hume famously declared in his *Treatise of Human Reason* (1740) that, 'Reason is, and ought only to be, the slave of the passions...' Yet instead of a hierarchical relationship between reason and passion as Hume suggests, most Scots have however, contrived to keep them well apart, if not totally separate. Thus reason has been designated to deal with the important practical affairs of life – such as scientific technology and commercial enterprise – while passionate feelings have been either totally suppressed, or only allowed to manifest themselves through the less necessary agency of the arts – usually in a safe and sentimental way. Hence, Scottish visual art has been regarded by its patrons and its public as mainly a convenient vehicle for escape from the harsh realities of modern industrial and urban life. This manifested itself in the 19th century through the ubiquitous nostalgic Highland landscape with not a trace of modern Scotland in sight; or in the 20th century, by the studio-bound claustrophobic still life in the regulation modernistic *belle peinture* style. That at least was mainly the case up until the Second World War, but as we have set out to show in our exhibition of *The Scottish Endarkenment*, since 1945 there has certainly been a marked change in the nature and attitude of progressive Scottish art. A new serious sense of purpose and awareness began – and still continues – to fire the ambitious post-war Scottish artists. They have immensely broadened their cultural and artistic horizons and have become a notable feature in the international art scene.

Many of the earliest artists in our exhibition were involved in the war effort and saw first-hand the devastating after-effects of the conflict. The 1940/50s brutalist sculptures of Eduardo Paolozzi and William Turnbull bear witness to the traumatic memories of the war years – as does Joyce Cairns' more recent *Shoes from Majdanek* (2002–03) as a reminder of the Holocaust's unspeakable crimes against humanity. Furthermore, the nuclear threat of total annihilation that emerged with the Cold War – and still continues into our precarious present – is addressed by a number of artists. These include Paolozzi again, with his *Mr Cruikshank* (1950) named after a robotic dummy created in the MITS laboratories to test the human capacity to withstand radiation, Ian Hamilton Finlay's memorial relief sculpture, ominously entitled *Et in Arcadia Ego* (1976) – usually translated as 'Even I, Death, am in Paradise' – and Kenny Hunter's tabletop atomic mushroom, ironically entitled *I Love Rapid Change* (2005) – is a satirical reminder that though nuclear weaponry may seem more controlled and invisible, the threat of total annihilation has not gone away, despite our convenient amnesia. Of course what concentrates our minds in our present troubled times are the spectacular violent terrorist attacks on our cities and their citizens, and John Kirkwood's awesomely prescient series of photomontages *Capital of Capital* (1987–90) are much too close to current events for complacent comfort.

Other selected artists – in their own distinctive ways – take up Thomas Carlyle's dire warnings concerning the consequences of the overtly materialistic nature of our career-obsessed and consumer-driven contemporary society. Matthew Ingles' (1985) ladder of *Success* turns the pursuit of that tantalising and elusive glittering prize into a fetishist object of desire for which we might be prepared to perform any humiliating stunt to gain its approval and reward. Similarly Beagles and Ramsay in their specially commissioned work *Parallel Incremental Sophistication (All Hail the New)* (2016) have created a man-made tyrannical god satirising our world of endemic consumerism and the ubiquitous supermarket which has now become our designated place of ritual devotion and worship.

The complex relationship between the material and the spiritual, the rational and the irrational at the heart of James Frazer's anthropological studies in *The Golden Bough* acknowledges the continuing power of superstition and magic which is still a force that we rashly ignore or intellectually dismiss at our peril. Alan Davie releases these primordial forces from our collective psyche, in his explosive *Woman Bewitched by the Moon No. 2* (1956). Unlike the Apollonian Enlightenment, the Scottish Endarkenment is illuminated by a lunar, rather than a solar, light. This form of illumination, popularly associated with madness, lupine transformation, and female hysteria induced by Selene, the moon goddess is witnessed not only by Davie, but also in a different manner, by women artists such as Pat Douthwaite in her moonstruck *Dancing Nude* (1973), and with Georgia Horgan's embroidered textile work *Witch Hunting Accusations* (2015).

A gigantic moon hovers over the goddess of wisdom's northern Athenian citadel in Jock McFadden's *Calton Hill* (2014). In this painting the minuscule architecture below – the Observatory, the classical temple buildings and monuments to the great men of the Scottish Enlightenment are bathed in a ghostly lunar aura. In contrast a very different nocturnal view of the Calton Hill is presented in Peter Thomson's *Little Foxes* (2009). Hidden in the shadows cast by those worthy emblems of intellectual authority and establishment respectability, all kinds of nefarious and frightening activities are ruthlessly pursued by the suppressed forces of sexual attraction and repulsion within the Scottish divided self and its society. It would appear thus that the visionary utopian society of mutual understanding and integration as envisaged by the optimistic idealists of the Scottish Enlightenment is sadly still a pipe dream.

For most, the Scottish Enlightenment embodies such qualities as reason, clarity, mathematical order, moderation, certainty and a belief in the human capacity to understand and direct the historical process to a mutually beneficial future. *The Scottish Endarkenment*, on the other hand, is deeply involved with passion, mystery, organic growth, excess, necessary doubt and a faith in the power of myth to connect us with our authentic selves. Yet these two contrasting aspects of human thought and feeling need not be seen as antipathetically opposed to each other. In nature – as in art – they are there to combine and create the *chiaroscuro* by which we make visual sense of the world and our relationship to it. *The Scottish Endarkenment* therefore, is just as vitally necessary as its enlightened counterpart to define and enrich our individual wellbeing and give us a fuller understanding of ourselves and the world we have created for ourselves.

This essay was published in *Scottish Art News* (issue 25, 2016) to accompany the exhibition *The Scottish Endarkenment: Art and Reason 1945 to the Present*, shown at the Dovecot Studios, Edinburgh in 2016.

SCOTTISH ARTISTS IN VENICE

WHEN THE PHRASE 'Scottish Art Home and Abroad' comes up, Venice does not usually spring to mind; rather, it is other great cities of culture – Rome or Paris – that more readily seem to fit the bill. In the 18th century for instance, the Scottish aristocratic Grand Tourist looked mainly on Venice as merely a pleasurable – in many cases as an erotic – diversion. It was in the Eternal City that the high aesthetic desires and needs of that 'culture vulture' were fulfilled. Needless to say to meet such demanding aspirations there was a whole colony of eager young Scots artists on call in Rome, where the all-powerful Gavin Hamilton was at the centre of an international network of artistic promotion and patronage. Later, in the 19th/20th centuries, it was modern city of Paris who took over as the major artistic attraction for young aspiring Scottish artists. This is borne out for example, by the fact that a whole generation – from The Glasgow Boys to post-war Scottish artists – made for the French capital. For instance both William Gillies and Jack Knox attended at one time or another, Andre Lhote's Parisian studio academy in the later 20th century.

In order to draw the attention of the wider world back to the city, Venice established the first Biennale in 1895 and since then, its reputation has grown immensely throughout the international art scene. It is not surprising then that Venice was very determined to reinstate as quickly as possible its hard-won artistic and curatorial status after the hiatus of the Second World War. This they succeeded in doing by 1948 and over the next decade or so the Venice biennale became an important launching stage for the international careers of three Scottish modern artists – Alan Davie (1920–2014), Eduardo Paolozzi (1924–2005) and William Turnbull (1922–2012).

Alan Davie had attended Edinburgh College of Art and was awarded his Diploma in 1940. After his war service however, he was unsure what direction his creative life would take –whether it would be poetic, artistic or musical. In 1948 however, an Andrew Grant travelling scholarship allowed him, and his new wife and constant companion Bili, to visit the great art centres of Europe. This richly rewarding experience was to have a profound and lasting effect on Davie.

In April 1948 Davie set off on his own personal grand tour of European culture in a very defiant and iconoclastic frame of mind, as seen from his letters and journal of the time. Of the art scene in London for example he dismissively wrote 'that which I am seeking is not here... what a mass of ugly rubbish on show under the name of Art.' Furthermore, when he got to Italy he was equally unimpressed by Renaissance and Baroque art and architecture – of St Peters in Rome he declared 'words cannot express my horror on seeing this wonder of the world. I can only say that it is the most hideous of monstrosities ever thrown up by mankind' – harsh words indeed! To find the inspiration he was desperately after Davie needed to seek out a different kind of art and he discovered this in the form of the mosaic religious icons to be found in the Venetian churches. For him such works were not sullied by the insidious fakeries of Renaissance and Baroque pictorial illusionism. These early Christian images by contrast were created through the open display and flat patterning of the mosaic medium, where form and background were as one, holding the holy imagery within an eternal vision. Davie's own inspired response to such visual mysticism can be seen in such powerful work as his radiant *The Saint* (1948).

Davie's visit to Venice coincided with the Biennale of 1948 where, through the auspices of the great American patron Peggy Guggenheim, he had his first opportunity to see recent American painting – including the work of Jackson Pollock. The Biennale's wide-ranging display of modern art was so mesmerising for the young Scottish painter that according to his journals he visited it seven times and wrote that 'at last I can say that my whole life is completely absorbed in art and painting.' This outburst of creative activity resulted in Davie having his first exhibition in Florence in September and another in Venice at the Galeria Sandri in November/December 1948. Well received critically in the local art press, the second show drew the attention of none other than the great modern art patroness, Peggy Guggenheim herself. She initially thought Davie's paintings were the work of an unknown American artist, and was so impressed that she purchased one work, *Music of the Autumn Landscape* (1948) for her peerless collection of 20th century art. Even more of a boost for Davie's burgeoning career was her recommendation to seek out a highly regarded London gallery which resulted in the first of his many exhibitions at Gimpel Fils in September 1950. Furthermore, though the Guggenheim connection Davie later visited the USA in 1956, where he met up with most of the major Abstract Expressionists, and also had his first American exhibition at Catherine Viviano Gallery, from which MOMA purchased *Magic Box* (1955). As a homage and token of his gratitude he felt towards his first patron Davie entitled one of his most important early works *Peggy's Guessing Box* (1950–52).

Like Alan Davie, when Eduardo Paolozzi and William Turnbull finished their war service and set out on their post-war artistic careers they were similarly disappointed with the art scene in Britain. In an interview for *Scottish Art News* in 2013 Turnbull told me, 'When I got demobbed I enrolled at the Slade. It was one of the biggest let-downs I had experienced. So I went to Paris because I wasn't interested in the artists in London, I was interested in the artists in Paris.' There in the late 1940s he shared a studio with Paolozzi and both had access to meeting, and seeing the work of, the great modern sculptors such as Brancusi, Giacometti and Dubuffet. Naturally such direct contact with these most renowned exponents of modern sculpture had an encouraging effect on the early experimental work of these two young Scottish artists. When they returned to London in 1950 they immediately sought out the circle of the progressive artists and patrons who were linked to the ICA which had been set up by Guggenheim, Roland Penrose and Herbert Read as a centre for progressive and innovative art and ideas.

Paolozzi in particular quickly created an interest in his work and was commissioned for the prestigious Festival of Britain to make his first large public sculpture entitled *Fountain* (1951). More importantly however both Paolozzi (with *Cage, Bird, Forms on a Bow* and *Large Form in Concrete*) and Turnbull (with *Mobile Stabile, Head* and *Horse*) were included amongst the group of new generation sculptors that the British Council chose to represent Great Britain at the Venice Biennale of 1952. This was the famous exhibition *New Aspects of British Sculpture* selected by Herbert Read. For the exhibition catalogue Read wrote his controversial 'Geometry of Fear' essay, implying that this group of young British sculptors were a homogenous movement – all committed to an 'iconography of despair' – which most of them certainly were not! It should be also be pointed out, that the philistinism which Davie and Turnbull noted after the war was still very much a dominant force in British society, as shown by the *Guardian's* art critic who questioned 'why are we sending to Venice the bronze biscuits and plaster pies by William Turnbull and Eduardo Paolozzi?'!

In Venice – on the international art scene – the reaction to the British pavilion was thankfully very different, where for instance, Alfred Barr, renowned director of MOMA, declared it the most powerful display of modern sculpture on show and purchased four works – including one by Paolozzi – who also caught the attention of Guggenheim during his visit to Venice. With this important success and acknowledgement from such powerful figures in the international art world, the British Council was quick to support and sponsor younger emerging artists like Turnbull and Paolozzi by buying their work for their collection and also regularly including them in their worldwide touring exhibitions. Yet at the time he was showing at the 1952 Biennale Turnbull told me himself, he was 'completely broke and working the night shift at a Lyons Maid ice cream factory and couldn't afford to go to Venice.' After that important success however, he was soon offered a teaching position by William Johnstone, Principal at the Central School of Art in London. He then also became – along with Paolozzi – a leading member of the newly formed, and soon to become, the highly influential Independent Group at the ICA, as well as regular exhibitor with the Waddington Gallery. It was the charismatic Paolozzi however, who benefited the most from British Council patronage, resulting in him having the whole of their sculpture pavilion at the Venice Biennale of 1960. This gave him an important opportunity to present a carefully selected group of his 1950s art brut figures, including his forbidding *His Majesty the Wheel* (1958) and *Krokadeel* (1956). This won him the Bright Foundation Award for the best sculptor under 45. Even more significant for his subsequent career Paolozzi met Gabrielle Keiller in Venice. She quickly became his most important patron and collector, and could have on occasions more than 75 Paolozzi sculptures on display in her extensive garden at Kingston Hill, London.

Through the aegis of Edinburgh College of Art Rachel Maclean is now representing Scotland at this year's Venice Biennale and is at a similar stage in her career as these earlier Scottish artists who showed in Venice between the Biennales of 1948 and mid-1950s. Hopefully like them, she will go on to have a major international career. Finally it should also be remembered that it was through the dedication and generosity of collectors like Gabrielle Keiller – and the three artists themselves – with their bequests to the Scottish National Gallery of Modern Art – that we now have access to see and appreciate one of the most outstanding episodes in the history of Scottish modern art.

This essay was published in *Scottish Art News* (issue 27, 2017).

SECTION 3

Essays on Scottish Abstract Painting

MAKARS OF BEAUTY
Scottish Contemporary Abstract Painting

Painting or art generally, as such, with all its technicalities, difficulties and
particular ends, is nothing but a noble and expressive language.
John Ruskin, *Modern Painters*, 1843–60

MAKAR IS THE Scots literary term given to a 'maker' of poetry in the 15th and
16th centuries: the most revered of the Makars were Robert Henryson and
William Dunbar. The term was revived in the 20th century by the leading
Scottish modernist writer, Hugh MacDiarmid to describe those of his fellow
poets who chose to write in Scots rather than modern English. Whether
medieval or modern, what distinguishes the poetic language of the Makars is
its emphatic sense of the opaque materiality and essential tangibility of their
verse. In such work the Makars' words, with their strong sonorous resonance
and visual distinctiveness, are never treated as merely transparent semantic
metaphors through which meaning passes like light passing through clear
glass. On the contrary their approach to language was like that of a maker of
things who skilfully works the material of his or her craft into a well-made
object of touchable beauty.

It could be argued that abstraction more than anything brought the ethos
of the Makar back into the art of Western painting which had been lost since
the end of the Middle Ages. It was the great Renaissance theorist Alberti
who perceptively noted the transparency of post-medieval painting when he
likened it to 'a window on to the world' – but it has to be remembered, that a
window not only protects, but also separates. With emergence of the modern
world and the rise of Modernism, the medium – the material tactile stuff of
paint –now began to reassert itself again as a crucially important collaborating
agency of expression. As Clement Greenberg observed in his essay *Modernist
Painting* of 1961, 'Whereas one tends to see what is in an Old Master before
seeing it as a picture, one sees a Modernist painting as a picture first.' This
undoubtedly is the case with most abstract painting as can immediately
discerned by the works in this exhibition.

All the artists in *Mark of Beauty* are acutely aware – through their deeply
serious attitude and considered approach to their work – of the complex and
shifting relationship between paint as a physical entity, and painting as an act of
communication. At every stage in their demanding practice they are faced with
the challenge – how does the painter negotiate between the dual demands of the
medium and the message. This balancing act has to be achieved in such a way that
something meaningful is created, but never at the expense of the visual means by
which this is achieved. To examine this vitally important dialectic between plastic

form and rhetorical content it is necessary to examine what is meant by the nature and use of language as it is expounded in the art of abstract painting.

All text with aesthetic authority, including painting, is multi-layered and there are at least four distinctive levels of visual language operating within pictorial communication. Firstly, there is what might be termed the subliminal operation of language, which in the case of painting involves its own basic building materials – space, shape, colour, line etc. The early abstractionists founded their faith on the particular ability of abstract art to release the authentic power of this innate language of profound significance and spiritual enlightenment. While the original mystical associations surrounding abstraction have now receded, many contemporary artists, especially those with a strong expressionist emphasis in their painting, create work which seeks to draw upon this fundamental level of visual communication and make direct and visceral impact on the somatic and psychological sensibilities of the viewer.

Language at its secondary level of operation is where we discern different varieties of formalised semantic systems, such as English or Scots in literary and spoken communication. In the visual arts we are also able to identify different languages of painting such as Impressionism and Cubism for example. Interestingly, at one time it was generally thought that abstraction transcended this level of language and it was hoped that it might become the universal Esperanto of artistic expression. That utopian ideal however, has not proved to be the case, and abstraction is now generally regarded as specific artistic language in its own right operating at a secondary level of visual communication. As a consequence viewers need to be practiced and conversant in the language of abstraction, with its own particular pictorial conventions, to be able to respond appropriately to abstract paintings – in the same way as they need to know English in order to understand Shakespeare or Scots to appreciate Dunbar.

At the third level language is found to be much more particular in character than the earlier two. It is here that internal variety and differences within a mode of communication come into being as witnessed for instance by the innumerable variations on spoken 'English' found all over the world. In modern art this can be seen for example in Cubism with the difference in means of formal expression between the analytical and synthetic languages of cubist painting. Within the area of abstraction sub-languages of pictorial articulation have also evolved – gestural action painting as opposed to formal hard-edge composition for instance. In practice most painters are drawn towards their own particular choice of pictorial language through a number of factors such as, personal temperament, artistic education, inspiring influences and the community of fellow practitioners with whom they keep company.

Finally, the fourth level of pictorial language is the most individual and specifically nuanced. It is here that the personal 'voice', 'handwriting' or 'brushwork' of the author/creator is recognised and its unique characteristics are critically examined and aesthetically savoured. At this level the artist's own distinctive style and mode of expression comes to the fore, and it is this particular visual quality which allows us to have a much more appreciative and rewarding experience with a work of art. Being aware and sensitive to these different levels of visual language can allow us to experience a fuller and deeper range of experiences in front of a work of art – from an initial fairly open and instinctive reaction through to a much more focused and intimate relationship in which the painting seems to 'speak' directly to us at a profoundly emotional and psychological level. When something like that does occur then the personal and the pictorial become as one and all four levels of language are in perfect unison with each other.

That being said however, abstract art for some people can still be a difficult challenge – for it can sometimes seem rather overwhelming and disorientating – until you have found your critical bearings and developed an approach which suits you best. Through this process it is hoped that *Mark of Beauty* will in the end be an enjoyable and rewarding experience for the attentive and responsive viewer of this exhibition. The highly creative and accomplished work of the seven artists involved allows for a pertinent and hopefully comprehensive appreciation of the range and variety of contemporary Scottish abstract painting. The grouping of these abstract painters, who are at different career stages – from early to mature – in their artistic development, reveals significant similarities and decided differences in their approach and practice. For instance the commonalities – such as their application of pigment and gesture technique – to be found in all their work are mostly linked to the two primary levels of the pictorial language of painting as outlined above. On the other hand the recognisable marks of a distinctive style and unique personal vision in each of the individual artist's work – in the way they arrange compositional space and create colour harmonies for instance – are the outcome of their sophisticated and highly skilful articulation of the two superstructures of pictorial language.

As with the inherited visual language of painting which these artists draw upon, their own work is also multi-layered in its power of expression, and thus can be appreciated in a variety of different ways depending on what the viewer brings to each aesthetic encounter. Yet it has to be remembered however, that for all this talk of language, the authentic experience of true painting – and this especially applies to abstraction – is not translatable into words. No more than poetry can be turned into prose without great loss to its unique power of expression – so too with the visual arts. Complex works of art – such as the paintings in *Mark of Beauty* – are never mere vehicles for semantic meaning or conceptual interpretation. By their arresting and engaging presence, they contain and convey their own significant ethos within themselves through the process of their own making. Furthermore, that significance must be true to itself and so unconditionally visual; for any such meaningful experience always has to be an aesthetic revelation.

This catalogue essay was written for the exhibition *Mark of Beauty* shown at the Union Gallery, Edinburgh in 2012.

THE BEHOLDER AND THE BEHELD
A Philosophical Approach to Scottish Modern Painting

Beauty is taken from the idea raised in us.
Francis Hutcheson, *Inquiry* (IX, 34), 1725

*The sentiments of men often differ with regard to beauty and deformity of all
kinds, even while their general discourse is the same.*
David Hume, 'Of the Standard of Taste', 1757

*It is therefore contrary to the universal sense of mankind that…'beauty is not
really in the object, but merely a feeling in the person who is said to perceive it'.*
Thomas Reid, 'Beauty and Common Sense', 1764

ALTHOUGH THE GERMAN philosophers such as Baumgarten, Kant,
Schopenhauer and Hegel are usually given the credit for founding the ongoing
discourse on modern and contemporary aesthetics, it was the Scots literati
who were also the pioneers in this particular area of intellectual and critical
enquiry. The most important and influential writers in this field included
the three major Scotch philosophers – Francis Hutcheson, David Hume and
Thomas Reid. By looking at their ideas and writings on beauty and taste we
all should become more enlightened 'beholders' in the never-ending argument
over whom – and for what reasons – should be granted the power to award
the laurel crown to the beauty of their choice. For as both Pierre Bourdieu and
Terry Eagleton in recent times have convincingly argued, beauty is as much a
social class and ideological issue as an aesthetic one in what might otherwise
be called the tyranny of taste.

A philosophical interest in the ways works of art impact on human
sensibilities and attitudes goes at least back to the writings of the Ancients
– most notably in Plato's *Republic* and Aristotle's *Poetics*. With the coming
of the Christian era however, the issue of aesthetics was forced to take
up a secondary position in relation to ethics and theology within Western
discourse until it returned to the philosophical agenda with the Renaissance,
and even more so with the emergence of the Enlightenment. This early
modern secular era in the 18th century was established by the new scientific
rational investigations into our world and its place in the universe by natural
philosophers such as Isaac Newton. Newton's empirical method of enquiry
undoubtedly had a profound influence on the philosophical and scientific
ambitions and approaches of the major Scottish Enlightenment figures,
including the philosophers – Hutcheson, Hume and Reid.

Aiming to break free from what they regarded as the religious extremist
dogma and superstitions of the recent turbulent sectarian religious past these

Scots felt it was now possible to examine the workings of the human mind and senses in the same objective and independent manner as Newton had mathematically traced the movements of the Earth and the planets. Amongst a wide range of different aspects of human and social behaviour all three philosophers were each drawn to examine why certain natural phenomena and man-made objects – especially works of art – can cause us pleasure or displeasure in the beholder.

This idea is well expressed in Hutcheson's early treatise *A Sense of Beauty* where he writes 'it plainly appears that some objects are immediately the occasions of this pleasure of beauty, and that we have senses fitted for perceiving it.' Clearly Hutcheson believes that it is our innate 'sense of beauty' which gives all of us feelings of aesthetic pleasure. Furthermore, without this programmed response in human nature, the experience of beauty would not exist, for he goes on to say, 'Were there no mind with a sense of beauty to contemplate objects, I see not how they could be called beautiful.' Thus for Hutcheson it is not God the Father, or Mother Nature, or even the Artist who creates the sensation of beauty, but some impulse in our make-up which involuntary stimulates our additional 'sixth sense' – almost in an automatic Pavlovian manner. For Hutcheson nature has certain qualities which make us instinctively appreciate its beauty. These qualities are rather vaguely described by him as 'uniformity amidst diversity'. Furthermore these critical attributes should also be sought after by the artist in order to stimulate the pleasure principle in the beholder, who is genetically programmed, rather than culturally conditioned, to respond to such aesthetic experiences.

While Hume read Hutcheson's ideas on these matters with a good deal of interest and sympathy they must have seemed over-imposing and formulaic for his open and tolerant outlook. Hume was seeking an approach to the question of taste and beauty which was more open to democratic discourse, but without falling into discursive anarchy. He presented his own particular perspective on these issues in his greatly influential *Of the Standard of Taste*. Strategically Hume shifted the goalposts in this debate from abstract questions concerning the nature of beauty, to the more social and critical-orientated ones as to why certain works of art are preferred to others. He was looking for an agreed objective standard of aesthetic beauty using the Newtonian 'experimental method of reasoning'. In matters of aesthetic taste however, this was a formidable challenge, for as Hume observed 'the sentiments of men often differ with regards to beauty and deformity of all kinds.' This view is further echoed in Hume's agreement with Hutcheson that 'beauty is no quality in things themselves: it exists merely in the mind which contemplates them: and each mind perceives a different beauty.' This latter statement verges dangerously close to romantic solipsism – 'beauty in the eye of the beholder' syndrome that could easily lead to critical chaos – something which a social utopian like Hume would always try to avoid like the plague. Thus throughout his deliberations on these aesthetic matters Hume needed to steer a careful course between the Scylla of universalism and the Charybdis of individualism in order to reach the calmer waters of communal consensus. The guide for this journey of critical exploration and aesthetic discovery is not The Good Shepherd, but Hume's secular counterpart – The Good Critic.

Hume agreed with Hutcheson that we all possess – to a greater or lesser extent – an aptitude to appreciate aesthetic qualities in works of art. The true aim for Hume however, was not instinctive appreciation, but sound critical judgement which would carry consensus with all art lovers of taste. As might be expected a sizable part of Hume's writing on these matters is taken up with listing the required qualities which were essential to the practice of good criticism. Hume felt that a convincing cultural authority must display the following five attributes for cultivated society to concur with their pronouncements. A good critic first and foremost, must obviously have a 'delicacy of taste' and consequently abhor the grosser attractions of folk and popular culture. Secondly, Hume held that critical judgement was a serious business and needed constant exercise – 'where he is not aided by practice, his verdict is attended with confusion and hesitation.' Thirdly, a good critic needs to be knowledgeable in order to make relevant comparisons with ancient and modern artistic achievements and also between good and bad contemporary art. Fourthly, a good critic's opinions should always be free from any personal prejudice or self-interest – a central issue in Kant's later 'impersonally personal' theory of aesthetics. Finally, the good critic must possess a 'strong sense' in order to present a convincing justification for any aesthetic judgement.

Reid, like his illustrious predecessors, also took a philosophical interest in aesthetic matters and particularly in the visual arts; for instance, writing a treatise *The Craft of Painting*. It is however, in Reid's other major work on aesthetics – *Beauty and Common Sense* that he radically challenges the views of both Hutcheson and Hume. Reid, being an ultra-empiricist, set out to refute Hume's claim that 'beauty and deformity... belong entirely to sentiment'. Reid felt that Hume was too beholden to Cartesian dualism where there is always the tendency to internalise things when in fact they are, according to Reid, to be found in the outside world. For Reid beauty was not an inner sensation of pleasure, but existed in the attributes of the external object itself, and this beauty was perceived and experienced through the senses. According to Reid, when I say for example, that a painting is beautiful I am talking about the painting and not about myself. For as Reid points out in his dig at Hume:

It is contrary to the universal sense of mankind... 'that beauty is not really in the object, but is merely a feeling in the person who is said to perceive it'. Philosophers should be very cautious in opposing the common sense of mankind for when they do, they rarely miss going wrong.

On the whole I find Hutcheson's position too essentialist with its exclusive concentration on our innate responses to aesthetic stimuli and denial of external beauty existing in its own right. Furthermore, although Hume's proposals seem reasonable and balanced in theory, I fear that the power games within the art world can too easily turn and hijack his optimistic aims for more informed, detached aesthetic discourse into a canon of institutional pronouncement and authority over matters of aesthetic quality. It is therefore Reid's common sense phenomenological approach to aesthetics, which is most in accord with my feelings on these matters. Like Reid, I am much more concerned to focus my visual attentions on the work of art itself and be aware of its effect on my sensibilities, rather than evaluating my critical judgements against those of others and the canon of taste. Hume places 'taste' over 'sentiment' – Reid reverses that aesthetic order of values. Reid is committed to the centrality of fundamental consciousness in aesthetics; but, unlike Hutcheson and Hume, that consciousness is not a cerebral deductive process, but a physical embodied experience. Ultimately Reid differs from Hume in that he does not seek out an intellectual engagement with a work of art, but rather, a direct and somatically authentic one. It is interesting to note that Reid's nascent existentialism was fully developed in the 20th century writings on aesthetics by Modernists critics, such as Roger Fry and Clement Greenberg.

This essay was published in *Scottish Art News* (issue 17, 2012) in response to the exhibition, *The Eye of the Beholder* shown in 2012 at the Talbot Rice Gallery, The University of Edinburgh.

A POINT IN TIME – THE ETERNAL NOW
Abstraction in Scottish Modern Painting

I remain intrigued by the fact that it's the four Scots at Stockwell studios…
that are alone in England – if not in all Europe – in bearing down on
painting as a high art.
Clement Greenberg, *Four Abstract Artists*, exhibition catalogue, Fruitmarket Gallery,
Edinburgh, 1977

IT MAY COME as a surprise to many of my fellow Scots – including some of
those who might consider themselves informed 'art lovers' – that there is such
a thing as a history of abstraction in Scottish modern painting. Not that they
are really to be blamed for such a remiss. For there has never been any marked
recognition of this particular history – either through a major publication or
exhibition – focusing exclusively on this distinctive aspect of Scottish modern
art. There have of course been numerous exhibitions and accompanying
catalogues on the work of individual Scottish abstract painters – I have
curated and written some myself. Yet on the whole, their artistic achievements
have been seen in relative isolation, and never within the wider context of a
recognised history of Scottish abstract art. Even with the Scottish National
Gallery of Modern Art's up-and-coming exhibition *A New Era; Scottish Art
1900–50* abstraction will have to take its allotted place alongside a number of
other accompanying modern movements such as Fauvism and Surrealism.

When are we then to be given the opportunity to see, admire and celebrate
the particular nature and specific history of abstraction in Scottish modern
painting? Who knows? My article however, sets out to go some way to rectify
this lamentable neglect and encourage a change in attitude to abstract painting
in this country.

Before starting I think a couple of qualifications are necessary. Firstly,
there will be the purists – including some abstract artists themselves – who
will be unhappy to see abstraction and national identity linked together. In
their favour they could cite Jackson Pollock, who famously argued that you
might as well talk about American mathematics as American abstraction.
For them their fundamental belief that abstraction is a universal – or at
least a Transnational language of communication and expression rejects
any nationalistic colonisation. In response to this; I would point out that
I am careful, as my title shows, not to conflate the two terms – Scottish
and abstraction. Rather my intention here is to trace the broad historical
development of abstract painting – as created by individual artists – without
any ultimate claim that there is such a cultural phenomenon as Scottish
abstract painting – I leave that for others to argue. Secondly, what qualifies

as abstract painting? At its most basic abstract art is non-figurative: this frees the viewer from the pictorial illusionism of perceived reality – what Malevich called 'liberating art from the tyranny of appearance.' This of course does not mean that abstract art is non-representational, it can represent and express, a whole range of experiences – from conceptual ideas to emotional feelings – but in a different manner to that of mimic representation.

One final qualification should also be pointed out between 'hard' and 'soft' abstraction. While all abstract art is non-figurative, 'soft' abstraction can be still tangentially linked to its source of inspiration from nature in the outside world – say through the title for example. On the other hand, 'hard' abstraction is pure and autonomous – 'a realm unto itself governed by its own laws proper to it alone' as Kandinsky claimed. Scottish painters are to be found in both camps.

It was a Scottish artist, William Johnstone, who in the 1920s, did more than any other to introduce and pioneer the art of abstract painting in Britain. As much a radical modernist as his great friend, the poet Hugh MacDiarmid, Johnstone was committed to creating a new mode of painting which would visually complement the poetic innovations of MacDiarmid. Although much of the art of both painter and poet was rooted in the landscape of their native Border hills, they were also committed internationalists. Thus Johnstone's career was one of much travel – constantly going from his homeland and returning to it. Firstly to Paris in the mid-1920s where he came in direct contact with European Modernism. There he encountered and became deeply involved with surrealist biomorphism which allowed him to develop a deeper, more psychological, relationship with his atavistic feeling for landscape. He was later to say – 'I am part of nature and nature is part of me'. Secondly, during the inter-war years, he was one of the first British modern artists to go and work in America, and long before Jackson Pollock, he discovered Native American art and noted commonalities with Pictish/Celtic art – 'When I studied those Indian paintings, so simple, with such depths of intensity in the abstract patterns, I was reminded of the old Scottish and Pictish carved stones.' The abstract paintings which Johnstone evolved from the later 1920s onwards were therefore a rich eclectic mix of modern and ethnic sources. Furthermore, he would work on what was deemed an epic scale for the time with such paintings as *A Point in Time* (1929–37) which critic Paul Overy was later to describe as 'a masterpiece of surrealist-abstraction unrivalled in scale and ambition in British painting in the 1930s'. Johnstone continued to develop his abstract painting throughout his long career, adapting different approaches and experimenting with new techniques, but almost always using nature as his primary source of inspiration.

In the immediate post-war period three Scottish painters shared a similar attitude and approach as Johnstone to their own abstract, or near-abstract, painting. They were Wilhelmina Barns-Graham, Joan Eardley and William Gear. All of them used their experiences of natural phenomenon – be it

metrological or geological – as the starting point for their highly personal
approach to abstract painting. As Barnes-Graham succinctly put it 'I'm very
affected by nature. Nature is a tremendous informer.' Barnes-Graham in
Cornwall and Eardley at Catterline both painted within their chosen costal
environments – the former mainly taking rock formations as the impetus
for much of her work – such as *Glacier Crystal* (1950): while the latter
preferred to confront the sublime power of the North Sea and capture its
awesome force in the bold sweeping gestural brushstrokes of her late abstract
expressionist inspired paintings such as *The Wave* (1961). By contrast Gear,
who reinterpreted the intricacies of Cubism more imaginatively than any other
post-war British artist, sought to capture those intangible aspects of nature –
such as shifting sunlight and shadow – and abstract these fleeting effects into
complex rhythmic patterns of highly coloured decorative compositions in his
dazzling paintings, as seen in such works as *Trellis* (1952).

All the painters covered so far can be seen as 'soft' abstractionists where
– as indicated by their titles – there is a traceable connection between their
paintings and some aspect of the natural world. Alan Davie's work however,
is more problematic, especially from the fact that he did not regard himself as
an abstract artist. Being a mystic – as were all the early pioneers of abstraction
– Davie did not even see himself as an artist at all. He claimed 'I don't practice
painting as an Art but as a means to enlightenment.' On the other hand Davie,
whether consciously or not, drew deeply upon the conventions and language of
post-war abstract painting. In particular Davie's paintings of 1950/60s – when
he was hailed in *The Times* as 'The most remarkable British artist to emerge in
recent years' – were closely associated with surrealist automatism and Abstract
Expressionism. Yet for Davie painting took place within a shamanistic ritual
in which the artist loses all sense of self and becomes a spiritual medium,
through which cosmic forces pass, leaving traces in the form of inchoate
marks, amorphous shapes and archetypal symbols on the canvas stretched out
flat across the studio floor. As Davie exclaimed, 'The work of art seems to be
something thrown off – a by-product of the process of being and working', and
his most powerful paintings do have that raw immediacy of some newly formed
creation just coming into being – such as in *Disintegrating Target* (1960).

Although Alan Davie and William Turnbull were both recruited by
William Johnstone to teach at the Central School of Arts and Crafts in
London in the 1950s there was little love lost between them. In an interview
I did with Turnbull in 2011 – the year before he died – he stated 'Alan Davie
had a very high opinion of himself which I didn't share'. They did however,
share a very open approach to their artistic practice, based on intuition and
improvisation. 'I've never believed in planning what I am going to make' was
Turnbull's working mantra; but while Davie saw pictorial space in cosmic
terms, Turnbull, 'thought about "space" as almost an object.' This material
attitude reflects Turnbull's dual role as sculptor/painter who 'always thought
of the paintings in three dimensions'. After his early highly simplified 'Head'

paintings Turnbull shed the image all together and became a truly 'hard' abstractionist where his 'paintings, after 1957, don't refer to anything else, only to themselves.' Turnbull described his highly innovative and challenging paintings – which are just titled by date and numbers – as 'a dialogue between the artist and his material' where the truly epic scale of his all-over monochrome canvases 'acts outwards into our world'. Turnbull was greatly admired by leading critics such as Lawrence Alloway and Frank Whitford who regarded him as 'a key figure in the development of British painting' in the 1960s.

In the 1960/70s the most serious abstract painting by Scots was carried out in London. Four Scottish abstract painters – Douglas Abercrombie, Alan Gouk, John McLean and Fred Pollock – were all associated with the studios and the important annual exhibitions at the Stockwell Depot, a former brewery in south London. They were each engaged in their different ways with their own individual response to the recent American post-painterly abstraction of Noland and Olitski, but as McLean put it 'They've done their paintings and we ought to be able to do ours, and still acknowledge that what they've done is good.' They were visited in their studios, and, as can be seen by the opening quote of this essay, supported and encouraged by the leading American champion of abstraction at the time – Clement Greenberg. Yet they all were determined to develop their own independent and personal engagement with recent aspects of abstract painting. Gouk for instance, strove in his painting to 'allow colour maximum richness in relation to surface through painterly facture', while Pollock – whose painting was greatly admired by Anthony Caro – took a more 'sculptural' approach – 'my work must contain an illusion of the third dimension, giving a sense of some colours projecting forward from the picture plane and others appearing to recede'. At the same time John Mclean experimented with a range of painting techniques to create a directness of application and lightness of touch that is pure *sprezzatura*. As he said of his work 'There is nothing about my paintings that, if you look hard enough, you cannot see for yourself. They are not obscure. Their directness hides all the hard work.'

Back in Scotland in the 1970s there began to emerge a very different approach to abstract painting. One of the main impulses for this was a strong reaction amongst the Scottish younger artists against the *belle peinture* style which was still a predominated feature of modern painting in Scotland since The Colourists. This new generation of painters had had enough of picturesque landscapes in a sub-fauvist style and sought a radical alternative through minimalist abstract painting. Like Turnbull they wished 'to charge the canvas with maximum meaning through the minimum of means.'

An important exponent of this highly austere and intense approach at that time was Kenneth Dingwall who painted with a limited range of colours – blue, red, black and grey – all of which in his painting alluded to, and evoked, profound emotional associations. Although much of his work appeared to be monochrome, on closer examination, little breaks in the paint revealed layers of different colours underneath the final surface, suggesting hidden depths of complex feeling and profound expression. As the critic Paul Overy wrote 'Dingwall's paintings give little away at first. Meanings seep out of them slowly.'

Another abstract artist from this period who also took a highly pared-down approach to his art was Alan Johnston. Using the simplest of means – pencil markings on a canvas or a wall which were held together within some loose non-Euclidean geometric shape – Johnston's minimal interventionist approach required highly perceptive and sensitive awareness in the attentive viewer. Johnston's fugitive and ethereal art – forever hovering between presence and absence – emanated from a wide range of philosophical and esoteric sources – from Merleau-Ponty's phenomenology to Japanese Zen.

In contrast to Johnston's graphic approach, Callum Innes' art is deeply concerned with revealing the range of physical properties in paint as a material substance. Innes prefers to work in ongoing series which are differentiated by the process of their making and unmaking; for example his *Exposed Paintings* – as the name implies – are as much about removing colour pigment as applying it. There is a high risk element in Innes' art, resulting in the destruction of a notable percentage of his canvases as not up to the required standard of satisfactory execution. Innes' finely balanced approach to painting involves intuition and experimentation, accident and control, yet with the ultimate aim 'to create an image that is somehow natural, that exists in its own right.'

In 1998 Callum Innes was part of a multinational group exhibition shown in Houston's Contemporary Arts Museum which was entitled *Abstract Painting, Once Removed*. The exhibition set out to show that good abstract painting was now being produced, not only in the major art centres like New York or London, but anywhere and everywhere across the globe – even in Scotland! Unlike their predecessors, for instance, Innes, Johnston and Dingwall are based in Scotland. Furthermore there is now a whole generation of younger and emerging artists working in Scotland, who are investigating and extending, in their own individual way, the range and creative possibilities of contemporary abstract painting – from the intriguing organic pictures of *Abstract Critical* prizewinning Zara Idelson to the 'everyday abstraction' of Kevin Harman's double glazing window constructions.

In conclusion it should be asked: has this concise historical survey of abstract painting by Scottish artists – (there could and should be many more excellent painters included) – revealed any unifying features? Yes, I feel that one important common characteristic has emerged. Abstraction for Scottish artists came later than for their European counterparts, and thus, unlike the pioneers of abstract art, the Scots were not touched by the mystical or utopian ideals that dominated the early stages of abstraction. Scottish abstract painters were therefore rarely motivated by Platonic ideals. They were much more Aristotelian in their outlook – less concerned with the transcendental and immutable, more with the immediate phenomenological impact of colours, shapes, textures, and scale on the human senses, what William Turnbull termed the 'eternal now'. For inspiration they preferred to look to nature and their own place in it – even Alan Davie took some of the impetus for his art from flying and swimming – rather than seeking after some otherworldly experience.

The historian Christopher Kissane recently wrote in the *Guardian* that 'Historians must take it upon themselves to increase engagement with broader audiences, spreading awareness of the content, diversity of their subject.' This I feel, equally applies to art historians in particular and art institutions in general. I have not written this article to promote the reputations and careers of these important Scottish abstract painters – individually they hardly need it, as seen from the critical responses quoted throughout. Rather I have been motivated to write this article in order to 'increase engagement with broader audiences' who have still to be given a full and proper opportunity to appreciate the overall history and collective achievement of this important aspect of Scottish modern art.

This essay was publish in *Scottish Art News* (issue 28, 2017).

SECTION 4
Essays on Scottish Figurative Painting

BODY POLITICS

Representation of the Figure in Recent Scottish Painting

Bodies are like time slices through the fabric of social lives; bodies tell a contested political history.
Donna Haraway, *Contested Bodies* (1987)

IN SCOTLAND WHEN we talk about 'union', sex is usually the last thing on our minds. After football, the Union (with a capital letter) is the most contested political issue amongst the Scots. Yet, I would contend that that word – Union – within a sociopolitical British framework, is in fact a contradiction in terms. The whole process surrounding this crucial historical engagement has never created a meaningful cultural 'coming together'; rather it has caused and reinforced deep and lasting divisions. This is clearly and repeatedly revealed in the poetic and pictorial language of the arts. The history of the representation of the figure in Scottish art, for example, bears witness to this.

Many have been surprised by the way that the figure and the body have become such a central theme in recent Scottish art. This is particularly the case with the great upsurge in neo-figurative painting in the 1980s and early '90s, but is now also true of the more recent neo-conceptional work of such Scottish artists as Christine Borland, Julie Roberts and Douglas Gordon. The deconstruction of the social and gender meaning within the representation of the human figure has become a major issue. And although few of these artists have explicitly brought their 'Scottishness' into their creative discourses, I would contend that they are all involved in ideological struggles which lie deep in the Scottish psyche and a long way back into the country's cultural history. As Rosemary Betterton rightly points out, 'These representations of self and others assert, this body, the particularity of this history, against prevailing gender and racial stereotypes' (*An Intimate Distance: Women, Artists and the Body*, 1996).

Today much is made of the notion that we now live in a postcolonial world and more and more attention is correctly paid to emerging third world cultures. Yet rarely is one of the oldest colonised countries – Scotland – discussed in this context. This might be because the Scots in fact do not always see themselves as thus. They have always had a very complex attitude towards their subservient position within the imperial system of the United Kingdom of Great Britain and its Empire. Didn't we Scots start the whole thing in 1603 with the first British monarch coming from north of the border?

Ironically it was the top dogs from Scotland – the Stewarts and their hangers-on – who were the first to run this new nation. With all the self-asserting swagger which they liked to project in their baroque portraits by the likes of Mytens, Van Dyck and Rubens, they could not wait to subject their uncouth Scottish bodies to a quick respray of Anglifying gloss paint. This instant cultural transformation can be witnessed by King James (VI and I) proudly displaying a St George medallion on his chest in a portrait by Isaac Olivier; while his successor, Charles I went one better and had Rubens portray him in actual guise of the patron saint of England slaying the dragon of his inherited Scottishness.

With the later political and economic merger of Scotland and England in 1707, the subservient attitude of the Scots began to percolate right through the social classes. For instance, one only has to think of Boswell's grovelling apologies to Dr Johnston for his country of origin and his attempts (along with many other of his yuppie fellow countrymen) to eradicate all traces of the Scottish vernacular from his speech, to get the picture. Yet in Boswell's defence, it should be pointed out that after the 1745 Jacobite rebellion it could be rather dangerous to assert your Scottishness, without also reasserting your loyalty to the British crown at the same time. A superb example of this duality of national allegiances is displayed in the Grand Tour portrait of Col William Gordon of Fyvie (1766) who has his swashbuckling pose swathed in tartan plaid. Yet clearly shown underneath is his red-coated uniform which is much closer to the body which will fight and die for British supremacy – especially over those 'knavish Scots' to quote the recently composed national anthem.

By the early 19th century the stereotyping of Scottishness was beginning to come into full operation. The first spectacular display of this long ongoing process was Walter Scott's stage-managed triumphal entry of George IV into Edinburgh in 1822. The grossly over-corpulent figure of the British monarch, girthed in a tartan kilt, parading itself through the adoring streets of the Scottish capital demonstrated that the Scots clearly knew their place and role within a now secure and stable United Kingdom. A little earlier, the differences between Northern and Southern cultural attitudes were shown by two portraits of Walter Scott by David Wilkie. In the first Wilkie presents *Scott at Abbotsford* (1817) sitting and blethering amongst his family and retainers as was his natural Scottish disposition. Such close and informal bodily contact between high and low caste however, was offensive to Wilkie's London audience who were outraged by being presented with 'a common clodpole and his rude associates'. Needless to say, Wilkie, knowing which way the wind was blowing, redressed his faux pas and repainted Scott as the 'elegant poet', after the appropriate manner which Reynolds had exemplified in his portrait of Oliver Goldsmith. Thus Scott was now placed with the great tradition of English letters.

Throughout the 19th century, with Scotland now completely integrated into British imperial and industrial expansion, the Scots were visually represented not as individuals, but as 'rude associates' of their more sophisticated neighbours – hence the rise of Scottish Victorian genre (or kailyard) painting. Here the Scottish body was no longer glorified as action man in tartan regalia, but as a 'common clodpole' who could cause tears to flow when over-exploited, or mouths to guffaw when over-intoxicated. This caricature of the Scottish figure reaches its apotheosis with the renowned stage antics of Sir Harry Lauder – the displaced, couthy, fawning Scot incarnate.

With the disengagement of popular culture from the high art of 20th century Modernism, Scottish art jettisoned its connections with earlier Victorian kitsch. The representation of the figure in Scottish culture had become so compromised and contaminated with 'false consciousness' that it was now almost impossible to address the issue in a meaningful fashion. Not surprisingly most Scottish artists tended to avoid the figure like the plague – the conservative ones retreating into the safe refuge of picturesque landscape; while the more progressive pioneered the development of British abstract art. William Johnstone, the best example of the latter group, certainly had strong feelings about the erotic power of the human body, but was always inclined to submerge that in his paintings.

In the immediate post-war period the body in its nude and naked form began to emerge as a powerful, but complex presence in contemporary Scottish art. Up until then the nude had been conspicuous by its almost total absence in the history of Scottish art – no William Etty here. The first controversy over this contentious subject centred on Joan Eardley's one and only venture into this minefield of aesthetic and gender prejudices. Her painting *Sleeping Nude* (1954/55), which showed the naked body of her fellow artist Angus Neil, caused great critical offence ('miserable realism') and public outrage ('Oooh, this sleeping man has no clothes on'). More interestingly one critic compared Eardley's figure to the 'emaciated victims of Belsen'. Interestingly this theme of victimisation was very much in tune with the way the human body was also treated by the two major figurative artists of post-war Scottish art – Eduardo Paolozzi and John Bellany.

In the depressive atmosphere of the cold war years, Paolozzi subjected his shattered and fragmented totemic figures to the ruinous effects of the legacy of industrial exploitation and technological indifference. Paolozzi's critique of modern materialism turned the broken bodies of his sculptures in the 1950s into icons of martyrdom by their identification with such religious figures as St Sebastian. Bellany, by contrast, comes from the other side of the great schismatic divide in Scotland. The deeply traumatised figures in his earlier paintings are terrorised by vengeful demons created by Presbyterian self-loathing. The pain and punishment that is inflicted on their physical being comes from internal forces of religious guilt and persecution which sees the body as the main cause of the fall of man into the pit of despair. Thus the body is both the source of sin and the agency for its punishment. If Paolozzi's figures suffer from too little spiritual sustenance, Bellany's men and women have it with awful over-abundance.

With Scotland being politically paralysed during the Thatcher/Major years, the arts played an increasingly important role in Scottish cultural life through the 1980s and '90s. In painting, Glasgow certainly took the initiative with figuration now the central area of artistic expression. Undoubtedly the major force in this neo-figurative movement was the New Glasgow Boys – Steven Campbell, Peter Howson and Ken Currie.

Howson and Currie tended to continue the theme of the victimised figure in their work, but instead of treating their human tragedies as universal mythic sagas, they attempted to focus down on the distressing signs of their own social times. As Donald Kuspit observed of Howson's paintings, 'they are explicitly social narratives', which portray the ruined lives of the casualties of post-industrial Thatcherite Britain. Both artists played with the stereotypical image of the West of Scotland working class; which is predominately gendered in the masculine and psychologically conditioned in the self-destructive mode. Certainly, Howson exploits this caricature image to powerful effect, by playing off all the clichés of Scottish Victorian genre painting against a monumentalising treatment of his figures, which gives them a kind of 'sculptural immobility'. At his best, Howson's tragic-comic characters can induce a response which Baudelaire described as 'the laughter caused by the grotesque which has about it something profound, primitive and axiomatic'.

There is also a prevailing Baudelairian attitude in Currie's work – he is nothing if not 'passionate, partial and political'. And all of these forces are powerfully at work in his treatment of the human body which is the central focus and target for all the social and moral injustices that are visited on ordinary working people. There is an almost Old Testament severity in the obsessional manner in which 'brutality and persecution' stalks every footstep of Currie's haunted figures. For them there seems to be no escape and no end to their historically ordained role of victims and victimisers.

If Currie presents us with a Darwinian world of endless struggle for survival, Campbell turns that worldview on its head and allows us to fall into an Alice in Wonderland experience, where all such conflict is changed into slapstick and farce. Campbell treats his figures to the full impact of the other side of the Scottish character – satire and ridicule. To great comic effect, Campbell exploits the intrinsic theatricality of group figure painting. Yet whereas in the past, history and genre pictures had some coherent meaning through the academic conventions of body language and gesture, in Campbell's paintings the sign and its significance have become uncoupled and so semiotic mayhem breaks out all over the place. In Campbell's work the humour lies in the discrepancy between the high seriousness of the heroic treatment and the low burlesque of the bathetic narrative content – as Stuart Morgan observed, 'For Campbell the sublime and the ridiculous are always near neighbours'.

Not totally surprisingly, not one of the Scottish male artists has shown any real interest or ability in representing the female figure, revealing yet another clear division in Scottish genderised culture. The female body has become the exclusive property of Scottish women artists. Yet what strikes a male critic like myself is that even here there is a division between those artists who focus on that figure as a battleground of contending issues and those who use the body to reconcile 'difference' through the harmonious sensuality of the physical presence. In the first camp I would place Lys Hansen and the Glasgow Art School trained Jenny Saville and in the second Gwen Hardie and June Redfern.

Lys Hansen treats her subjects in an allegorical and overtly expressionistic manner. In her work the female experience is represented by the distortion and disfigurement of the body, which echoes the overall thematic character of her painting, *The Divided Self* (1985). Hansen's women seem to be torn, both by the external forces of social role-playing (mother, lover, saint, artist), and internal personal doubts and thwarted aspirations. Everywhere there is a pervasive atmosphere of suppression which is expressed through the self-imprisoning posture of her figures, acting as a metaphor for the wider context of social disjuncture within the body politic. The deeply divisive effect that this personal civil war of sense versus sensibility can have, is dramatically expressed in Hansen's painting where head and body are literally tearing each other apart.

In contrast to the highly expressionistic nature of Hansen's manner of painting, Jenny Saville seems to take a more detached approach. The unmitigated realism of her art does give some justification for comparison with the work of Lucian Freud. However, because she always uses herself as subject-model there is a constant process of self-examination involved. In a Burnsian mode of 'seeing ourselves as others see us', the perception/conception duality is at the core of her work. This is most clearly demonstrated by the monumental scale to which she subjects the representation of her body (up to 9 x 7 ft canvases). Thus the viewer has to accommodate two distinct experiences in front of her pictures – up close, the immediate tactile physicality of painting as female skin (and vice versa), and then from a distance, the fully coherent referential imagery of the picture itself. Thus Saville confronts and disturbs us with what Betterton describes as the 'vexed set of relationships between painting, gender and embodiment'.

Gwen Hardie also addresses these relationships, but has worked towards resolving them in a more harmonious fashion. Over the last decade Hardie's treatment of her own body as subject, has moved from the earlier opening up and exposing the inner physical and sexual self, to a minute examination of the outer barrier of surface forms and skin tissue. These latest near abstract paintings, with their subtly modulated textured surfaces and lyrically shifting atmospheric effects have a seductively meditative appeal, which offers the possibility of reconciliation between our physical and spiritual state of being.

If Gwen Hardie's micro/macrocosm presentation of her self-subject turns the body into a human landscape, June Redfern's paintings transport us to a mystical landscape world – half remembered, half imagined. She takes us back to a time long before and beyond the 'civilised'. Here we are with human community before all the disharmony of man-made progressive society. In these evocations of idyllic arcadia, the human body is presented through a whole spectrum of different postures to reflect the varying aspects of the changing human and natural condition. These figures seem to be endowed with a perfect state of equilibrium and grace. They are beautifully poised between the gravitational pull of their sustained attachment to the ground beneath them, and their freedom to move with ease through the space which permeates the world around them.

So maybe it is only the poetics of painting that can body forth such dreams and desires of innocent sensual delights. Maybe it is only there that we can experience such a true, unified harmony and, with our bodies free from 'contested political history'. Alas, as we say in Scotland, 'In your dreams, in your dreams'.

This essay was published *Contemporary Visual Art* in June 1998.

THE NUDE AND THE NAKED TRUTH

The Representation of the Female Figure in Scottish Contemporary Painting

To use the body of a woman, her image or person, is not impossible,
but problematic...
Mary Kelly, *Post-Partum Document XVIII*, (1985)

LET ME BEGIN by dispelling any suggestion that the seven artists I have chosen for this feature form in any way a self-conscious, coherent group. We are not dealing with some macho Magnificent Seven here. Although these artists must be aware of each other's work, I doubt if there is much, if any, direct professional contact between all of them. What does link them, however, is the fact that they are all women figure painters with strong Scottish connections – all were either born, taught, or still work north of the border.

Unquestionably, the theme of the body has become a dominant one in contemporary art. Yet what is striking about this subject in the context of Scottish art is that a medium commonly perceived as redundant – namely oil painting – is the one which has most successfully been deployed to address and challenge this crucial topic. Life painting still lives (if not rules), OK! Why this should be particularly so in Scottish art is too complex a subject to engage with here, but it must surely be partly due to a strong reaction against the repressive attitudes to most things female and feminine which pervaded patriarchal Scottish society and art until fairly recently. In a culture which tended to be hostile to the visual anyway, the aesthetic subtleties of the difference between 'the naked' and 'the nude' cut little ice. For in Scotland the nude was always in a no-win situation. The figure could not be allowed to emphasise the erotic, for that would stimulate men's carnal desires. Yet if it remained chaste it was not doing its reproductive job, and could then be condemned for providing merely unproductive decorative pleasure. Either way, John Knox had you by the short and... One of the achievements of these artists is that they have succeeded in breaking this vicious moralising circle.

I realise that according to certain extreme feminist art circles I have no right even to discuss this subject. I should be condemned before I open my mouth. I must be a misogynistic Scottish art critic, woefully gendered in the male. Well, besides all that, I am also conditioned to be cowardly, so I am going to hide behind another male art critic who has had many feminist potshots aimed at him. I refer to John Berger, whose highly influential (if now unfashionable) book *Ways of Seeing* (1972) remains a promising starting point for any discussion on figure painting. The two major contributions that Berger made to this debate concerned the intrinsic nature of oil painting and the dominant conventions governing the representation of the female figure in that medium.

Firstly, Berger pointed out that there was an 'analogy between possessing, and the way of seeing, which is incorporated in oil painting'. Secondly, he also, most famously pointed out, that 'Men act and women appear. Men look at women. Women watch themselves being looked at ... Thus she [the woman] turns herself into an object and most particularly an object of vision: sight'.

To ascertain just how pervasive Berger's views have become in the gender politics of contemporary culture one only needs to see how his ideas reverberate through the writings of leading feminist theorist Laura Mulvey, who similarly declared:

> In a world of ordered sexual imbalance, looking has been split between active male and passive female. The determining male gaze projects its fantasies onto the female figure which is styled accordingly. In their traditional exhibitionist role women are simultaneously looked at and displayed, with their appearance coded for strong visual and erotic impact.

All seven of the artists I wish to discuss here address, and in different ways subvert, the dominance of the 'male gaze'. Each, with varying strategies and from different perspectives, develops a critique of the possessive properties of oil painting and of conventional representations of the feminine within the traditions of that highly respectable medium. In marked contrast to their contemporaries who choose to work in more fashionable media, these painters do not set out to change their subject on view through Alberti's 'window'. They do, however, radically reframe and readjust that view so that the critical issues surrounding gender assumptions and reassessments are brought into play, challenging the previously secure position of the spectator looking onto this woman's world. This recolonisation of a familiar subject can certainly have a transgressive agenda – one which forces the audience to move away from the logocentric objective approach of the dominant male attitude, with its scopophilic tendencies; to one in which a sensual, tactile embodiment takes over the spectator's subjective and visceral experience of the painting.

Despite all the controversy surrounding her work, Jenny Saville – who trained at Glasgow School of Art and is currently one of Charles Saatchi's favourite female painters – probably has the most conventional approach to figure painting when considered alongside the other artists under discussion. She certainly impresses through her use of scale (with canvases up to 9 x 7 ft), but her monumental paintings with their unmitigated emphasis on female corporeality could still readily be placed within the realist tradition going right back to at least Courbet. Within that realist context, Saville's work forcibly demonstrates that the body is as much a social as a biological construction. She has turned 'fatness' into a weapon in order to assault stereotypical social and academic notions of the female body beautiful. The real threat posed by these paintings issues from their lack of fixed aesthetic parameters (the ideal), and the disturbing underlying menace of a female body that is not controllable normal pictorial conventions.

Whilst the realist paintings of Saville are always palpably close, those of June Redfern are forever evoking the faraway horizon of a long-lost landscape. She is fundamentally a romantic artist, but unlike her male counterparts Redfern does not take the view that man is omnipotent over nature. The poetry of her paintings lies in the way they hover between nature and culture – beyond and before the 'civilised'. Here the human body seems to be endowed with a perfect state of equilibrium and grace. Such an idyllic condition is out of reach, yet our yearning for it is made tangibly real by the sumptuous way the richly coloured impasto paint is abundantly applied to the picture surface. Near and far are simultaneously stimulated for the mobile viewer in these evocative, and tantalising, works.

With Gwen Hardie we return to the single figure, but because of its pressing proximity to the picture surface her paintings appear to slip between figuration and abstraction. This ambiguity is crucial to Hardie's work up until 1996, in which she used her own torso to eloquently critique the complex relationship between Modernism and the female subject. Here modern painting's greatest triumph – the aesthetically pure and socially uncontaminated picture surface – coalesces with the presence of the artist's body, which disturbs and questions the autonomy Modernism claims for itself. The tinted atmospheric aura which hovers around Hardie's female forms increases their sublime, indefinable qualities and makes their very nearness even more ungraspable.

Such an expansive lack of spatial definition is in marked contrast to the claustrophobic oppression which permeates the paintings of Lys Hansen. Alberti's open window has been replaced by a spy hole onto a cell in Bedlam. Everything is now turned in on itself: entrapment replaces openness and 'female' emotional hysteria overthrows 'male' rational logic. Again the spectator's normally safe position of control, is seriously endangered as *The Divided Self* (1985) of one of Hansen's female figures begins to disintegrate totally before our very eyes. Yet like the surrealists' fascination with sensual metamorphosis, Hansen can equally suggest that her seemingly pathetic victimised figures are also simultaneously capable of turning into the monstrous female aberrations which haunt the dark corners of the male psyche.

If Hansen's paintings are overtly disturbing, Alison Watt's work appears, on the surface at least, to be the epitome of cool, objective elegance. The smooth inviolable finish of Watt's paintings re-enacts the classical tradition of the female nude. Yet their studied theatricality, with all their props and poses, attends to Mulvey's notion that 'the feminine is a masquerade'. In her art, Watt discourses on the tradition of Western iconography – a tradition which equates 'woman' with 'image'. The 'image' presented to us as the paragon of pictorial perfection is for Watt, Ingres' Odalisque. However, even as Watt is reconstructing this academic ideal, she is simultaneously dismantling its mythical status: her draperies seem to cover over hidden cracks in the edifice, and her still life accoutrements do not celebrate voluptuousness, but rather, bear witness to mortality and decay.

If academic painting looked to Classicism as its badge of cultural authority, then modern art sought out the primitive as its access to the truly authentic. The lure of the savage was of course very much associated with Western, patriarchal, imperial notions of the 'natural' – innocence and unconstrained sexuality. Helen Flockhart's painting mocks this aspect of Western male mythology and self-deception. Her pictures may appear to be primitive in style, but their thematic content is certainly not innocent. Using what is regarded as the male prerogative of satire and irony, she presents, through allegory and symbolism, a damning critique of conventional images of female sexual, domestic and spiritual beauty. Flockhart's intense icon-like pictures may be small in stature, but their awkward robustness gives them a hard won authority which has infinitely more to do with women's lived experience than primitive innocence.

The paintings of Watt and Flockhart are steeped in the iconography of the history of art; by contrast Julie Roberts seems to distance herself as much as possible from that kind of referential dependency. Her pictures, with their blank opaque backgrounds, avoid any overt stylistic allusions and appear as neutral and impersonal as forensic photographic records of a violent event after the victim has been removed from the scene of the crime. The 'absence of presence' is crucial to the undercurrent of ominous threat which permeates Roberts' work. As she says, 'I don't feel my work has to look like traditional painting to tell a story… I deal with the body all the time. The fact that it is removed doesn't mean it's not there'. Ironically, the 'scene of the crime' settings in many of Roberts's paintings are social welfare institutions – such as hospitals and mental asylums – which appear not to operate for the wellbeing of the body (male or female), but to facilitate its painful inhuman constraint and its ultimate final departure.

The sheer range and inventiveness of the work of these seven female artists makes a lie of the current belief that painting is due to make a quick exit. If painting is on its last legs in other parts of the art world, then that's their problem. In Scottish art, there is still plenty of life left in the old dog yet – the women see to that.

This essay was published in *Contemporary Visual Art* (issue 21, 1999).

OBJECTS OF DESIRE
Scottish Modern Still Life Painting

If content is something that is contained, then it seems to me that the work of art is not a container; that it does not contain, but is something that allows something to pass through to someone in sympathy.
JD Fergusson, *Modern Scottish Painting*, 1943

THE MAJORITY OF people in Scotland would probably concur with the notion that the most fruitful place to look for the source of their national identity is the Scottish landscape. This still prevalent romantic idea was made extremely influential through the writings of Walter Scott who propagated the popular notion that every hill and river of Caledonia resounded and reverberated with echoes of Scotland's turbulent past. On the other hand however, before the creation and avid consumption of Scott's historical novels most inhabitants of rural Scotland would have had a very different view. Most would have regarded the fractured landscape of Scotland as clear evidence of the split nature of the nation's social and cultural identity. Previous to Culloden and the Clearances the northern Highlands was home to the separate Gaelic communities with their own distinctive social customs and language; while in the southern Lowlands the Sassenach Scots pursued a way of life very different from the Gaels. By the later 19th century however, Walter Scott's most illustrious successor, the exiled Thomas Carlyle – cut off from his native abode – no longer looked to landscape, but the heroic history of Scotland as the inspiring examples of true Scottishness. Carlyle's exemplar Scots – gendered exclusively in the masculine – were of course carefully selected from the great and the good. These inspiriting examples were, for Carlyle, a permanent reminder of national greatness, and for whom he strove successfully, to have a temple built to their immortal memory in the form of the Scottish National Portrait Gallery. In more recent contemporary times a new attitude has emerged where the elusive Holy Grail of national identity is sought for, not in the achievements of heroic patriots, nor in the stirring settings of their great deeds, but in the physical *things* that history has left behind.

We now live in an age of material culture where we Scots make our pilgrimage to national or local museums of Scotland, to seek out a cornucopia of absorbing artefacts which stir and excite the national memory and which helps us to find and celebrate the roots and nature of our intrinsic selves as a common cultural community. Furthermore, within artistic context, it is now just as likely that the humble still life painting, rather than the swaggering portrait or the sentimental landscape, will stir our imagination and hold our attention in our continuing quest to find out who we are, and what moves us most deeply.

In the modern era, the intellectual and aesthetic discourse on the growing impact of materialism goes back to the 18th century and the Enlightenment in Scotland. It was the radical ideas of the Scottish literati, and especially the philosophical scepticism of David Hume, which focused rational attention more and more away from the realm of the metaphysical and the transcendental, and towards that of the mundane experience of the everyday which Roland Barthes described in his essay *The World as Object* as 'man and his empire of things'. The figure who was most responsible for pioneering a new scientific enquiry into the complex experience of this world of tangible objects was Hume's renowned contemporary, Adam Smith. Today he is mainly remembered for his monumentally important work *An Inquiry into the Nature and Causes of the Wealth of Nations* which could be described as a blueprint for the emerging Western capitalist system and consumer society. From this profoundly influential economic discourse some have seen Smith as another Doctor Frankenstein creating a new creature – the *Homo Ecomonicus,* who only lives by the desire for financial profit and the pursuit of self-interest. This one-sided view of Smith's philosophy is however, a gross misunderstanding and distortion of his ideas. Smith in fact, was not just concerned with the production of goods and the market price of desirable things, but more importantly with their true value through how they might be used and enjoyed for the full benefit of a caring community. This attitude is most clearly seen in Smith's other major publication *The Theory of Moral Sentiments*. In this work the Scottish philosopher powerfully argues that what binds a civic society is not the ruthless pursuit of self-interest and gratification; but rather, the sympathetic bonding of each of its citizens to each other and the mutually beneficial material world which we can create for all. It is those feelings – or 'moral sentiments', which, through the power of the human imagination and fellow feeling, allows us to have an empathic relationship with the experiences of other people, as well as our connectedness with the unique nature of the objects which also have their being in the same world as us. As JD Fergusson points out, all true modern art is based on this sympathetic bond, and this is especially the case with still life painting where the relationship between the creative subject and the inspiring object, can be so personally intimate and perceptively direct.

Even though throughout most of its history still life retained a lowly reputation within academic circles, it always had a secure, if relatively unimportant, position within the Western canon. With the European academies' inordinate respect for the taste of the Classical world the fact that still life painting was admired and keenly sought by Greco-Roman connoisseurs established and sustained its reputation for subsequent generations. Furthermore, the fact that Pliny the Elder's 1st century Latin text, *Natural History,* included admiring stories of how celebrated ancient artists such as Zeuxis could paint a bowl of grapes so convincingly that birds tried to peck his pictorial fruit sanctioned the inclusion of still life painting in the collection of any serious art lover. Such painting was however, still seen as more to do with skilful craft, rather than uplifting art. This was mainly due to the fact that while other kinds of pictures – for example portraits – were individually commissioned by a patron, still life paintings were usually produced for the mass demand of the marketplace, like any other commodity. Thus still life was regarded as having more to do with material base commerce, rather than artistic high culture. There were on the other hand critical attempts to raise the intellectual status of still life by reading the objects in the pictures symbolically, and not merely mimetically. The most famous example of this was the *vanitas* type still life, which usually included such items as fading flowers and burning candles along with human skulls to remind the viewer of the brevity of life and the certainty of death. It was however, not still life's conscripted role as pictorial sermon which gave it lasting popularity, but rather its very lack of challenging intellectual and moralising content. Unlike other types of art the humble still life usually only required the viewer to use their eyes and admire the artist's mimetic skills in convincingly rendering the detailed appearances of everyday reality. It was the Dutch painters of the 17th century who were generally regarded as the supreme masters of this visual feat of pictorial illusionism. Up until the mid-19th century the democratic and egalitarian character of still life, where everyone, from a marquise to his maid, could equally enjoy such amenable images, tended however, to work against its reputation and make it easy to dismiss it as of little serious cultural consequence.

Things began to change radically by the end of the 19th century, with the rapid development of the modern urban and industrial era, where man-made objects increasingly became the predominant feature of the new bourgeois world. Now quotidian material reality had to be urgently addressed by modern artists in all its visual complexity. From Manet and the Impressionists onwards many modern painters tackled this new aspect of social reality in their own individual way through the aegis of still life. These modernists used the rich interpretive possibilities of still life in more and more complex ways, culminating in the almost impenetrable density of the layered pictorial iconography found in the cubist works of Picasso and Braque. Ironically by the beginning of the 20th century the reputation of still life had turned full circle – from previously being regarded as the least demanding and most accessible genre, to become the most challenging kind of painting to understand and critically appreciate!

The paintings in this exhibition are all examples of modern still life – and this qualification is important. The academic still life of the previous art historical era was, like all the other artistic genres, defined, not by stylistic interpretation, but by subject content – or what Fergusson terms 'the container'. With modern still life on the other hand, what the artist presents to the viewer is not a depiction of an everyday subject in a highly illusionistic manner as in the past, but something infinitely more important – a highly personal response and expression of the artist's own perceptive and interpretive relationship and attitude to that subject. Again it was a member of the Scottish Enlightenment, Thomas Reid in his *The Craft of Painting* who drew our attention to the crucial difference between objective and subjective perspectives in the rendering and understanding of picture-making like that of still life. Reid warned:

> I cannot entertain the hope of being intelligible to those who have not acquired the habit of distinguishing the appearance of objects to the eye, from the judgment which they form of their colour, distance, magnitude and figure. The only profession wherein it is necessary to make this distinction is that of painting.

Furthermore, it is those very essential elements – colour, distance, etc – in modern still life which should primarily and consistently hold our gaze and intellectual attention. This certainly was the view of Reid's 20th century follower, the French phenomenologist, Merleau-Ponty who in *Art and the World of Perception* boldly stated 'thus the work of art resembles the *object of perception*… So painting does not imitate the world but is a world of its own, creating on the canvas a spectacle which is sufficient unto itself.' In other words modern painting must communicate with us in its own unique and distinctive language of visual representation and interpretive expression.

Modern artists have now freed themselves from the 'containing' tyranny of *trompe l'oeil* illusionism and the need to present the image of the material world behind a veil of appearances of likeness that plagued the role of previous still life painting. No longer is the meaning of the still life picture solely contained in its mimetic relationship with its outside subject; but rather, is to be found in the imaginative and aesthetic experience that the artist expresses and conveys to the viewer in the language and specific requirements of painting itself. This idea was succinctly expressed by one of the greatest Scottish painters of modern still life, the late Craigie Aitchison, when he explained to one of his interviewers 'I do invent things if I have to… but they would have to be taken out if they weren't right.' Being a superb master of the art of modern still life Aitchison nearly always got it 'right'. That is when he, the artist, found the moment where he could fully identify with his painterly interpretation of his still life subject. I hope, in their own individual way, this is also the case with most of the very varied examples of Scottish modern still life painting in this exhibition.

This catalogue essay was written for the exhibition *Scottish Modern Still Life* shown at the Lemon Street Gallery, Truro in 2010.

SECTION FIVE
Two Scottish Art Colleges

SCHOOL'S OOT!
Glasgow School of Art

THE TERM 'SCHOOL', both as a collective noun and as the verb to teach and instruct, has a wide range of meanings and connotations. In the history of art however, this concept is usually involved with the notion of a recognisable stylistic mode that unifies, however loosely, the work of a group of artists. It is the generally accepted belief that art, unlike science and technology for example, does not progressively improve, but rather changes and mutates under different sociohistorical circumstances. Thus scholars and critics therefore feel required to impose convenient order and unity on their subject by retrospectively breaking up the history of art, not only into chronological eras, but also into various geographical and historical stylistic schools of art. It is this particular classifying process that makes the art world go round. We are all familiar with exhibitions and book titles such as *Masterpieces of 15th Century Flemish Painting* or *Highlights of Florentine Quattro Cento Sculpture,* where Flemish painting or Renaissance sculpture is as much a stylistic school as an historical period. Implied in all this academic and aesthetic categorisation is that there is some commonality of visualising technique which overlays the whole body of work of the various artists within a certain imposed grouping. If any artist's work should unfortunately not readily fit into this stylistic categorising system because of too much individuality in their particular practice, then they are usually expelled from the school, either as troublesome mavericks or invisible nonentities. Later, in some cases, to be deemed as unique geniuses.

Not surprisingly in the modern period the more rebellious artists began to take matters into their own hands and resisted this imposed system of classification by creating their own ready-made schools of art. From the early 20th century these modern artists began to see themselves much more within a transnational, neo-historical dimension that required them to gravitate towards one of the international modern metropolises like Paris, London, Berlin or Moscow. There these disparate artists' colonies exchanged and shared their innovative ideas as well as experimental practices and thus cohered into such avant-garde groupings such as, the futurists, the constructivists, the dadaists and the surrealists. These modern schools of art also demonstrated to the rest of the art world their shared commitments through the publication of manifestoes and periodical journals. Such a practice of declared theoretical and artistic unity was the avant-garde's own strategy of turning individual vulnerability into group counter-attack against hostile criticism in particular and bourgeois society in general.

How then does Scotland and Scottish visual culture fit into this complex concept of 'schools of art'? Unfortunately from an art historian or critic's point of view, not very readily. Metaphorically speaking, if Scottish artists were placed in a school classroom they would most likely turn out to be a rather unruly bunch of independently minded individuals. Interestingly, the issue of nationalism as an artistic concept has, for various reasons, never has had much appeal to most Scottish artists compared with Scotland's writers. On the other hand however, there have of course, been attempts by others to pigeon-hole them into convenient groups, creating such art market labels as the Glasgow Boys, the Scottish Colourists, the Edinburgh School; and recently, in true postmodern fashion, the New Glasgow Boys and Girls!

Is this exhibition then yet another example of the same dubious practice? Well, yes and no, would be the probable answer. Yes, in an Aristotelian manner, because any group exhibition needs to have some core thematic purpose in order that significant similarities and differences between the works on display can be noticed and critically analysed and interpreted. No, because, as with Wittgenstein, there is no attempt at prescribing or superimposing a process of unification here. Rather this exhibition aims to give an opportunity for stylistic family resemblances between works to reveal themselves and be observed by all those who attentively want to engage with the paintings on display.

There is however, one specific unifying, but crucially important, factor that brings this very diverse group of artists together for this occasion. They have all, at one time or another, had some connection with Glasgow School of Art; either as students or teachers. Charles Rennie Mackintosh's unique building was enthusiastically described by the modern art journal, *Studio* as 'one of the most complete and best equipped art schools in the United Kingdom' when it was erected at the turn of the 20th century. Since then it has remained at the centre of the city's cultural life and through Glasgow School of Art's illustrious portals have passed some of the finest and most important Scottish artists of the modern and contemporary eras. What these creative individuals variously gained from their contact and experience there would be of a distinctly personal nature; but, consciously or not, the whole environmental ethos of Mackintosh's building would certainly play some part in forming their artistic outlook and practice. For in the essential design of that building Mackintosh brilliantly resolves the challenge that confronts all ambitious artists working in a small modern nation like Scotland. In its richly innovative structural design and decorative features Glasgow School of Art skilfully accommodates and integrates both, the distinctive elements of Scotland's own vernacular architectural traditions and also the radically experimental approach that is the hall mark of all great modernist achievement. This enriching dialectical process between the past and present, which is at the heart of the best of the 'Glasgow Style' – between reconnecting with an indigenous cultural heritage and responding to the radical challenges of international Modernism and postmodernism, is also an essential feature of the best painting that has come out of Glasgow School of Art. The particular balance and emphasis of this mutually rewarding dialogue between the inherited and the innovative will of course vary from artist to artist included in this exhibition. Yet it is this creative dynamic of internal/national and external/international perspectives that has been one of the main forces which has driven the development of Scottish modern painting throughout the 20th century – with Glasgow often at the forefront.

Another dialectical tension, more local this time, which also requires to be taken into consideration is the civic and cultural rivalry between Glasgow and its near neighbour, Edinburgh. Probably no other country but Scotland has its two main metropolises in such close proximity to each other. So it is hardly surprising that a climate of keen cultural and artistic rivalry has long existed which has brought about advantages and disadvantages for both communities. In the Scottish modern art world this urban competitiveness goes back to the later 19th century when the up-and-coming young Glasgow painters rightly felt that the old 'glue pots' of Edinburgh were monopolising the Royal Scottish Academy in the Capital. In true Glaswegian style they took matters into their own hands in various ways – by setting up their own exhibiting institutions like the Royal Glasgow Institute, by helping to create a booming art market in Scottish and European modern painting through dealers like Alexander Reid and collectors such as William Burrell and by providing the best education for student artists and designers anywhere in the United Kingdom at Glasgow School of Art. Out of this rich mix of entrepreneurial and artistic activity emerged a whole range of internationally acclaimed achievements, including the work of the 'Glasgow Boys' and the 'Glasgow Four' who were the first generation of modern painters and designers in Britain.

Contrary to their critically imposed group name the Glasgow Boys rarely drew their subject matter from their city, but, like their Romantic predecessors, preferred to look to the Scottish landscape for inspiration. What was radically different in their approach however, was that these aspiring modern painters turned their back on the then clichéd Highland scenery of misty mountains *et al*, and concentrated their *plein air* attention on rather non-descript rural farming districts such as East Lothian. Then, in a similar manner as their French Realist and Impressionist counterparts, they treated the act of painting itself to as much vigorous attention as the visual description of their subject content. Thus it no longer mattered so much what subject was pictured, but rather, how it was painted – or in our contemporary critical jargon, the medium was beginning to assert itself over the message. The inherent decorative and directly expressive qualities of the tactile materiality of paint were now foregrounded for particular attention on the surface of the pictures of these innovative Glasgow painters. Yet it should also be recognised that the pictorial image was rarely eradicated completely from Glasgow painting. (Interestingly, in this context, the three pure abstract artists in the exhibition have pursued their careers elsewhere in London). As a distinctive phenomenon, Glaswegians are usually highly articulate conversationalists and this element of their social character passes over into their pictures which usually have a bold figurative narrative theme and visual presence at the heart of their pictorial compositions.

The modern painters of Glasgow at the time of the opening of Mackintosh's School of Art were as aware as anyone in Britain as to what was going on amongst the avant-garde circles in Europe. This was due to their immediate contact with progressive dealers like Reid and also having ready access to the collections of resident rich industrialists which included the latest works from the Continent. Furthermore, many of the more enthusiastically committed individuals, also travelled abroad and worked alongside their European modernist contemporaries. Up until the outbreak of the Great War in 1914 the Glasgow modern art scene was extremely active and this is demonstrated in the colourful exuberance of the work produced during the early period of Scottish Modernism. However after the social and economic devastation of the 1914–18 mass conflict, there was a traumatic change in the condition and outlook of the renowned 'Second City of the Empire' No longer the workshop of the world, its glorious imperial and industrial days were swiftly slipping away and an austere economic climate was severely setting in. This drastically affected the much more sombre art scene of the inter-war years. Now decorative colour and bravura technique were replaced by architectonic composition and precision draughtsmanship and under such conditions, not unexpectedly, a number of the best Glasgow artists of the period also turned out to be superb black and white printmakers. Contact with international Modernism was also less available, but some of the ambitious painters of that period did for instance, absorb aspects of pictorial Surrealism into their more challenging work.

Remarkably, and, in marked contrast to the disastrous impact of the First World War and its debilitating aftermath, the 1939–45 conflict laid the foundations for the long-sustained revival of the post-war Glasgow art scene. As a result of the Second World War many important artists, including JD Fergusson, Stanley Spencer and continental refugees such as Josef Herman and Jankel Adler chose to move there and make important contributions to the revival of Scottish Modernism. The stimulating and inspiring presence of such figures encouraged and directed the aesthetic aspirations and artistic ambitions of the next generation of young students emerging from Glasgow School of Art – such as Colquhoun and MacBryde and Joan Eardley, the latter, who although English was so enamoured by her adopted city that she opted to develop her career there. Furthermore through the aegis of travelling scholarships Scottish artists were again making direct contact with the international art scene as evidenced by their creative response to such post-war movements as Art Brut, Tachisme, Abstract Expressionism and Neo-Figuration.

In the immediate post-war period much of its former vigorous energy returned to Glasgow painting, but this time, with a marked urgency which gave a powerful momentum to its subsequent development throughout the second half of the 20th century. This new optimistic situation was also accompanied by the re-establishment of a much more supportive art gallery scene in the city led by the indomitable Cyril Gerber, and later joined by Roger Billcliffe. Fortunately at Glasgow School of Art there also was a series of inspiring head teachers in the painting school – such as David Donaldson, Jack Knox and Sandy Moffat; each with their own particular art educational approach, but all encouraging their students to develop their own individual creative potential within a Scottish and international art context. Thus, for instance, when the reign of late cosmopolitan Modernism began to wane Glasgow's contemporary figurative painting, in all its individual modes, was well-placed to assert its powerful presence on the British and international art scenes.

Today of course the ever-changing contemporary art world is infinitely complex, and painting now has to find its own credible and assertive place amongst a plethora of new types of rival media and alternative means of expression. Yet despite this daunting situation Glasgow painting has constantly managed to rise to the competitive challenge and demonstrate that it can hold its own and still make its distinctive and much sought-after, contribution to the visual culture of our age. The main reason for this is the sheer variety of different kinds of work constantly being produced by the painters from Glasgow today. So whether you are looking for paintings to delight your senses, pictures to lift your spirits or images to disturb, but at the same time stimulate your thoughts and attitudes, you will certainly find what you are looking for in this rich display of painting that owes its origins, in one way or another, to Glasgow School of Art.

This catalogue essay was written for the exhibition *The Glasgow School of Painting*, shown at the Lemon Street Gallery, Truro in 2008.

THE ANTHENIAN WAY
Edinburgh College of Art

You must yourselves realise the power and beauty of Athens, and feed your eyes upon her from day to day until love of her fills your hearts.
The Athenian Oration of Pericles, Thucydides, *Peloponnesian Wars* (Book 2, 34–46)

AS ITS NAME clearly indicates Edinburgh College of Art (ECA) has strong ties with its parent city. This historical relationship goes back to the setting up of its predecessor, The Trustees' Academy in 1760, and has continued over the next 200 years. Furthermore, the visual bond between 'The Athens of the North' and ECA was clearly underlined with the building of the College during the opening decade of the last century, when Edinburgh made its last significant attempt to revisit and recreate the inspiring architectural and sculptural glory that was Periclean Athens. This zealous classifying ambition had begun around the time of the establishment of The Trustees' Academy in the middle of the 18th century. Then the Enlightened Scottish capital so enthusiastically committed itself to such a rigorous urban building programme of Greek Revivalism that it was then that it gained the international reputation of being 'The Athens of the North'. In true Janus fashion this highly self-conscious reinvention of 'Auld Reekie' as a modern city was achieved by looking back to the example of ancient Athens. Through antique military grid town planning and neoclassical architecture, the New Town was permeated with dedicated archaeological ambitions to recapture and revive that model of civic excellence and democratic reason which the Enlightenment ideal attributed to ancient Athens. For the historically informed, but progressive citizenry of 18th century Edinburgh, the visual appearance of their utopian ideal was founded on the freshly discovered examples of Greek art and architecture and the growing scholarly exploration of its ancient writings which fired the imaginations of artists and architects and educated public alike.

Unfortunately however, despite the worldwide acclaimed triumph of its splendid New Town the momentum of the Greek revival in Edinburgh began to falter and dissipate throughout the 19th century due to the impact of urban and industrial modernity and the growing nationalistic appeal of Romanticism and the Gothic Revival. Edinburgh's international-orientated neoclassical movement had however one last splendid flowering in the building of its new Art College at the outset of the 20th century.

One of the important reasons why the city's art education institution was moved from the Royal Scottish Academy building on Princes Street to its new site at Lauriston Place was to create much more accessible and appropriate accommodation for its exceptional collection of cast historical sculptures. The city was justifiably proud of this invaluable cultural asset and planned to have it displayed to its greatest advantage, both for the student body and interested members of the public who still have free access to the Collection today. This is clearly demonstrated in the architectural design for the ECA building which, although Beaux-Art classical on its monumental exterior, is laid out in the interior to simulate similar spatial and optical relationships between architecture and sculpture as those found in the original Parthenon Temple itself.

The dedicated collecting of Antique and Renaissance casts for the improvement of art education and public taste was vigorously carried out during the first half of the 19th century with the Athenian pieces, mainly cast from the British Museum and Lord Elgin himself, forming the jewel in crown of the then Trustees' Academy's Collection. The sculptural casts' central role in the fine art teaching at the Academy and the RSA School unfortunately soon began to wane after 1858 when the highly rigid 'South Kensington' mechanical method of instruction and examination of art and design was disastrously introduced into the Edinburgh curriculum. Furthermore by the time ECA was established and fully functioning in the early 20th century the life class had also began gradually to supplant study from the antique. Thus it is not entirely surprising when we look at the first installation photographs of the interior of the new Lauriston Place building that they seem to suggest that those sculptural presences, for which the College was built to house, were already turning into ghostly traces from a distance past which for most modernists would soon become redundant, if not, almost invisible.

Edinburgh's return to 'The Athenian Way' also had some unforeseen and unwelcomely similar dimensions as the ancient Greek city. For instance, just when Periclean Athens was glorying in its newly achieved imperial and civic triumphs, the storm clouds of the impending disastrous Peloponnesian Wars with Sparta were already ominously beginning to darken the celebrations of the Athenian citizens. Similarly the initial euphoria attending the protracted completion of Edinburgh's first purpose built Art College was quickly superseded by growing apprehension and fear as the nation slept walked into the nightmare of war in 1914. During the terrible conflict of the Great War ECA lost around 100 of its staff and students and to commemorate this terrible loss, along with the Panathenaic sculptures, the College's own war memorial still holds a place as a remembrance vigil over the main atrium.

Thus the first generation of painters who emerged as a distinctive force from ECA were all touched, to a lesser or greater, degree by their war experiences. This undoubtedly had a profound impact on the direction and character of the Edinburgh School of Painting during the inter-war years. Some chose to see Modernism and modernity as synonymous; and because modernisation had had such a calamitous impact of destruction and radical change, many tutors took refuge in escaping into the seemingly safe and secure values of academic practice. On the other hand, the dominant ECA group of artists/tutors decided on a middle way between radical and conservative values. Most of these painters benefited from the travelling scholarships which were made available after the war. They all spent a good deal of time studying abroad, especially in the studios of the modern masters of the Paris School where they learnt the new pictorial languages of Fauvism, Cubism, Futurism and even early Abstraction. It was this group of artists who dominated the Edinburgh School of Painting for the next generation. In their College studios and throughout the Scottish countryside they sought to reconcile modern techniques of painting practice and pictorial form with conventional subject content. Unlike the work of the continental avant-garde – from Matisse and Picasso to the Surrealists – the Edinburgh School mostly chose to turn their backs on the Greek classical example and avoid the human figure in their art. Instead they were drawn to the decorative and sensual appeal of landscape and still life rendered in a richly tactile and freely expressive manner. Finally, as with any institution, there were a few individuals of a more resistant and rebellious nature. The more ambitious of these usually pursued the future direction of their career outwith Scotland and went on to make their own distinctive contribution to the development of British modern art within the London cosmopolitan scene.

Figurative art had not of course completely disappeared with the Edinburgh School and it manifested itself most fully in the public art projects carried out in the 1930s. Following in the footsteps of the civic-minded Athenians, Edinburgh had a long distinguished history in beautifying the important buildings of the city through grand decorative schemes. In the early modern era this was very much linked to the Scottish capital's commitment to the Arts and Crafts movement. The finest example of this was the National War Memorial in Edinburgh Castle which involved the contributions of a number of the staff from ECA. Furthermore at the time when public art for the community was encouraged and promoted by the city, the College was very much involved, especially through the painting of educational, inspiring murals for some of the local primary and secondary schools.

By the later 1930s ECA was seen by most people to be an important cultural and communal asset to the city, but again, its long term future was drastically disrupted and had to be put on hold for the period of the Second World War and its immediate aftermath. As before, a further generation of young artists had to rethink what should be the future course of Scottish modern art in general and their own in particular. After 1945 some of the older figures of the pre-war Edinburgh School still held a dominant position and influence within the College and the Royal Scottish Academy. Not surprisingly then, a number of the younger members of the painting school decided to build on the example of the previous generation by further developing and intensifying the particular qualities of decorative and expressionist painting of the Edinburgh School. On the other hand, there were a few restless individuals who, after their wartime experiences, and their inspirational contacts with the wider post-war art scene in Europe and America, set out to extend the visual power and semantic possibilities of their art by incorporating into their challenging modernist work the language of arcane symbolism and gestural abstraction. Following on a little later, some of the more progressive members of the College staff who emerged in the 1960/70s pursued their own mode of severely austere, minimalist abstraction which was, amongst other things, in marked contrast to the colour saturated canvases of the previous Edinburgh School of Painting.

By the turn of the 1960s Modernism, especially the formalism of pure abstract painting was the triumphant force on the international art scene which had now become highly institutionalised. Yet this was soon to be challenged by a range of counterculture strategies and the almost ubiquitous Pop Art movement. At ECA however, the most significant resistance to High Modernism took a very different form. Amongst a few of the more rebelliously committed students (and with the sympathetic support of some of the tutoring staff) there was a return to a re-examination of the depiction of the human figure in a range of different generic and historical contexts. Modern realist and expressionist paintings were executed, some on an epic scale, full of human conflict and compassion that matched the universal themes of struggle and resolve to be also found in the Athenian works which graced the College's central sculptural court. By the 1980s, such was the power of this approach that the return to figurative painting made a powerful impact on all the Scottish art colleges. Furthermore, on this occasion, Scottish modern art was also at the forefront of the international art scene where Neo-Figuration reigned supreme from New York to Milan. This relatively brief, but spectacular return to figure painting, encouraged at ECA a body of fine painters. This was especially notable amongst the growing body of emerging women artists, a number of whom would use their perceptive skills to re-examine and represent the visual depiction of the female figure in Western art.

Since the turn of this century however, there has undoubtedly been a clear shift in artistic and critical attitudes, with painting no longer holding its former dominant position in the contemporary art scene. A whole new array of alternative modes of visual communication and engagement has emerged to challenge painting's former central role at the forefront of aesthetic and theoretical debate. This situation is now all-pervasive from the powerful institutions of the international art world to the standard art college curriculum. Whether this change should be welcomed or not is open to debate. Yet it does provide the opportunity for the practitioners and supporters of one of the longest surviving art forms to reconsider the new and relevant social and cultural roles that painting might be able to claim for itself in the vast multimedia world of the new millennium which beckons before us.

In age of constantly accelerated progress it is easy to forget that the future is always dependent on how we regard and respect the past. Whether we like it or not the past is always with us. At ECA for example, they have recently achieved the securement of an important grant from the Heritage Lottery

Fund to help them restore their classical sculptural cast collection. This of course includes their unique Athenian pieces copied from the Parthenon which are integral to the original design of the College's interior space. After decades of neglect and disrespect, these magnificent works will soon be revealed to us again in all their former glory. Hopefully this time they will stir and sustain the creative powers and artistic ambitions of staff and students alike.

These Panathenaic masterpieces, and the ringing words of Pericles, demonstrate to all ages that art should on the one hand, pursue its own concept of the ideal; but, on the other hand, remind us that that ideal must always be born out of the circumstances of its own historical age and particular artistic heritage. All art that aspires to be worthy of that illustrious name – as with the Panathenaic sculpture – should always strive, to reveal 'the power and beauty' of the whole of the community which it is ultimately there to serve.

This catalogue essay was written for the exhibition *The Edinburgh School of Painting*, shown at the Lemon Street Gallery, Truro in 2009.

ALAN DAVIE

Jingling Spaces

Have you ever considered yourself as an abstract painter?

No, not really [...] I've never felt attracted to pure abstraction [...] However in a painting by Mondrian, for example, I always felt this isn't abstract art, this is sheer magic [...] It takes me into mysterious spaces.[1]
From 'An interview with Alan Davie', Bill Hare and Andrew Patrizio, 1995

ALAN DAVIE (1920–2014) must surely be regarded as the most otherworldly major artist that Scotland has ever produced. Evidence of this abounds, for example, in such statements as 'The artist was the first magician and the first spiritual leader, and indeed today he must take the role of arch-priest of the new spiritualism.'[2] The subject content of his work, as well as his artistic practice, with its allusions to esoteric phenomena like Jungian spiritual psychology, Zen Buddhism and occult shamanism, is shrouded in mysticism and mystery (such as, at its best, in the work of Michael Tucker).[3] Furthermore, Davie's own writings on his art practice have set the agenda and been profoundly influential on the subsequent critical debate surrounding his painting. This approach to Davie's work is best exemplified by the critical writings of Michael Tucker. Davie's claim that 'I do not practice painting as an Art' but rather 'to find enlightenment and revelation'[4] has established the view that as an artist, Davie is someone set apart – virtually a being unto himself, a medium through whom creative forces from an alternative universe flows. Davie firmly holds the view that 'Self-expression is something contrary to Art' and 'Art just happens,'[5] thus, by implication, his art should not be discussed within the usual historical and critical perspectives that apply to others. This paper wishes to challenge such a view and show that important aspects of Davie's art practices can be opened up to fruitful discussion by placing them within a range of historical and cultural contexts.

At least one of these very general shaping pressures on a cultural level is, we suggest, a new approach and attitude to space – both as a phenomenological experience and as a philosophical concept. The 20th

1 A Patrizio and B Hare, 'An interview with Alan Davie', *Alan Davie: Works on Paper*, London: 1995, p11–14
2 A Davie 'Towards a new definition of art. Some notes on (NOW) painting, Catalogue of the Alan Davie exhibition at the Galerie Charles Lienhard, Zurich, April–May 1960', reprinted in *Alan Davie*, A Bowness, ed. London, 1967, p16
3 M Tucker, 'Music Man's Dream' in *Alan Davie*, London 1992
4 A Davie, 'Notes by the Artist', *Alan Davie*, Whitechapel Art Gallery, London 1958, reprinted in Bowness (n.2), p.11
5 Davie (n.4), p.10

century saw an exponential expansion of spatial regimes, whether it be in science or politics, that produced new psychogeographic maps and contested territories, mediated by highly pervasive media and visualising technologies that both orbited and inhabited the earth. Furthermore a multifold crisis over space became a dominant concern in post-war artistic practice and critical attitudes where a radically new fluid relationship was sought between the spatial and the temporal. There was now an urgent need to challenge and overthrow the grand *linear* narratives of Enlightenment history and treat them as the 'bunk' they were. The present had to be freed from the oppressive burdens of the past in order to revitalise and invigorate our sense of self in the new and immediate dynamics of spatial experience in the contemporary world.

* * *

Davie was born in 1920, into the age of modern tyranny. Suppression of individual and mass freedoms was not only to be found throughout the imperial empires stretching around the globe but was practiced in its more sophisticated oppressive forms under European totalitarian dictatorships and other kinds of sociopolitical and economic hegemonies. Under such dictatorial regimes their subjects were not only forcibly instructed on how they should live socially, but more insidiously, how they should think politically *and aesthetically*. In the case of architecture they were required to live in regularly ordered spaces within a rationally planned dystopia. Within the area of artistic production and aesthetic consumption they were expected to admire academic, idealised naturalism and monumental Neoclassicism; and conversely their disapproval was insistently directed against the monstrosities of Modernism – most infamously exemplified by Stalin's and Zhdanov's policy of Socialist Realism in the USSR and Hitler's Munich exhibition of Degenerate Art of 1936 (for which Davie's work would have been suitably qualified!)

Under such historical circumstances, it is not surprising that Alan Davie's early artistic career had to be put on hold as he, like millions of others, was sucked into the maelstrom of yet another self-destructive ritual of catastrophic, near apocalyptic, disaster. This mass tragedy was most powerfully expressed by the great Beat poet Allen Ginsberg's opening lines of *Howl* – 'I saw the best minds of my generation destroyed by madness, starving hysterical naked.'[6]

All the various subversive movements to emerge after the shattering traumas of the previous era – from Art Brut, COBRA and Absurd Theatre in Europe to American Beat Literature, Bebop jazz and Independent Cinema – were fired by a fiercely independent spirit of iconoclastic anarchy. Davie, spiritually sustained during his period of military service by his readings of the poetic eulogies to the freedoms of the *Body Electric* which he found in

---

6 A Charters, ed. *The Penguin Book of the Beats*, London 1993 p.62

the writings of his beloved Walt Whitman, must have sensed a new dawn
was breaking over mankind as he toured around war-ravaged Europe on
a postgraduate Edinburgh College of Art travelling scholarship in 1948/9.
Academically trained at ECA (1937–40) he now felt that he needed to redirect
and ultimately reinvent the whole procedure and purpose of his art. To
achieve this he began to realise that as a practising painter he must not only
refuse to bow down to, but destroy and replace, that most powerful symbol
of conventional authority – the mimetic image with all its formal and spatial
illusionism and exhausted discredited narrative content.

Davie's incipient iconoclastic urges began to express themselves in his
letters and the journal that he kept during his visits to the great art centres of
Europe. Of the art scene in London he dismissively wrote 'That which I am
seeking is not here... what a mass of ugly rubbish on show under the name of
Art'[7] and even more antipathetic was his reaction to the Italian Renaissance
tradition of religious art and overblown Baroque architecture on his visit to
St Peter's in Rome: 'Words cannot express my horror on seeing this wonder
of the world. I can only say that it is the most hideous of monstrosities ever
thrown up by mankind.'[8] To find inspiration appropriate to his newly realised
purpose Davie needed to turn his back on the Age of Reason and seek it in
the earlier Age of Faith. In Venice and later visiting Sicily, he found what he
was initially looking for in the form of the Byzantine mosaic icon. Such work
would have a special appeal for Davie's quest, as it had not been sullied by
the insidious deceptions of Renaissance linear perspective and chiaroscuro.
Rather the image was created through the open display and flat patterning of
the mosaic medium itself – form and content were as one. Davie responded in
well-known early works such as *The Saint* (1948).

In June 1948, Davie encountered contemporary American painting
showing at the Venice Biennale through the auspices of Peggy Guggenheim
to whom Davie later sold *Music of the Autumn Landscape* (1948) from his
second one-person exhibition at Galleria Sandri in November of that year.
What impact the work of Jackson Pollock *et al* had on Davie has always
been open to dispute but, interestingly, as Douglas Hall points out, such
painting 'hardly rates a mention in the journal. He pays more attention to
Ernest, Klee and Arp.'[9] Davie's later work undoubtedly has links to Surrealist
biomorphic forms and the overall pictorial surface manipulations of Klee.
The critic David Sylvester understood the spatial innovations of Klee in a way
entirely sympathetic to that of Davie. 'The last works of Klee undermine your
perceptual habits [...]. In late Klee, the end is the beginning. The picture is
limitless, like space and time.'[10] Interestingly, Sylvester was a major supporter

---

7 D Hall, 'Introducing Alan Davie', *Alan Davie*, London 1992, p.10
8 Hall (n7), p14
9 *Alan Davie*, London 1992, p16
10 D Sylvester, 'Late Klee' (1948), in *About Modern Art: Critical Essays 1948–96*, London 1996, p35, 38

of Davie at the outset of his career.[11] Davie's writings during this time clearly indicate that he feels himself part of a seminal moment of change within which he must make his own contribution – 'It is my belief that we are all on the verge of fundamental changes, in life as well as art. This is a period of destruction, a blowing up of old edifices for new construction. All I can do is to keep working.[12]

It was not until Davie finished his tour of the Western European art centres and he and his wife Bili had returned to live in London that he began seriously to develop his radically new approach to painting. Like the innovator and practitioner of Art Brut, Jean Dubuffet, who claimed 'I have broken with art, style and talent,'[13] Davie also felt that he needed to begin afresh and so cut himself off as much as possible from the domination of canonical Western art. Only then would he be able to discover new and relevant possibilities for painting in the fractured and fearful Cold War world. As he wrote later: 'No new or prophetic image can possibly come forth from knowledge of the past – rather it comes from sudden realisation of the NOW and a knowing from beyond knowledge – knowledge that comes through intuition and meditation.'[14] Davie clearly reveals his bond with the predominant attitudes of the international post-war avant-garde – all of whom, to various degrees, broke with received conventions. Davie's innovative attitudes can also be found within a wide range of other contemporary innovative art practices. For example, Jack Kerouac and the Beat writers' assaults on the syntactically narrative order of literary form as expressed in *Essentials of Spontaneous Prose*.[15] Or Charlie Parker and the bebop jazz performers' transformation of melodic structure and headlong dive into free-form improvisation. Or John Cassavetes (to whom we will return later) and other independent filmmakers who explicitly rejected Hollywood's script and director-dominated cinema. (This was borne out by Cassavetes' constant mantra-like injunction to his actors – 'Nothing cute! Nothing cute!')[16] This generation of dissatisfied and rebellious individuals all rejected the received ideologies and academic practices of the past and wished to return to condition zero where no preconceived ideas existed. As the Scottish sculptor, William Turnbull, in true existentialist fashion put it, 'I began to make a piece of sculpture to find out what a piece of sculpture should be like.'[17] This is echoed in Davie's statement,

One must concern oneself with the activity of painting, be it a physical one

---

11 'Abstract artists I especially admired were Alan Davie, Gerald Wilde and Victor Pasmore in England', in D Sylvester, (n10), p15
12 D Hall (n7), p18
13 S Wilson, 'Paris Post War: In Search of the Absolute', in F Morris, ed., *Paris Post War: Art and Existentialism 1945–55*, London 1993, p32
14 D Hall (n7), p20
15 Charters (n6), p57
16 In R Carney, ed. *Cassavetes on Cassavetes*, London 2001, p.xv
17 D Mellor, 'Existentialism and Post-War British Art', in Morris (n13), p53

(like a dance) or an improvisation with ideas and concepts, and we must contrive to pay as little attention as possible to the end towards we are moving – allowing the end to come when it comes...[18]

Or as the legendary Neal Cassady of *On the Road* urged Kerouac – 'just write Jack, write! Forget everything else.'[19] (This ties closely with at least one pedagogic strategy used by Davie with art students – namely to try from the outset to avoid making 'good' art at all, described by the artist thus: 'Another important request was for them (his students) to make a series of abstract compositions using specific elements with the aim of making bad compositions... Each person had to work the whole surface and use all the colours... To everyone's surprise the results often turned out to be quite extraordinary and a group of quite dynamic compositions would result.')[20]

This crucially urgent approach to the destructive/creative act immediately began to manifest itself in the paintings Davie produced in his new London studio. In tune with Dubuffet's belief that 'The essential gesture of the painter is to cover a surface'[21] we see in works like *Jingling Space* (1950) and *Birth of Coloured Organisms* (1950) that all traces of mimetic figuration have been swept away. Such sweeping pictorial iconoclasm involved a radical change in Davie's whole attitude and approach to the creation of pictorial space. This necessitated abandoning conventional easel painting and the security of the spatial certainties of Alberti's rational system of linear perspective. Davie now had to find out for himself as a painter that the world is 'round me, not in front of me' as Merleau-Ponty put it.[22]

With the evidence we have from his wife's documentary film of his studio practice, Davie worked simultaneously on any number of pictures – some lying on the floor and others propped on the walls surrounding him. This undoubtedly created an entirely different spatial orientation to his practice. Instead of painting just with his arms and wrists Davie was required to be acutely aware of the involvement of his whole body in the creative performance. Alberti's 'window onto the world' needed to be smashed and so allow a free-flowing spatial relationship to exist between the painter and the painting like the 'continuous chain of undisciplined thought' in Kerouac's writings.[23]

The nature of this new spatial freedom however brought with it new existentialist challenges and sublime terrors. The free-floating artist now

---

18 A Davie, (n4), p11
19 Charters (n6), p188
20 In 'Towards a philosophy of creativity – a lecture delivered by Alan Davie on the occasion of the retrospective exhibition', *Alan Davie Drawings*, Brighton 1997, unpaginated. This echoes his 'Notes on Teaching': 'Dynamic results are obtained when students are urged to try for bad compositions... the outcome of proper exploration of the unknown.' In Bowness (n2), p14
21 Wilson (n13), p. 33
22 M Merleau-Ponty, *L'oeil et l'esprit*, (1964) in D Macey, ed. *The Penguin Dictionary of Critical Theory*, London 2000, p247
23 Charters (n6), p189

had to find his bearings in a world without a pictorial horizon and the fixed security of a distance vanishing point. Lacking the orientation of a horizontal marker the artist needed to locate where he stood physically in relationship to everything within this post-Newtonian universe. It required body and mind to be as one – as Dubuffet put it, the artist must 'leave as imprints the most immediate traces of *his* thoughts, the rhythms and impulses that beat in his arteries and run along his nerves.'[24] This is most clearly demonstrated in works such as *Footprint Image* (1952) and other paintings with footmarks like *The Blue Triangle Enters* (1953) or the handprint in *Yes* (1955) where the physical presence of the artist has been left as the trace of an indelible presence on the picture surface. Thus, once the artist has established an 'authentic' phenomenological relationship with the picture surface – 'body to body'[25] – the intellectualisation of painting no longer applies and it can return again to being a performance or, in Davie's phrase, 'like a dance.'[26]

As a painter highly attuned to the modern crisis around creativity that we have set out, Davie had to establish the dominant coordinates that would allow him to paint as he wished. This surely had to be done within 'the extended, disconnected, bewildering world of phenomena'. This ringing phrase is Wilhelm Worringer's, from his prescient 'Abstraction and Empathy' (1907). According to Worringer, one of the functions of the lineage of rationalism from the Renaissance onwards, was to stem man's feeling of being lost in the universe. The civilised peoples of the East, whose more profound world-instinct opposed development in a rationalistic direction... they alone remained conscious of the unfathomable entanglement of all the phenomena of life, and all the intellectual mastery of the world-picture could not deceive them as to this. Their spiritual dread of space, their instinct for the relativity of all that is, did not stand... *before* cognition, but *above* cognition.[27]

The turn to the East, heralded by Worringer, is a well-observed inclination evident in artists such as Davie and many others later in the 20th century, such as Mark Tobey, but we should not ignore the signal it offers to a Western crisis around space. The non-dualism inherent in Davie's thinking finds early echoes in Pascal's *Pensées* that, 'Nature is an infinite sphere whose centre is everywhere, whose circumference is nowhere,'[28] and leads to Worringer's 'spiritual dread of space', and of 'being lost in the universe' and, we suggest, pre-empts the much more familiar formalist critique of pictorial space in art associated with Clement Greenberg and American abstraction.

---

24 Wilson (n13), p33
25 Wilson (n13), p33
26 A Davie, (n4), p11
27 W Worringer, 'Abstraction and Empathy' (1907) in F Frascina and C Harrison, eds. *Modern Art and Modernism. A Critical Anthology*, London, 1982, p161
28 B Pascal, *Pensées*, fragment 199. There is a prehistory to this phenomenologically inclined reading which has its origins in Western scientific thought in the Alexandrian 'Corpus Hermeticum' in 3rd century BC, and goes through Alain de Lille in 12th century 'God is an intelligent sphere whose centre is everywhere and whose circumference is nowhere' to Pascal in the 17th century

Greenberg's assertiveness and confidence in his view of modern painting .was, somewhat ironically, in inverse proportion to the uncertainties and anxieties of the artists he lauded. For example, Rothko described his paintings as 'unknown adventures in an unknown space'.[29] In 'Abstract, representational, and so forth' Greenberg asserted that

> No matter how richly and variously he [the painter] inscribes and folds this curtain, and even though he still outlines recognisable images upon it, we may feel a certain sense of loss. It is not so much the distortion or even the absence of images that we may mind in this curtain-painting, but rather the abrogation of those spatial rights which images used to enjoy back when the painter was obliged to create an illusion of the same kind of space as that in which our bodies move. This spatial illusion or rather the sense of it, is what we may miss even more than we do the images that used to fill it.[30]

Rather than concentrate on Greenberg's aspiration for a 'balanced, Apollonian' restraint in art[31], we draw attention to the terms Greenberg uses such as 'loss', 'distortion', 'absence', and 'abrogation of rights'. The existential flavour of this passage captures, perhaps accidentally, some of the key anxieties around post-war artistic practice. Everything seems up for play in an era when humanity's capacity for evil seemed all too evident. Although this is a highly partial extraction of Greenberg's phrasing it serves to illustrate too that rarefied notions of pictorial flatness are entirely irrelevant to an artist like Davie. His art neither required extreme flatness nor representational depth but rather a different kind of space altogether, constructed around a shallow proscenium-like format, yet one that was, as we shall see, immanent in the forms and figures that populated that organic space, for example in *Opus D.617* (1953), rather than predetermined as found in the mathematical formulation of Alberti.

As said above, Davie's studio practice from 1950 onwards challenged orthodox spatial orientations. The somatic presence of the artist, the canvas and other materials, and the space of the studio were locked into a different and more intense kind of relationship. Greenberg captured this in part:

> The picture has now become an entity belonging to the same order of space as our bodies; it is no longer the vehicle of an imagined equivalent of that order. Pictorial space has lost its 'inside' and become all 'outside.' The spectator can / no longer escape into it from the space in which he himself stands.[32]

29 M Rothko, 'The Romantics were Prompted...' (1947) in C Harrison and P Wood, eds. *Art in Theory 1900–1990. An Anthology of Changing Ideas*, Oxford, 1992, p563
30 C Greenberg, 'Abstract, representational, and so forth' in *Art and Culture*, New York, 1961, p136
31 C Greenberg, 'The Present Prospects of American Painting and Sculpture', in *Horizon*, Oct 1947
32 Greenberg (n30), p136–7

But in reality, Davie seems just as unconvinced that a painting is to be considered primarily as an object in our space any more than as a three-dimensional spatial illusion (analogous to the non-sequitur that sheet music might be conceived as an object in space, rather than as a means to creating art in another dimension altogether). A more common rationalisation concerning Davie's performative studio practices, and one which distances it from Greenberg's formal purism, is to connect it with the writings of Harold Rosenberg and the term 'Action Painting'. Rosenberg's *The American Action Painters* (1952) is one of the classic position statements: '...the canvas began to appear... as an arena in which to act... What was to go on the canvas was not a picture but an event.'[33] This is not far from Davie's 'One must concern oneself with the activity of painting... and we must contrive to pay as little attention as possible to the end towards we are moving.'[34] As Rosenberg says: 'The image would be the result of this encounter.'[35]

Davie would soon directly put pen to paper to oppose this reading as himself as 'Action Painter', as we will see, but the reformulation of the artist's and the artwork's space in the process of art-making proposed by Rosenberg still contains important insights for connoting Davie's work as 'event' and a radical improvisation aimed at changing our perceptions. (Recall that Davie was indeed a performer in the jazz halls around Edinburgh long before he was a painter. The performative creative act was not an affectation and Davie continued to make advances in improvisatory jazz well into the 1970s). Both Davie and Rosenberg set out phenomenological accounts of material meeting material, through the body of the artist, which results necessarily in a communicative image. Moreover, Rosenberg echoes the destructive thread we found in Davie's earlier statements in the 1940s, cited above, when he says: 'what counts is [action painting's] special motive for extinguishing the object'.[36]

Yet Davie sought to distance himself from the label Action Painter as early as 1958, at the very epicentre of Britain's encounter with the new American painting. In 'Notes by the Artist' he wrote:

The popular term Action Painting is generally tagged on to my work and the writers imply in the term the outward show and expression of the artist's physical activity and emotion. Nothing could be further from the truth... Self-expression is something contrary to Art.[37]

Those familiar with Davie's oeuvre will realise that existentially inflected self-expression is antithetical to his practice. He continued,

33 H Rosenberg, 'The American Action Painters' (1952) in Harrison and Wood (n29), p581
34 A Davie, (n4), p11
35 Harrison and Wood (n29), p581
36 Harrison and Wood (n28), p582
37 A Davie, (n4), p11

one has no aim, striving, or expectation… Our painting does not convey
the drama of the moment of creation. Perhaps a better term for our purpose
would be 'Non Act Painting' implying more accurately that the true artist is
basically against acting and that he accepts the relative reality of existence
and therefore is not infatuated by the images of himself as above it.[38]

The action of an artist in a studio, making a painting, is akin to the practice
of a Cassavetes style 'method actor' losing themselves in the character they
are playing (as opposed to a theatrical actor drawing attention to their
performance). In this relative reality, they are no more important than the
materials with which they work. Physical effort and manipulation of material
is that through which art happens.

As has been noted above, the live creative process was seen by Davie and
his wife as important enough to record on film, as the compulsive footage
of Davie painting in his studio shows. We believe that in considering the
durational and active medium of film, and filmic space, we can approach
new readings of Davie's project. Again recall the underlying filmic metaphors
within Rosenberg's writings: 'Since the painter has become an actor, the
spectator has to think in a vocabulary of action: its inception, duration,
direction – psychic state, concentration and relaxation of the will, passivity,
alert waiting. He must become a connoisseur of the gradations between the
automatic, the spontaneous, the evoked.'[39]

'The artist works in a condition of open possibility' acting 'as if he were
in a living situation', as Rosenberg writes.[40] This is closely echoed in Davie's
(unerringly consistent) statements from over three decades – 'You can't see life
if you're in it'[41] and 'Painting is a continuous process which has no beginning
or ending.'[42] Rosenberg's performative aesthetics relies fundamentally on
open and dynamic techniques of artistic production, uppermost is perhaps
improvisation.

In this context, we might compare Davie with the methods of experimental
filmmaker John Cassavetes. Despite there being no direct historical connection
(they seem to have never met), comparison throws up some illuminated
insights. Cassavetes' quasi-improvisational techniques were non-teleological
and of an unfolding nature.

I want to do a film that would allow the actors the time and room to act. What
I try to do is anticipate the movement of the scene, let the actors be as free as

38 Davie (n4), p11
39 Harrison and Wood (n29), p582
40 Harrison and Wood (n29), p582
41 A Davie 'Artist's Statement for monograph by Michael Horovitz in Methuen 'Art in Progress' series,
1963, in Bowness (n2), p18
42 A Davie, unpublished lecture, delivered February 1992, University of Edinburgh

possible in space… We generally lit a room so we could shoot 360 degrees.[43]

Before the final credits of Cassavetes' film *Shadows* (1961), it seemed important enough to the director to announce that 'The film you have just seen was an improvisation'. (The improvisational strategies of the actors and director were also emphasised through the pervasive incidental music of jazz legend Charlie Mingus, an icon in the pantheon of Davie's musical sphere). In both cases, for Cassavetes and Davie, improvisation is far from anarchic, unfettered expression. As Davie reflected in 1991 'In order to create new forms and new ideas you have to curb your freedom. By all means you had to use freedom in the gestation of the process but working within restrictions can be so much more productive.'[44] Cassavetes, belying the totalising improvisational myth, offered structures and boundaries for his actors just as Davie's loose grid-like spatial architecture contained exuberant mark-making within, for example in *Kaleidoscope for a Parrot* (1960). The core aspiration that lies at the heart of improvisation is that it permits access to a level of reality that otherwise would not be possible, certainly not through conventional mimetic techniques. If Davie, in distancing himself from Action Painting, writes of acting as a kind of falsehood, then it is clearly the striving for more 'reality' that drives the artist. This is not so distant, in fact, from Rosenberg's view that 'Art as action rests on the enormous assumption that the artist accepts as real only that which he is in the process of creating.'[45]

As an extension of our argument, we find in the perhaps surprising source of Gilles Deleuze a compelling discussion of Cassavetes, particularly in relation to a radical rethinking of space. As Deleuze writes in *Cinema 2*,

> The greatness of Cassavetes' work is to have undone the story, plot, or action, but also space, in order to get to attitudes as to categories which put time into the body, as well as thought into life. When Cassavetes says that characters must not come from a story or plot, but that the story should be secreted by the characters, he sums up the requirement of the cinema of bodies: the character is reduced to his own bodily attitudes, and what ought to result is… a 'spectacle', a theatricalization or dramatization which is valid for all plots… As a general rule, Cassavetes keeps only the parts of space connected to bodies…[46]

This extraordinary passage on Cassavetes as a filmmaker applies equally to Davie as a painter. For Deleuze, Cassavetes puts time into the body by having the plot 'secreted' through the characters. Cassavetes is presented as a consummate filmmaker who has developed strategies that undo normative

---

43 R Carney (n16), p152–3
44 Patrizio and Hare (n1), p16
45 Rosenberg, (n33), p584
46 G Deleuze, *Cinema 2. The Time-Image*, London, 1989, p192

categories and ways of working with time, plot, story and, above all, space. The parallel with art is not that the artist secretes the painting, but that the painting secretes meaning within a spatial environment created by the forms painted therein, as an inevitable yet non-teleological process of improvisatory creation. The relatively consistent shallow pictorial envelope that almost all of Davie's paintings feature throughout his entire career – never expansive and Albertian yet equally never flattened and Greenbergian – similarly 'keeps only the parts of space connected to bodies', as Deleuze says.

Looking back on Davie's career, it is perhaps becoming clearer to see continuities, particularly with regard to a radicalised view of space and agency, rather than the common distinctions often highlighted in Davie's career and overall progression. A purposely reined-in improvisatory strategy locked within a shallow proscenium and grid-like space is his key approach, for example in *The Studio No. 30* (1975). Existing literature has cooperated with the artist in exclusively focusing on supposed mystical and 'universalist' intentions behind Davie's work. Rather than reasserting this ahistorical view, this paper has attempted to demonstrate that Davie's paintings embody an aesthetic order rooted in a specific historical moment where awareness of a particular crisis around spatial experience was the dominant issue in 20th century discourse.

This essay was jointly written by Andrew Patrizio and Bill Hare for the *Journal of the Society of Art History* (vol. 15, 2011).

EDUARDO PAOLOZZI
Master of the Universe, 1989

As Newton numbered the stars, and as Linnaeus numbered the plants,
so Chaucer numbered the classes of men.
William Blake, *A Descriptive Catalogue*, 1809

JAMES JOYCE CLAIMED that the Dublin of 16 June 1904 could be fully replicated from the portrayal of 'Bloomsday' in his novel *Ulysses*. A similar claim, but on a much more epic scale, was lodged by the science fiction writer JG Ballard – a long-time admirer of the artist – who proffered the seemingly outrageous notion that if the whole of 20th century civilisation was wiped out, later archaeologists would be able to reconstruct it from all the information contained in the vast work of Eduardo Paolozzi. Whether this piece of supreme hyperbole has any justification to it is of course open to debate, but the artist does appear to portray himself in this late sculpture as the master creator of all things.

Such claims are by nature metaphorical, and it was through the imaginative and creative use of metaphor – and its visual equivalent, collage – that Joyce, and later Paolozzi, radically developed fresh languages of representation to describe and critically scrutinise the multi-faceted aspects and complex workings of our brave new modern world. These innovative textual and visual languages with their endless permutations of equivalents allowed Paolozzi for instance, to formulate an encyclopaedic lexicon of new forms and highly flexible syntax, endowing the artist with the imaginative intellectual power to build and evolve his own vision and version of contemporary reality. Thus everything that grew out of, walked on, or flew over the earth's surface could now be reshaped and re-presented in different forms through the artist's awesome creative power of metamorphosis. Like a modern-day Linnaeus or Chaucer, Paolozzi could number the plants in his own botanical empire; and list the different types of creatures, men and deities in his animal and human kingdom – from insects, reptiles, mutants, monsters, heroes and gods. He could even match Newton – not with astronomical stars – but with cinematic ones, who as the Hollywood studio MGM claimed, even outnumbered the heavenly constellations.

Master of the Universe is the evolutionary apotheosis of Paolozzi's self-created chain of being which began with his early brutish creatures and figures of the 1950s. These he cobbled together from the debris and detritus left behind after the destructive waste of the preceding war years. These inchoate figures tottering on their shaky spindly legs, still possess a raw energy and primitive aura to them as though they have just emerged from the primordial swamp and are attempting to stand upright for the first time and walk forward into human history. By the 1960s Paolozzi's figures had evolved into beings of a very different character. Still using his much favoured, highly adaptable collage approach he now drew his source material from factory mass-produced units which were rearranged into different permutations to give his latest state-of-the-art figures a much more hard-edged abstract appearance. Furthermore, in tune with the mood of the 'swinging sixties' and the Pop Art era, Paolozzi also emblazoned much of his sculpture of that time with bright jazzy colours.

After his controversial 1971 retrospective exhibition at the Tate Gallery, Paolozzi produced relatively little figurative sculpture for the next decade or so, but by the end of the 1980s he had returned to the figure with greatly increased enthusiastic energy and a new attitude and approach. He now envisaged his sculptural creations as being figures of notable public status and cultural importance within the noble classical tradition. Appropriately many of these sculptures were commissioned to be placed in important civic sites – the most famous being his *Newton* prominently raised and situated outside the British Library in 1997. Paolozzi's method for the creation of these late figures was again an innovative variation on his collage-sculptural technique. Following the example of Rodin, whom he admired greatly, Paolozzi began building up an enormous store of plaster figures cast from a variety of high and popular cultural sources – from Michelangelo's *David* to Walt Disney's *Mickey Mouse*. These plaster figures then could be pulled out whenever needed in order to be cut into different anatomical sections. These fragmented bodily pieces could subsequently be rearranged and reconstructed to supply an endless variety of reassembled figure compositions in a Doctor Frankenstein manner.

Master of the Universe comes out of such a complex and protracted process. It began with Paolozzi's longstanding fascination with William Blake's famous satirical print of the great scientist Isaac Newton. He is depicted by Blake as naked, sitting on a rock under the sea of materialism, and bent over a scroll over which he holds, as his mathematical attribute, a pair of compasses. Paolozzi admired what he saw as the duality in Blake's image 'presenting to us simultaneously nature- and science-welded, interconnecting, interdependent' – significantly, the same notable characteristics and concerns of Paolozzi's own art. He initially translated Blake's *Newton* into a plaster relief of a highly mechanised figure from which developed his subsequent series of small scale plaster and bronze maquettes. For the later public commissioned versions of this work Paolozzi greatly enlarged the figure, giving it a more muscular physique, while still retaining elements of its mechanised form, through its plated and bolted surface. He also introduced a self-portrait head to the figure. There are however subtle differences between the various versions – for example, whereas *Newton* of the British Library has eyes after Michelangelo's *David* and weilds a giant pair of compasses, our *Master of the*

Universe is eyeless and holds a flat triangle in his hand. The statue is situated near the garden entrance to the grounds of the Scottish National Gallery of Modern Art's Mod Two. Appropriately it is in close proximity to a sculpture by Paolozzi's early studio partner and former Independent Group associate William Turnbull, entitled *Gate* (1972). Turnbull's work with its shiny burnished stainless steel surface and its open geometric minimalist abstracted composition makes a striking contrast to Paolozzi's *Master of the Universe*.

In the 1950s when Paolozzi was still experimenting with different ways to develop his art he observed that 'a plastic iconography is as difficult as a language.' Four decades on in the 1990s Paolozzi had mastered those difficulties and could draw upon an infinite range of sources to give undoubted authority and substance to his work, 'My own readings of source material is largely that of previous art works, technical magazines and books, a world of intricate problems and a lucid language.' *Master of the Universe* is a superb example of this, where the protean figure carries within it a history of Western figurative art from Hellenistic/Roman idealised bodies with portrait heads, to the medieval image of God the Geometer, to Michelangelo's figure of Abias on the Sistine ceiling, to Blake's *Newton,* to Rodin's *Thinker,* to Frankenstein's monster and through to a comic strip Nietzschean Superman.

Finally with that Nietzschean concept in mind it is interesting to compare the attitudes of James Joyce and Eduardo Paolozzi to the issue of the master artist/creator. While Joyce stated that 'The artist, like the God of Creation, remains above his handiwork, invisible, refined out of existence, indifferent, paring his fingernails', Paolozzi did not assume such an aloof and detached attitude to his own universe, 'I'm interested in the total idea of being an artist. I like the possibility of perhaps working on several levels, and I like the idea of a challenge.' Thus the *Master of the Universe* is never fully satisfied with his handiwork, but forever looking to create and bring into being yet more brave new worlds.

This essay was written for *Paolozzi at Large in Edinburgh: Artworks and Creative Responses* (Luath Press, Edinburgh, 2018).

WILLIAM TURNBULL

Large Horse (1989)

DUNDEE BY BIRTH, but London-based by profession, William Turnbull rarely showed north of the Border. Most Scots are still not familiar with his work. I first came in contact with his sculpture when *Large Horse* (1989) was on an extended loan to the Scottish National Gallery of Modern Art and had the work displayed in their grounds.

Right from my initial encounter I found that *Large Horse* invited and encouraged you to move around and through it. From a distance you are struck by its striking profiles which play off allusions to an adze axe motif against that of a plumed Greek helmet. Then moving closer its protective, self-supporting, two-piece architectural form draws you into its internal space. There, as you look out through the two large eye holes, you are imaginatively transported back to Ulysses and his fellow Greeks inside the Wooden Horse before they take Troy.

That ancient Greek connection is appropriate, as it was the *Horse of Selene* (438–432 BCE), from the east pediment of the Parthenon – on display in the British Museum – that stimulated Turnbull to embark on his lifelong creative engagement with the theme of the horse in his sculpture. It begins with his cubistic *Horse* from 1946, but the Greek classical dimension is clearly underlined by *Pegasus* of 1954. It is however, his corrugated textured *Horse* piece from the same year which, with its grounded arch form of neck and head that makes a clear connection to the similarly formatted *Large Horse*. There are also subtle differences between these early and late horse sculptures, but the main one of course, is scale. Yet although *Horse* would be completely dwarfed by the later *Large Horse* that does not mean it is less significant. As Turnbull himself said, 'Monumentality is a value, not a dimension.'

This essay was written for *William Turnbull, International Artist* (Lund Humphries, London, 2022).

JANET BOULTON

Remembering Ian Hamilton Finlay's Little Sparta

*And the earth, anchoring in the perfect harbours of Aphrodite, meets with
these in equal proportions, with Hephaistos and Water and Gleaming Air…*
Empedokles, *Poem on Nature*, Fragment 98

JANET BOULTON WORKS equally successfully in a range of different mediums,
but for this short essay, I have concentrated on her watercolours.

As one of the curators of Edinburgh College of Art's renowned classical
art cast collection I was particularly keen to witness the impact that Janet
Boulton's three-pronged Spartan assault would have on one of the main
citadels of the Northern Athenians. Many will know that Edinburgh College
of Art's Sculpture Court, where Janet Boulton's *Remembering Little Sparta*
took place, was specifically designed to present the ECA casts of the Parthenon
sculptures in as an authentic manner as possible. I was therefore very
interested to see how this cultural clash between the two opposing Greek
city states, Athens and Sparta would be played out. It was however, another
dialectic which soon diverted my attention. At the centre of the Sculpture
Court the artist had placed the presiding presence of the Medici Venus, a
plaster cast monument to Aphrodite herself. Thus unlike Ian Hamilton Finlay's
Spartan domain, where Apollo, that fearful force of reason and terror, holds
awesome sway, Janet Boulton's *Remembering Little Sparta* chose to dedicate
itself to a very different aspect of the power of the divine presence.

With this seemingly minimal, yet profoundly challenging intervention,
Janet Boulton provokes dialectical debate worthy of the Master of Stonypath,
Ian Hamilton Finlay, himself. Now this time the issue of gender was the focus
for consideration. For instance, we are again reminded that the initial Little
Sparta collaborative project was a joint one – between Sue and Ian Hamilton
Finlay, where a complex combination of feminine horticulture and masculine
culture combined to create one of the great art works of our age. Still, one
might ask however, what came first – the garden or its contents? The force
of nature has been around infinitely longer than our tenuous civilisation, and
it was only through the control of its mythic and physical powers that the
creation of human history and culture was made possible. Thus in the great
scheme of things it is the Garden of Love – Aphrodite's empire of the senses
– that creates the setting and possibility for Apollo's world of the mind and
Hephaistos' platform for human art and technological endeavour.

Psychology and feminism have revealed to our modern age that gender is
not merely a biological phenomenon, but much more importantly, a socially
and ideologically constructed one. The genderisation of most sociocultural

activities has also had strong influence on the visual arts, as witnessed by the Arts and Crafts debate, for example. Janet Boulton's long and sustained engagement with Finlay's garden in all its varying character also raises issues of artistic gender relationships. Little Sparta is a masterly 20th century reworking of the 18th century landscape garden where the Apollonian power of masculine reason controls and triumphs over the unruly forces of the natural world – for as the 18th century Augustin poet Alexander Pope declares in his gardening manifesto *An Epistle to Burlington*, 'Still follow sense, of every art the soul'.

Yet sensibility also found its proper place in the lower hierarchies of Enlightenment aesthetics; with the practice of watercolour painting for instance; which, until the professional romantics like Girtin and Turner came along, was deemed the prerogative of women and amateur artists. So it is all credit to Ian Hamilton Finlay to realise what an important additional visual contribution Janet Boulton's watercolour practice could make to the many other kinds of views and interpretations of Little Sparta that have been produced over the years.

In *Remembering Little Sparta* Janet Boulton, with sure technical skill and acute sensitivity, uses the so-called feminised medium of watercolour to create a very elusive, yet alluring vision of her absorbing subject. Although she does include Finlay's sculptural and textual poetics throughout Little Sparta, their presence pays a less prominent role in these richly atmospheric and subtly translucent dream-like images which recall Watteau, rather than any of his neoclassical successors. As with the magical paintings of the great rococo master, these delightful works of Janet Boulton, with their concentration on sensual involvement and emotional response, seem to deflect and defer the immediate need for rational thought and explanation.

This gives added significance to the Proustian aura suggested by the exhibition's title. Mnemosyne, the ancient Greek goddess of memory and the mother of the Muses, takes us back to before the reign of Apollo and the creation of reason and art, when humankind was imagined to be in immediate contact and complete union with the natural world. That previous existence persisted in the memory of the Greeks down the civilising generations as it still continues to haunt our collective unconscious to the present.

The Little Sparta watercolours of Janet Boulton poetically evoke this eternal yearning which we have for our lost arcadia. Yet in her pictorial world of the imagination, we are closer to Aphrodite's Isle of Cythera where 'Et in Arcadia ego' alludes not to the finality of death, but rather to the regenerative power of love.

This essay was published in *Scottish Art News* in 2012.

Joan Eardley

Street Kids and Stormy Seas

WHY WAS THE Joan Eardley exhibition given the elbow from its intended venue at the Scottish National Gallery to make way for Picabia this Festival? I keep asking myself that question. It couldn't have been because the letters of the latter's name conveniently slot into the spaces between the eight columns for display above the entrance to that august building. On that score Eardley would have equally fitted the bill. Was it something to do with the theme of this year's Edinburgh Festival? Hardly. The chameleon-like Picabia, claimed to be many things but never to my knowledge that he was Neopolitan. I can only surmise then that Picabia was preferred by those at the Scottish National Gallery who now make the decisions as to the use of the RSA Gallery, because he was regarded as a much 'bigger' (if not longer) name than the Scottish painter. That may be so in some quarters, but speaking to people without an art history degree, most had not heard of Picabia. There were even some who thought it was the name of a drink, and the exhibition was a return of the dreaded art of wine label design which was inflicted upon us a few years back.

Despite losing the prime exhibition site on Princes Street, the Joan Eardley show proved a popular success at the Talbot Rice Gallery, Edinburgh University, and the basement rooms of the Royal Scottish Academy. Not only was the exhibition continually full of enthusiastic visitors, but also their enthusiasm for the Scottish painter's work was such that they were eagerly buying Cordelia Oliver's newly published book in great numbers. (I wonder how many Picabia catalogues were sold?). Undoubtedly, Joan Eardley strikes a chord with a wide range of people. Her popularity continues to grow as do the value of her paintings. All of which makes it increasingly difficult to assess critically her achievement as a mid-20th century painter working under extremely difficult circumstances in a remote part of Western Europe.

As everyone knows, the Scots are particularly addicted to heroes and hero worship; especially the tragic sort – Robert Burns, Hugh Miller, Benny Lynch. And, now Scottish art has its own in the windswept figure of Joan Eardley, photographed, forever battling to hold down in pigment the storm-tossed seas at Catterline. Her short life – she died at 42 – was the stuff of tragedy but also heroic courage.

Born in Sussex in 1921 she suffered the traumatic experience of the suicide of her father at the age of eight. She was then brought up by her mother and maternal grandmother and educated at a private school in Blackheath. As her diploma *Self Portrait* (1943) reveals, she was an introspective person, preferring the company of other women and children. But she was also strong-willed and the early discovered gift for art quickly became the main driving passion in her life. In fact, it does seem that the old cliche of living to paint, really did apply to Joan Eardley. She became a student at Goldsmith's Art College in 1938, but was soon evacuated from London to Glasgow where she continued her studies at the School of Art under the encouraging teaching of Hugh Adam Crawford. A prize-winning graduate, she quickly discovered that she was temperamentally unsuited to teaching, and it must have been at this time that she decided to attempt to become a full-time practising artist. This, in a rapidly declining Scotland, with little or no artistic support or patronage, was extremely hazardous, if not, in the case of a single woman painter, downright foolhardy.

At this point it might be helpful to look at one of the most important influences on Joan Eardley; that of Vincent van Gogh, whose example must have affected her course of action right from the beginning of her career. Sometime in their lives, usually during late adolescence, most people who come in contact with them, fall under the spell of van Gogh (or DH Lawrence), but then quickly grow out of it. In this respect Eardley never did grow up. Not only was the art of the great Dutch painter a presence in her work, but his life of sustained commitment against all kinds of obstacles, gave her a strong feeling of moral support throughout her difficult career. A late landscape, *Stubble Field* (c1960), not one of her best works, painted around the time when she was becoming aware of how ill she actually was, is clearly an act of homage, maybe even a kind of self-identification. The profound influence of van Gogh on Joan Eardley, is much more than certain stylistic similarities. Both shared a dedication to reveal through their art the bond of feeling that is generated between the human spirit and the ever-changing environment. The energetic power of van Gogh's paintings, and the best of Eardley's works, especially the late seascapes, are not depictions of uncontrolled chaos, but an expression through gesture and colour, of human creativity in harmony with the ultimately unifying vitality of natural forces.

Yet, it has to be said that van Gogh's influence on Eardley's development as a painter was a mixed blessing. In her early work, for example, she is inclined to similar subjects as the Dutch artist, with jam-packed compositions of cosy interiors, workers in the fields or broken-down cottages, most of which merely reach the level of the picturesque. Still, on occasion, as with her first major work, *The Mixer Men* (1944), and the ink drawing *Study Of Harness* (1947), she could produce an image which assertively stands up for itself through its own ungainly awkwardness.

What Eardley required as an emerging artistic personality was a counterbalance to her natural inclination towards overexpression of her feelings for her subjects. She needed someone to direct her towards a more considered, analytical approach to her art, in order to allow the subject to speak for itself. Fortunately she found that restraining influence in the example and teaching of James Cowie. He was an independent-minded outsider on the Scottish art scene, who was warden of Patrick Allen-Fraser School of Art at Hospitalfield, near Arbroath, where Eardley went as a postgraduate student in 1947. Cowie had little time for 'the self-expression business'. He regarded painting as the intellectual pursuit of clarity and order in the manner of Poussin as his late *Self-Portrait (The Blue Shirt)* (c1950) demonstrates. Not surprisingly, Eardley did not hit it off with such a man as Cowie, but she was shrewd enough to take on board much of the advice she received at Hospitalfield.

Cowie's influence is most apparent in the early Catterline landscapes, but can immediately be felt in the drawings Eardley did on a GSA travelling scholarship she won the following year. The single-figure studies of Italian and French peasants (for example, *Old Italian Peasant Woman* (1949), are set against the neutral background of the untouched paper. Her drawings now have an intensity of undistracted focus, which while concentrating on the structure of interlocking forms, also, through the sensitive use of line shading, bring out the calm individual dignity of the subjects. Even the crowded landscapes and city views display a much more considered presentation than in her earlier work.

Despite her language difficulties, the people and street life which she encountered on her travels made a deep impression on Eardley. On her return she set about continuing with outdoor subject matter. In this she was fortunate to be working from a studio in Glasgow. For despite its geographical position, Glasgow has much of the character of a southern continental city, with its vigorous working-class street life or so it was in the early 1950s, before the bulldozers moved in.

Eardley's acquired mastery of controlled line and composition is most evident in her drawing of shipbuilding yards she began around the Port Glasgow area, as seen in *Shipyard With Cranes* (1951–52). Although less robustly dynamic, they are comparable with Muirhead Bone's well-known depictions of similar scenes. In Eardley's case, however, these studies of industrial activity and tenement architecture were developed into generalised backdrops for the early versions of an aspect of urban life for which her name has almost become synonymous – the street life and games of Glasgow kids.

Some of the best examples of her portrayal of this subject were achieved during this early period. Maybe this was because the art and the working people she had recently witnessed in Italy and France were still fresh in her imagination. She was able to infuse the experience of both into her vision of Glasgow life with which she wanted her art to be identified. Like Courbet, or Caravaggio, or Giotto, Eardley wished her art to endow the shared experience of the common life with the grandeur she felt it deserved. In the best of these works, especially *Children, Port Glasgow* (1952), which for Scottish art at that time is a large picture, great emphasis is placed on the outline of forms and the frank application of paint in broad slabs of local colour. These features, plus the shallow depth of composition, give the painting a monumental relief-like quality reminiscent of the great Italian frescoes and the 19th century French realist works which she had recently studied on her travelling scholarship.

Impressive as these works of the early 1950s may be, there are many people who find the main subject of Eardley's Glasgow paintings, especially the later ones, hard to take. She might have been wiser to have followed WC Fields' advice and stayed clear of children where in art the accusation of exploitation is never very far away. For, undoubtedly, the use of such subjects in painting can be a minefield of potential dangers, putting the artist's integrity constantly under threat. Why Eardley was so compulsively drawn to these kids is open to speculation. Most might accept her straightforward explanation that they were just there, coming and going through her studio, and so readily available. Others have felt that there was more to it than that: that there must have been some psychological reason for the constant use of such subject matter. A combination of both reasons is likely to be the case.

What is certain is that after her return to Scotland she rarely ever treated an adult theme. In fact this was a great pity, for on the odd occasion she did, Eardley produced some of her finest works, outside her great seascapes. This is certainly true of the four small pen and wash head studies she produced of *Jeannie* (1954). In these deeply affectionate portraits Eardley delicately manages to balance the push and pull of the van Gogh/Cowie influences on her. In almost Rembrandt manner she is able to give full attention to the individuality of the sitter, while at the same time conveying the universal character of old age.

The other adult to feature in a number of Eardley's best works of her middle period was Angus Neil who she had met at Hospitalfield. Like Jeannie, he possessed a childlike personality and his emotional dependency on Joan, made their relationship more like one of mother and son. Eardley portrayed him in a series of interior scenes, the last of which was probably *Sleeping Nude* (1954–55). This was the only work which brought Eardley public attention, outside the art scene in Scotland. When this painting was shown at the Glasgow Institute in 1955, the *Sunday Express*, that staunch guardian of Scottish morals and culture, could not, despite the classical precedent of Diana and Endymion, come to terms with the idea of a clothed woman observing an unaware naked man. With the Scottish macho image under such threat, there appeared an outraged article under, it has to be said, the rather wimpish headline, 'This sleeping man has (ooh!) no clothes'.

Amusing as that incident seems now, it does give an indication of the array of sexually inspired suspicion and rank philistine prejudices that a woman artist had to face during the 1950s in a backward country like Scotland. There is a certain irony, then, in that Lucian Freud, also shown at this year's Edinburgh Festival as the honoured artist at the Scottish National Gallery of Modern Art, should specialise in similar nude subjects, and be hailed as 'the greatest living realist painter' (whatever that might mean). However, he is a man looking at naked men, and also, of course, an English painter of the Establishment-promoted 'London School' of figurative painting, so the £300,000 forked out for one of his works for our Scottish National Collection must be well worth it.

After the *Sleeping Nude* controversy, Eardley must have realised that the Scottish public were unable to take such demanding paintings. Furthermore, no patron, as has happened to other artists in a similar situation in other countries, appeared to demonstrate their support by buying the painting. Not entirely surprisingly then, from this point, there begins a gradual change in the character and later a decline in the quality of her Glasgow kid paintings. This deterioration coincides with a growing taste for her work through such dealers as Aitken Dott in Edinburgh and Cyril Gerber in Glasgow.

It should be said that there are still some fine individual works, for example, a series of boys' heads *Boy in a Cap* (1956), which have a direct intense quality reminiscent of van Gogh's Nuenen peasant women portraits. But generally speaking from the mid-50s a marked contrast begins to appear. In the earlier Glasgow pictures, there is a respect for the psychological, if not always the physical, individuality of the children and their decaying city environment. But in the worst of the later works the subject is treated to a dose of Bastien-Lepage type sentimental realism. In these pictures Eardley appears stylistically to have come under the influence of Dubuffet and *art brut*. The figures, as with *Little Girl With Squint* (1961), are flattened out against graffiti covered walls in a pastiche of childlike drawing. Any physical defects, such a large ears, badly cut hair, or squint eyes are exploited for pathetic effect. These scenes of urban kailyard must have had special appeal to the bourgeois buyers who were now beginning to acquire her work. As John Berger pointed out in an essay on Millet, the capitalist cannot get enough of poverty and deprivation, as long as it is framed and he can hang it on his wall.

If the Glasgow paintings were all there was to Eardley's *oeuvre*, then she might, despite some fine work, have been little remembered. From the mid-'50s, however, she began to turn more and more to landscape as the area where she could seriously develop her creativity as a painter. She had 'discovered' the small fishing village of Catterline, near Stonehaven, and gradually began to regard it as her spiritual home. In the last years of her short life, Eardley's routine seems to have been to work in Glasgow during the summer months. Then for the rest of the year she would be in Catterline to witness and paint with great relish the glories of the Scottish climate in all its variable moods.

Coming across the later works of Eardley one might be excused for thinking that they were the product of two distinct personalities. But on a closer look there begins to appear a linking area between the 'graffiti' pictures and the great seascapes. This bridge between the two aspects of Eardley's last years lies in the treatment of most of the later landscapes around Catterline, which for all their free use of gestural brushwork and whirlwind compositions, (for example in *Beehives*, 1961), remain basically graphic in character like the Glasgow pictures of that period. Few of them really take off. With little feeling for atmosphere, they tend to remain static, illustrating a climatic condition rather than a natural changing process. They are theatrical rather than truly dramatic, with the sky now, not the city, as a flat backdrop; the artist acting more as a director than a painter, choreographing the landscape to reach sometimes stunning, but ultimately artificial, heights of virtuosity.

The seascapes are something else. In contrast to the expressionist gymnastics of the landscapes, all the best seascapes are distinguished by a mood of austere restraint. As with *Breaking Wave* (1960), all have the same basic compositional arrangement of classic simplicity. Within the horizontal format of each work – which was considered enormous for a Scottish painting at that time – there are three bands of varying tone or colour stretching across the picture plane; the middle and narrower one being the most active in character. The seascapes are almost abstract, but for their sense of actuality which is not fixed but in constant flux. Set at the meeting place between land and sea, the paintings are also on the edge between recognisable imagery transforming into the physical reality of paint laid over paint. They do not depict, but through the suggestive power of the act of painting itself, stimulate our imaginative powers to sense the awesome, roaring power of the North Sea. (In fact, every oil company boardroom should be required to have a Joan Eardley seascape hanging on its wall to remind its directors of how vulnerable their oil rigs are).

These late seascapes are Eardley's masterpieces. They do not transport the spectators to new vistas, but directly confront them with the immediate experience of intense dram and powerful action, which through the unique properties of painting are made tangibly real. In the end Eardley is not an heir to the romantic impressionism of MacTaggart but the realist materialism of Courbet.

The Edinburgh Festival exhibition to mark the 25th anniversary of Joan Eardley's death revealed a career of prodigious output but variable quality. The lapses in her work were as much to do with the sorry state of Scottish art in the 1950s as with any fault on Eardley's part. She really was the only younger full-time practising artist of any distinction working in Scotland at that time. Yet she had to contend with almost no serious critical assessment of her work, a small picture-buying public whose taste on the whole was crass, and a right-wing reactionary press who only sticks its nose into art galleries when it thinks it can sniff a good story for its moronic public. Despite all this, Eardley's career was a remarkable achievement, and within the narrow confines of the Scottish art scene of her time she now appears one of the few figures of real stature.

Finally, to return to the issue of the Eardley exhibition removal from the RSA Galleries. In no way am I advocating that Scottish artists should be promoted simply for being Scottish (although like other countries, a little positive discrimination would not go amiss). But if one of our major artists is to give way to an important international exhibition, let it be one.

Again, I keep asking myself an unanswered question. Why is it that London can manage to have one major exhibition after another all the year round, like the recent early Cezanne one or the late Picasso show, while Edinburgh, which prides itself on being a city of international culture, cannot organise or buy in even for the Festival one exhibition of equivalent status and popular appeal? Maybe Frank Dunlop or Timothy Clifford can tell us why.

This essay was published in *Cencrastus* (issue 31, 1988).

ANTHONY HATWELL
Maker of Metaphor

*I construct a metaphor for an object from the visible world, creating forms
which will articulate the space through plane and form relationships, implied
movements and spacial directions. I wish a tension to exist between the
polarities of the humanistic subject and the spacial structure, fused into one
elemental image which bestrides the perceived external world and the internal world of the imagination.*
Anthony Hatwell, 1983

IN OUR CONTEMPORARY art world, which at times seems completely enthralled
to the cult of youth and instant celebrity, it will comes as a surprise to many,
that after being Head of Sculpture at Edinburgh College of Art for over 20
years, and having a distinguished artistic career which includes a number
of prestige national group exhibitions, Tony Hatwell should choose to have
his first one-man exhibition at the age of 82 at the Talbot Rice Gallery, The
University of Edinburgh. The reasons for this long delay are certainly complex;
they are not only private and personal, but are also an extreme consequence
of the rigorously dedicated nature of Hatwell's committed artistic practice and
sustained aesthetic beliefs within a particular period of British modern art.

Hatwell is of that generation of artists who emerged after World War
Two into a British art scene very different from the one today. At that crucial
time the London art world was then in the throes of a fierce struggle for the
leadership of British modern art, which at long last, was coming into its own.
Established and emerging artists and their champions were forming themselves
into rival factions. The dominant movement, headed by Henry Moore and the
St Ives artists, was championed by the powerful figure of Herbert Read. There
were however, a number of other contending groups – such as the Independent
Group at the ICA, promoted by Lawrence Alloway, The London Figurative
School supported by David Sylvester, the 'Kitchen Sink' of British Realism
advocated by John Berger and the belated emergence of British abstraction
encouraged by the painter/critic Patrick Heron. The young Tony Hatwell
also became part of a modernist group – The Borough Bottega – which, by
contrast to the others, had a very low public profile and lacked the promotion
of influential critical voices and curatorial support. Hatwell, along with other
members of The Borough Bottega Group – such as Leon Kossoff and Frank
Auerbach – had studied under David Bomberg, who remained a profound and
lasting influence on Hatwell's future development. Bomberg, after his early
celebrated connection with Wyndham Lewis's Vorticism of around 1913/14,
had by the time he taught Hatwell in the early '50s become a relatively

forgotten figure and had retreated into 'almost monkish seclusion'. This sense of isolation however, resonated with his followers, for the group name, 'Bottega' means medieval workshop – an anonymous community.

Yet despite his lack of critical or curatorial recognition Bomberg was still an influential force through his position at Borough Polytechnic where Hatwell studied, before going on to the Slade. For Bomberg brought into the teaching and practice of British modern art a radically different approach from that of the conventional art schools. He thoroughly rejected the still predominant academic method of art instruction based on empirical mimetic reproduction, which he dismissed as 'superficial realism'. Inspired by Bishop Berkeley's 'philosophy of the metaphysic of mind and matter' and Cezanne's revolutionary 'interpretation of form', Bomberg shunned 'the decorative properties of attractive superficialities' and 'wilful distortion'. Instead he advocated an intense process of visual and tactile exploration and experimentation which would release and express the physical and spiritual inner unity of the artist's subject – which he famously termed the 'Spirit in the Mass'.

Deeply impressed with these challenging ideas Hatwell tenaciously pursued them throughout his subsequent career by attempting to translate Bomberg's ideals for modern painting into his own sculptural practice – particularly through the mediation of drawing. This extremely demanding creative process has been a long and painstaking endeavour for Hatwell. As he observed in a letter of 2007, 'Bomberg did not have much consciousness of how sculpture might be made, and did not teach sculpture. I attended his drawing and painting class and tried to interpret a drawing approach into sculpture, which I found very difficult.' Faced with this challenge, Hatwell set about seeking a way, to not only adhere to Bomberg's artistic tenets, but also develop a valid studio method in terms of his sculptural practice. Interestingly, Hatwell's experimental approach to his work seems to be close to that of his contemporary fellow sculptor, William Turnbull – with whom incidentally he showed in a group show at Thirty Queens Gallery, Norwich in 1956 – who stated 'I began to make a piece of sculpture to find out what a piece of sculpture should look like.'

Making sculpture with no preordained rules for guidance and no preconceived idea how the work will turn out, must be a daunting and protracted process. This is clearly indicated by the extended dates of production for some of the sculptural pieces in this Talbot Rice exhibition which in some cases can even span two or three decades. Yet despite the lengthy periods of intense critical meditation and experimental practise involved in their making, Hartwell's powerful sculptures always turn out to be vigorously robust and intuitively primitive in a truly mythopoeic way. This consistently comes about as a result of Hatwell's particular modernist approach which acts out a similar creative role to that of the first makers of things who had the power to perceive metaphorical connections between the natural and the human worlds and were able to express that vital connection in concrete form. Hatwell's authentic art is likewise invigorated by the organic power of visual metaphor which is ultimately the primary source of inspiration for the creative imagination.

Hatwell's art is never in pursuit of rational empirical reproduction. On the contrary his sculpture is always ambiguous, ambivalent, illusive and poetic. As he declared in one of his letters the hard-fought goal of his art is 'not the analytical reproduction of natural forms, but a representation – a quite different thing – a creative appraisal of the model or object from the outset, creating a totality…' Thus through the metaphorical power of his creative will the sculptor transforms the raw material of his sculpture into absorbing presences of a mysterious and mystical nature. His constructed and vigorously painted figures express the essence of human physical consciousness through action, movement and gesture. Thus with such organic and dynamic unity at the heart of Hatwell's sculpture, works like *Dancing Figure* – even after close scrutiny and appraisal – leave us pondering with the Poet – 'Who can know the dancer from the dance?'

This catalogue essay was written for the exhibition *Anthony Hatwell, Sculpture and Drawings*, shown at the Talbot Rice Gallery, The University of Edinburgh in 2013.

COLQUHOUN AND MACBRYDE
The Last Bohemians

I AM AWARE that in the world of academic research the anecdotal is regarded with deep suspicion if not downright contempt. I still however feel obliged to relate my chance encounter with Roger Bristow a couple of years ago at the opening of an exhibition of Scottish modern painting which I curated for a gallery in Cornwall. My selection for that exhibition included Robert Colquhoun's *Bitch and Pup* (1958) from the Edinburgh City Art Centre Collection. This immediately attracted the enthusiastic attention of Roger and is now the opening illustration to his new book. We naturally got into a conversation in which he told me that he was then working hard to bring out a publication on Colquhoun and MacBryde.

I have to admit at the time I did not expect too much. Over the last few decades or so there have been occasional attempts to revive interest in their work – almost solely in Scotland where ironically, 'The Two Roberts' hardly ever showed during their careers. These previous valiant efforts unfortunately produced little new research material. I was therefore very surprised, not to say delighted, when I finally acquired the monumental achievement of *The Last Bohemians* which matches up to its fly leaf citation of being 'The fruit of nearly 20 years of original research'. Over that time Roger Bristow appears to have dedicated himself to pursuing as much material as is physically and historically possible concerning the art and careers of these once celebrated Scottish painters. He has succeeded in this very daunting task through his close examination of the artists' personal correspondence and those who wrote about them; as well as by seeking out and interviewing innumerable acquaintances, both friendly and hostile, who had their lives touched in one way or another by this alluringly delightful, but deadly duo. Some will certainly feel that such anecdotal material is untrustworthy, especially so long after their deaths in the 1960s. Yet the accumulative effect of such primary research does create a vividly revealing biographical account of Colquhoun and MacBryde and the post-war London art world which they served and suffered throughout their brief and tragic lives.

With regard to contemporary art historical studies Roger Bristow's book will have little appeal to those of a more theoretical disposition. There is no post-structuralist textual discussion of the image or post-Freudian psychological or queer theory on the artists themselves. Some critics have been a little disappointed in Bristow's reluctance to be diverted from his predominately descriptive narrative approach. For instance in a mainly appreciative *Guardian* review (24.04.10) Frances Spalding bemoans that 'Bristow does not rid us of the feeling that the mask they (Colquhoun and

MacBryde) put up obscures more interesting tensions.' Rightly or wrongly, as Ms Spalding notes 'Bristow remains coolly observant'; his observations nevertheless are highly informative and revealing in themselves without being overlaid with critical interpretation. Even if the reader were not particularly interested in Bristow's biographical subject there are rich sources of information to be found in his book for the social art historian. In particular many aspects of the London art scene during those crucial decades, when British Modernism was finally established as the dominant movement in the 1940s and 1950s. Furthermore, through Bristow's painstaking research we are made to realise what an important part Colquhoun and MacBryde played in that cultural achievement.

Contextually *The Last Bohemians* goes a long way to explain how this unlikely event came about. In great detail, Bristow traces the careers of Colquhoun and MacBryde – from their immediate personal and artistic partnership forged at pre-war Glasgow School of Art, where they were quickly regarded by the supportive staff and their student peers as having exceptional talent; to their final stages of alcoholic self-destruction brought about by disillusionment and despair. Yet during their 'golden boys' decade – between the mid-'40s and mid-'50s – 'The Two Roberts' were a powerful force to be reckoned with on the London art scene. With the support of the shadowy, but influential network of ambitious dealers, wealthy gay collectors, supportive administrators, fellow artists and writers they successfully challenged the insular attitudes of English art by producing paintings which seriously engaged with the challenges laid down by international Modernism. They were soon recognised by the more progressive elements of the creative and critical metropolitan community as radical innovators who understood, and could utilise for their own distinctively austere purposes, the complex pictorial languages of Cubism and modern Expressionism. At the time many were influenced and attempted to follow their example, but for a whole range of complex reasons Colquhoun and MacBryde subsequently fell out of favour with the new 'you've never had it so good' consumer society of Britain which by the early 1960s found abstraction and then pop art more to its fickle taste. Ironically, despite the decades of critical neglect of their own achievements, the modern figurative tradition in British art – which Colquhoun and MacBryde did so much to establish – has gone from strength to strength through Francis Bacon and The London School as well as the art of John Bellany and much Scottish contemporary painting.

This essay was published in the *Journal of the Scottish Society of Art History* (vol 15, 201).

BOYLE FAMILY

Old Habits of Looking – New Ways of Seeing

*I have tried to cut out of my work, any hint of originality, style,
superimposed design, wit, elegance or significance. If any of these are
to be discovered in the show then the credit belongs to the onlooker.*
Mark Boyle, 1966

THE DESIRE TO enter an idyllic 'brave new world' envisioned by Miranda in
Shakespeare's *The Tempest* has tantalised and enthralled the human memory
and imagination since the dawn of civilised society. Such recurring yearnings
have manifested themselves in many different religious, philosophical,
scientific, political and especially artistic forms. To the classical eras these
feelings have been expressed through the Arcadian pastoral. To romantic
sensibilities they could only be fully satisfied by regaining the perceptive power
of the 'innocent eye'.

Now, in our modern technological, consumer age, we have perversely
become addicted to the lure of the primitive in all its various guises. Such
Edenic, utopian longings have undoubtedly been a powerful impulse to artistic
creativity through the ages. Poets and artists have continually provided us with
reassuring words and images to succour and protect us against our sense of
loss and alienation in our hostile historical world. Yet should that really be the
mission of art? Should artists be expected to knit cultural comfort blankets for
a society that wishes to avoid and escape from the actual realities of its present
situation? In truth, should we in the words of Bertolt Brecht, not try to 'forget
the good old days and focus on the bad new ones'?

On the face of it, Boyle Family's minutely detailed descriptions of our
world produced for their ongoing, and seemingly endless enterprise, *Journey
to the Surface of the Earth*, would appear to resolve these contradictory
roles of art – between nostalgic reverie and contemporary awareness. Their
work, on the one hand, appears to give us back the lost innocence of pure
uncontaminated vision, and on the other, presents us with a raw slice of
the world that is as real and unmanipulated as could be possibly envisaged.
When we look at and pour over these enthralling works it seems as if we can
become like the entranced Miranda, who suddenly sees the world in a fresh,
yet profoundly reassuring light. In fact, for those who find looking at Boyle
Family's work consoling and unproblematic, please do not read this essay
further. There is no need to raise difficulties where none exist.

Mark Boyle's declaration of intent, quoted at the opening of this essay,
seems to have turned the interpretive role completely over to what
EH Gombrich termed the 'beholder's share'. Thus for those of a more

adventurous and enquiring disposition, there are 'difficulties' here which, of course, can also be regarded as challenges that bring their own kinds of satisfaction and reward to the 'onlooker'.

Before beginning a discussion on the appearance, status and nature of these fascinating works; it might be helpful to have a word about the actual making of a Boyle Family 'painting' taken from a random site anywhere on the Earth's surface. Although the details of the process is kept a family secret, it basically involves the making, and then painting, of a transparent resin caste of that site. The process is not dissimilar to the making a death mask. This may go some way to explain why these works do not have the instant immediacy of a documentary image for the 'onlooker', but rather, emit a meditative aura of timelessness which can be absorbing and even hypnotic.

Let's now begin to address the issue of artistic status and start by asking, as one of Mark Boyle's 'onlookers', what are we really looking at? Already even at this basic level of enquiry we might not come up with a satisfactory straightforward answer. Right away we begin to perceive that for all their seeming openness, these apparent slices of reality are elusive and enigmatic. They certainly allow us optically to scrutinise freely their luxuriously austere surfaces and to stand back and admire their extraordinary verisimilitude. However, they also mutely refuse to give a simple answer as to what they might be. Are these 'paintings', as the Boyles call them, really paintings in the normal sense of the term? Or could they just as easily be regarded as collaged relief panels? Are they just as much polychrome, moulded sculpture as painting? Or could they even be seen as monumental, three-dimensional, super photographic replicas? Even as physical material objects, hovering between the sculptural, the mosaic, the photographic and the tableau, they continually evade being readily pigeon-holed into constricting categories.

If, however, we are determined to pursue this line of enquiry, we might for example try to test the identity of Boyle Family's paintings as cultural artefacts against the academic system of generic classification. With this approach for instance, one might suggest that these works are pieces of natural landscape, yet are presented to us on the gallery walls as still life. There may be something in this, as both these types of painting – landscape and still life – were traditionally placed at the bottom of the hierarchy of the academic genre system.

This was because they lacked intellectual input and were deemed by the cultural establishment to be 'easy', non-learned subjects which everyone, irrespective of their social status and education, could readily access. This type of classifying approach could also be applied to that other lowly type of painting – genre, which dealt with ordinary, everyday human activity and was suspected of being socially vulgar and politically too democratic. Undoubtedly the egalitarian and the demotic – as opposed to the elitist or populist – lie at the heart of Boyle Family's belief in the social role of art and its relationship and responsibility to the onlooker.

Another generic possibility of classification might be portraiture. Our

English word 'portrait' ultimately derives from the Latin, *protrahere*, meaning to pull or single out one individual from the masses – literally a face in the crowd. Similarly the Boyles, through their random means of selection, extract an arbitrary spot from the mass of Earth's surface and present it to us for the same kind of particular scrutiny as a Roman veristic portrait. In the end, however, any attempt at this kind of defining is futile. Even in the art world, categorisation is commodification under a more respectable name. Artists and their patrons colonise their subjects through the aegis of some act of cultural and material possession. Whereas in the art of Boyle Family their subjects select themselves through chance and indifference to any self-seeking, audience-pleasing, aesthetic or ideological motive – as shown by Mark Boyle's quote.

Let us now turn to the possibility of placing Boyle Family's painting within the context of modern and contemporary art. Here again we find that categorising is still extremely elusive and maybe ultimately futile. Initially one might wish to link these works with such aspects of 20th century art as collage, art brut, dadaist ready-made or junk art. Certainly in the 1960s, during the early stages of their careers, Mark Boyle and Joan Hills were very heavily involved with the counterculture art scene of that decade, employing avant-garde, neo-dadaist approaches to their work, which ultimately led to their epic, world-encompassing series of paintings. Yet always at the core of their art, whatever form it took, was a constant testing and shifting of different strategies of experimental engagement. This was practiced through a range of disciplines, from sculptural construction to scientific archaeology, from radical democratic theatre to popular musical entertainment. Thus their work was involved with a whole variety of challenging and subversive acts, including performance, land art, Conceptualism, relief sculpture and documentary serialism. Boyle Family's work could never be contained or categorised by any single one of these multi-activities.

Their art is as open and receptive as any, and the Boyles' identification with archaeology is crucially significant here. Archaeologists must work with the evidence of the past as they find it; everything is potentially of equal importance and use in their enquiring pursuit of knowledge. Similarly, the Boyles engage with the landscape of our contemporary world, without any pre-motivated intention on the one hand, and with an encyclopaedic curiosity on the other.

By contrast, if any attempt to categorise the paintings of Boyle Family is fraught with difficulties and contradictions and is ultimately doomed to failure, the viewing of their content does appear to be straightforward and open in a 'Miranda-like' fashion. The labels and captions attached to their paintings would seem to confirm this, with clear statements as to subject, locale, date, size, etc. To all intents and purposes it would appear that we have secure pieces of verifiable realism hung on the wall for our examination and contemplation.

Why then do we, the onlookers, experience so much profound pleasure and sentiment from such a seemingly obvious state of affairs? Surely at any time we can all see such things literally at the drop of a hat. If it cannot just be the subjects themselves that are so fascinating, then surely it must be due to the actual context in which they are presented and viewed by us. Although they may appear to be 'pure' reality, we inevitably encounter them within a historically and culturally conditioned situation and institutionalised tradition. Thus the frisson which these works create in us must be something similar to looking at any other painting or sculpture with a high degree of mimetic input: such as, for example, a 17th century Dutch still life by Willem Kalf or a Duane Hanson super realist figure. Yet Boyle Family's art seems to have a much more intense and fundamental effect on our heightened awareness than any piece of mere high illusionism. This must have much to do with the way the Boyles present 'the brutality of fact' to the onlooker; in particular, their reorientation of the normal horizontal relationship we have with the world to a vertical one. Some commentators on Boyle Family works have singled out this feature – the transferring of the horizontal surface of Earth onto the verticality of the gallery wall – as being one of the significant ways in which their paintings distinguish themselves as works of art, rather than pieces of reality. On the other hand, one might question however, whether this re-presentation of viewpoint invalidates in any way, the vital connection between these paintings and our perceptual experiences of the real world. Of course, standing on two legs as fully paid-up members of the Homo erectus species, we do look towards an horizon which is never found in a Boyle Family painting. Yet were we always so erect? The Sphinx's riddle to Oedipus reminds us that we all made our initial, tangible contact with Earth's surface on all fours. Thus it could be argued that one of the reasons why we immediately and instinctively have such an intense visual and tactile bond with these almost mesmeric surfaces is that they put us back in touch with our very early evolutionary, pre-adult, pre-erectus self. Then we were all receptive sentient beings, clawing and crawling around with our eyes and noses only a few inches off the ground.

This pre-Oedipal stage in the development of our optical/tactile relationship with the world is as crucially important as the later symbolic one in our personality evolution when we begin the process of acquiring verbal and textual language. Could it be that, psychologically speaking, our attitude to Boyle Family's work is relocated in this early, but very fertile and potential, pre-linguistic period of our human consciousness? Could this be a possible reason as to why their paintings, while seeming to be so open and accessible, are also so resistant to semantic interrogation and explanation? Such uniquely autonomous work not only challenges each individual onlooker's rationale, but the power and authority of the *logos* itself.

Boyle Family have always been committed to subverting conventional attitudes and practices and their work needs to be seen within the history of modern and contemporary art. From the outset, modern artists wished to challenge and even overthrow the traditional forms of representations of appearances as witnessed by the development of innovatory techniques from the impressionists through to the cubists and their subsequent followers. The second focus of attack by the avant-garde was concentrated on breaking the seemingly inviolable link between imagery and language. This particular aspect of radical modern art led to abstraction, but was also associated with Dada and Surrealism, especially in the subversive work of Marcel Duchamp and Rene Magritte. Thirdly, and maybe finally, not only has that possible hiatus between the visual and the textual been achieved, but with the work of Boyle Family (as with Jasper John's *Flag* paintings) the visual can and does resist, the colonising and mythologising process of iconographical language and the politics of representation. Thus, when the onlooker gazes at the pre-semantic worlds that the Boyles present to our linguistically conditioned eyes and brains, their nature directly confronts our culture; but this time, to our dumb amazement without the intervention of symbolic mediation acting as either a bridge or a barrier.

There is a certain irony that these mimetic works by Boyle Family should be so independent and resistant to the mythologising power of symbolic and linguistic authority. According to modernist criticism and theory as espoused, for instance, by Clement Greenberg and his followers, such autonomy should only be achieved through non-figurative abstraction. Only abstract art was deemed pure and uncontaminated through its power to withstand and transcend the very materiality and the historical conditions, which had brought it into being. In striking contrast, Boyle Family's ultra-descriptive painting achieves its own kind of independence, not by denying the realities of the world of which it is a part, but by completely embracing them. Instead of relying on the language of symbol or metaphor, which always leads us away to some significant 'other'; here by contrast, we are allowed to scrutinise and delight in the random, metonymic bits and pieces of the world that appear to describe and represent nothing but themselves.

If these works are really so autonomous and unique, how are they also so open and accessible to our human sensibilities at the same time? This is another intriguing aspect to the contradictory nature of Boyle Family's paintings. They appeal to us because they are, paradoxically, both so realistic, and yet so perfect. Their perfection, however, is the antithesis of normal aesthetic associations connected with that critical and philosophical concept. For Boyle Family, beauty and perfection lie in the supreme individuality of the thing itself, not in some abstract system of aesthetic order. Thus they equally eschew the selective idealism of classicism and the self-referential purity of Modernism. Boyle Family's empirical art reifies the appearance of the world to the onlooker, not as a culturally constructed image, but as a perfectly authentic fact.

This is not to imply that the Boyles literally bring the real, physical world to our attention. What they create for us is access to an exceptionally excessive description of the minutiae of material reality, which normally passes beneath our highly conditioned and selective notice. This optical engagement with the previously insignificant can be so unsettling, and even disturbing, that sometimes it feels as if we have inexplicably come across an uncanny parallel universe. What we encounter here is something akin to *déjà vu* – an intensity of vision and certainty of being which, if it were not so rooted in the material world, might be taken for being a metaphysical insight and revelation. Yet it is physical exactitude, not aesthetic idealism or spiritual enlightenment, which is the foundation for the sense of perfection in these works. This again brings us back to another paradoxical dimension to Boyle Family's work, where beauty of perfection is not based on some Pythagorean system of mathematical order and control, but on an open and receptive creative process that incorporates the unpredictable, but crucial role of chance. Each Boyle painting is more than an image. It is a unique event.

Chance and accident are frequently conflated, when in fact they are antithetical to each other. Accident is the ghost in the machine, the unpredictable threat to reason and control. It constantly refutes and destroys the security and intellectual optimism we desire to create for ourselves through the power of our rational ideas and actions. Chance, by contrast, is not an anarchist, but a terrorist. It does not simply wish to destroy, but to create an alternative to the logical, orthodox order of things. Instead of a man-made selective system operating to predetermine ends, with chance, selection and intent are replaced by the totality of natural possibilities. Thus with this immutable faith in the redemptive power of chance and its essential role in the all-inclusive creative process of their art, the accidental is completely eliminated and each work attains a perfect 'rightness' about it, which no amount of conscious intent could possible achieve. Now we onlookers become instantly enthralled by these aleatoric encounters manifested in Boyle Family's paintings which, along with their excessive descriptive displays of detailed reality, arrest our normal, hyperactive optical habits and transform our passing casual glance into an intense, concentrated gaze.

Our entranced optical and tactile engagement with a Boyle Family painting is infinitely more visceral than normally experienced in front of an example of illustrative figurative art. In fact the sensation engendered is more akin to looking at the well wrought surface of an abstract expressionist work. In a conventional imitative picture the artist sets out to recreate, through the devices of pictorial illusionism, the physical conditions we usually encounter in our familiar environments. The most obvious aspect of this process is the graphic recreation of three-dimensional objects in a continuum of receding space through the employment of such pictorial techniques as perspective and chiaroscuro. This illusionistic role of art aping reality was concisely summed up by the 15th century Italian Renaissance theorist Alberti, when he described painting as a 'window on to the world'. This trope, common to all post-Renaissance Western art, began to be challenged and undermined by the emergence of modern painting in the later 19th century. From Edouard Manet onwards, the shift of emphasis in painting began to shift the focus away from spatial depth to tactile surface. With each new phase of modernist painting more and more illusionistic depth was squeezed from Alberti's window-picture, until by the mid-20th century, progressive abstract painting had little space left, which could possibly contain a three-dimensional figure. 'Flatness' had triumphed along with American Abstract Expressionism. Boyle Family's paintings are of course not flat, yet despite being figurative, they do share the same non-spatial characteristics as abstraction. In their work there is no illusion of depth. Unlike a conventional figurative picture, where the pictorial image recedes from your eyes as you approach its surface, a Boyle Family painting, like the surface of a true abstract work, seems to come forward to greet you the more intimate your proximity becomes to it.

Such close optical contact with the surface of a Boyle Family painting can create a hypnotic hold over the onlooker, who becomes increasingly fascinated and intrigued as to how it has been made. The surface of these paintings however, is not there, as in other pictures – figurative or abstract – to display the skilful and expressive imposed presence of the artist. There is no bravura brushwork, angst-ridden distortion or cool manipulation of decorative and compositional design. In fact what we have here is modern art, which does not look 'modern'. The Boyles create works that are so 'frighteningly exact', as one writer has described them, that we, as onlookers, are initially compelled to scrutinise their surfaces in a vain attempt to locate the point where fiction and faction meet. This seems to be a perfectly normal reaction on seeing Boyle Family's paintings for the first time. This, however, should be quickly succeeded by the onlooker being taken on a sensuous journey of discovery towards the philosophical heartland of Boyle Family's existentialist art practice.

From the beginning of their careers, Mark Boyle and Joan Hills and later their children, Georgia and Sebastian, have consistently and relentlessly set out to challenge and break down the artistic, aesthetic, social, political and psychological barriers of established orthodoxy and control, which separates artists from the authentic experience of their subject in its entirety and totality. Thus, with the art of Boyle Family, there is a connectedness between form and formlessness, between the smallest detail on the surface of their paintings and the sublime all-inclusive possibilities of their boundless subject.

The basis of Boyle Family's philosophical belief and artistic commitment is scientific empiricism; and such an attitude is out of step with the dominant ideologies of our postmodern contemporary world. Since Nietzsche's pronouncement on the 'Death of God' at the end of the 19th century, modern philosophy has been obliged to formulate new paradigms in which the world is forever recreated by different forms of cultural representations. The previous Enlightenment belief that the appearance of the world shaped its representation has now been radically superseded by the intertextuality of postmodernism, where the former distinction between what is real and what is represented is an outmoded anachronism. Reality has become formulated and experienced through the all-pervasive presence of interconnecting sign systems of communication. Needless to say, Boyle Family do not subscribe to this current orthodoxy and emphatically oppose such semantic hegemony. Boyle Family's resistance to the contemporary politics of representation is in the area of visual and textual interpretation. Their art seeks to occupy that space between nature and culture before the visual is turned into a veil of images and secondary semantic meanings.

What distinguishes and marks out Boyle Family's art for particular critical notice is that it is prepared to confront this tyranny of textuality head-on. The ultimate triumphalism of postmodern theory is to conflate reality and fiction into the simulacrum. As with the 1956 film, *Invasion of the Body Snatchers*, the replica completely colonises and destroys without trace, that from which it has been replicated. We now have endless reproductions where no original exists. In our multimedia, electronically generated world, this replication process seems to have become so insidious that the medium has not only become the message, but the very subject / content itself – television aping life and life becoming television. Without any sense of there being an 'original' this quickly sets the assumption that there is 'nothing out there', allowing a contemporary philosopher provocatively to claim that the Gulf War, for instance, did not happen, but was merely a set of images on our television screens.

Boyle Family's work also deals in the process of replication and communicates with the onlooker through the visual language of mimetic resemblance. Yet no one is led to believe that these paintings are simulacra of the world itself. These are works of art and their content and appearance have to be considered within their relationship to their source and the context of their presentation – cut off, set apart and displayed on the gallery wall. Their presence, in such a distinctively cultural space, emphasises their difference and separation from their original abode. What we have is not simply simulated replication, but physical and conceptual transformation. Thus it would be deceptively misleading to regard Boyle Family's work as straightforward fragments of reality. These paintings are not the 'real thing', but are independent entities in their own right. Boyle Family's autonomous works stand neither for their creators nor their audience, but for themselves. Through the direct, unmediated power of their appearance, uncontaminated by any conventional image-making process, these representative paintings present to our notice those aspects of reality that have never been previously granted any recognition and acknowledgement in our civilised culture.

This again brings us back to the politics and languages of representation. All language systems whether oral, textual or visual, operate on the basis of differences and similarities. For example, the arbitrary sound, or written appearance, of the word 'dog' tells us that it is different from the word 'cat'. Furthermore, if a word has more than one meaning, the different contexts in which it is used will tell us, unless it is a pun, what meaning to apply. The representational visual arts on the other hand, have a markedly different method of communication based, not on difference, but on reference and resemblance. Thus we recognise a dog in a painting because it appears to look like one; for example, its image has enough of the same visual features as a dog in the real world to allow us to refer it to that particular animal. Yet, what if we are encouraged to doubt our security in the appearance of the real world? What if we are now told that a picture of a dog only looks like a dog because it resembles another image of a dog? What if finally we are told that our postmodern, hyper-real environment is merely a hall of mirrors, a complex interconnecting system of reflecting signage generated by the all-pervasive presence of the mass media? Is a Boyle Family painting then just another piece of replication in a world of continuous replicating imagery? Or do these paintings resist and challenge such a view of our present state of affairs?

There are, of course, no absolutes in the act of seeing. Despite all the Ruskinian rhetoric, the 'innocent eye' of pure vision is wishful thinking. Seeing is never straightforward, but a highly complex neurological activity with around 30 areas of the brain programmed to deal with the innumerable ways we optically respond to the visual world. Yet broadly speaking, it is possible to divide the process of looking into conscious and subconscious, or subliminal, ways of seeing. While the latter method merely registers the vast amount of visual information that is familiar and expected, the former type of observing is stimulated to focus on appearances which seem to be distinctive, significant and exceptional. Most image-makers in our postmodern world usually try to capture our attention by resorting to obvious arresting devices through some kind of mendacious manipulation. Appearances are then turned into spectacular images. Boyle Family's attitude and approach is the complete opposite of this circus of insidious visual fakery. They do not seek out unusual and bizarre subjects which are the stuff of the entertainment business, nor do they attempt to transform the appearance of things by formal rearrangement which is the hallmark of much modern and postmodern art. On the contrary, any transformation that does take place in front of a Boyle Family painting does not occur in the subject itself, but in the attention and attitude of the onlooker. The apparently insignificant subjects with which we are confronted in these works are the very ones which we would barely register through our subliminal habit of looking. Now, however, we are made to see for the first time this everyday world, which we merely take for granted. Boyle Family's seemingly revelatory art allows us to engage directly with the very fabric of the familiar and makes us suddenly and acutely aware that the ordinary is in fact quite extraordinary. As Francis Bacon, an ardent admirer of Boyle Family's work stated, 'If only people were free enough to let everything in, something extraordinary might come of it.'

How this mundane miracle occurs is open to speculation. Amongst other things, this profound change in attitude forces the viewer to make comparisons between what is found in Boyle Family's work and other means of depicting the appearance of the world. Thus, a final comparison should be made with the most ubiquitous image-maker in our contemporary world – photography.

Many would contend that it is the photographic image to which the art of the Boyles is most closely linked. There are undoubtedly some points of similarity with certain kinds of photography – through such features as documentary empiricism, high-detail recorded factuality and a contingent engagement with the world. On the other hand, however, there is a crucial difference between any photograph and a Boyle Family painting. This has nothing to do with obvious disparities in scale or surface, for example. The fundamental contrast again lies with the simulated and imaginary sense of space created in the image-making process. Photographs, like other kinds of picturing, present a view of the world as a continuum of space. Yet this has further implications in a photograph compared with a painting. When a photographic image is snapped it freezes the spatial flux of reality and transforms a point in space into a moment in time. Photographs by the particular spatial / temporal relationship they have with the world are forever locked into the split-second of their immaculate conception. At the very moment of their miraculous, mechanical creation they become instant history and immediate nostalgia. Boyle Family's paintings, by contrast, create an overwhelming sense of concentrated corporeality where time and space become one. Thus by expunging any pictorial illusion of both time and space, and eschewing narrative descriptions of reality, Boyle Family's paintings always remain in the eternal 'now' of their own presence and materiality.

Despite the layers of semiotic encrustation accumulated through the civilising process, we humans are still basically visual creatures and the way we optically engage with the world links back to our distant prehistory. Then we were an endangered hunting species with our eyes acting as our lifeline to survival. Human brain and eye had to work in self-supporting co-ordination in order to discern the nature of the surrounding environment. There was a constant checking between visual information and stored memory in the brain. Thus the sensation of revelation goes back to when our sight would pierce the camouflaged veil of appearances in the natural world and in a flash of recognition discern between friend and foe, between prey and peril. Ironically, we now call our revelations blinding insights in order to distance them from their primordial origins and elevate them on to a higher, otherworldly plane of mental and spiritual insight. The art of Boyle Family radically goes in the other direction. With their consistently all-inclusive, non-hierarchical, anti-aesthetic approach to art, their revolutionary work directs us to reconnect with the visual and physical world in order that we can see it for what it truly is. Reflecting intently on Boyle Family's uncompromising realistic paintings, the onlooker begins to realise that Miranda's 'brave new world' is in fact our courageous old one, which has always been here. Whether we are aware of it or not, we are all, including these paintings, part of this ever-changing world.

This catalogue essay was written for the exhibition *Boyle Family* shown at the Scottish National Gallery of Modern Art, Edinburgh in 2003.

JACK KNOX

The Art of Drawing

THE MARXIST ART historian Meyer Schapiro once observed that the main reason that the fine arts still hold their own in the 'age of mechanical reproduction' is that they are appreciated by capitalist society as the last remaining human practice where a high degree of manual skill is matched with individual human creativity. With such a view, however, there is always the danger that the traditional activities of drawing, painting and sculpture, will end up being regarded as merely high quality craft-making, and will be required to be artificially protected as an endangered species by some institution within the Cultural Heritage industry.

Ever since the appearance, in the earlier part of the 19th century, of its chief rival, photography, the fine arts, particularly painting and drawing, have been seen by many as very much under threat of extinction. The doom-laden lament, 'Today, painting is dead' has echoed down through the modern era, and these dire views are still very much with us as witnessed by the title of a recent symposium at Edinburgh College of Art *Drawing in the digital age: a necessity or irrelevance?* This is certainly a valid question, especially when it must be increasingly difficult for teachers and tutors to disregard the growing excuse, 'What is the point in drawing when we've got photography and computers to do it for us?'

Over the last two or three decades many art schools have in fact surrendered to this attitude and pretty well abandoned the teaching of traditional drawing skills. This is especially the case now with much art education in England for example. Yet here in Scotland however, the art institutions have retained a more conservative line, and up until now, still make the manual graphic practices a central core of their basic teaching. The reasons for this are complex (involving art politics as well as pedagogical considerations), but there are also distinctive indigenous character traits at work here. If philosophical speculation is the basis of the enlightened Scottish academic tradition, then the practice of drawing is the most important discipline where this is carried out in the area of visual thinking. Democratic intellectualism is not the exclusive prerogative of Scottish universities, but is (or certainly should be) also at the core of art education in this country. This should be most evident in the drawing class, where students are guided and encouraged, not only to test the empirical evidence of their visual world, but also to speculate on how to develop the most appropriate means to represent that world in all its distinct physical, emotional, psychological, social and historical characteristics.

Our late 20th century world has of course radically changed since the days when the art academies had an almost monopolistic authority over the training of art students. The central importance of the life model and the obsessive pursuit of ideal or romantic beauty are now thankfully, things of the past. Today artists have much more freedom. Still, it is a very daunting task to negotiate a way between the extremes of Ruskinian realist objectivity on the one hand – 'The representation of facts is the foundation of all art', and expressionistic subjectivity on the other, as advocated by someone like Kandinsky, who felt, 'drawing is a journey into the land of deeper understanding'.

Jack Knox, more than any other artist working in Scotland, has, over the last 30 years, demonstrated the crucial importance of the practice and art of drawing. Even though his subject for attention is nearly always the humble still life (or the occasional deserted landscape), he presents us with a distinct image of the way we Scots understand, enjoy and represent our relationship with the world we have created and find ourselves in. As the Ruskin/ Kandinsky dichotomy reveals, this relationship is a very complex objective/ subjective matter. It is however, through the study of the semantics of the varying graphic languages found in Knox's drawings, that a real appreciation of the resolution of this dichotomy can be seen.

It is necessary therefore, before looking closely at the broad development of Knox's drawing, to present a brief discussion on the role of visual language in the graphic arts. Because of the mimetic, iconic nature of conventional drawing, with its high degree of resemblance factor, most people take the image on the paper at face value as an uninterrupted transcription of what the artist sees. I suggest this may be common sense, but also a rather naïve view; for example, it may come as a surprise that Jack Knox for instance no longer draws directly from life, but from memory and imagination. No more than writing, drawing is not just the simple act of making marks on paper; but a distinct language of representation, with its own separate vocabulary and grammar, and its own ongoing history of conventions of communication. Thus artists are required to familiarise themselves through study and practice, with this inherited language of drawing, which has existed long before they ever picked up a pencil or a piece of charcoal. This is what semiologists, such as Saussure would identify as *language* – the universal language of graphic mark-making, which, as the American sculptor, David Smith, claimed, 'Came before song itself'. All types of communication, whether they be verbal, textual or visual, are culturally defined, and this is where *langue* (a particular language) operates. All artists must choose, consciously or unconsciously, a particular form of visual language, whether it be academic, cubist, realist, abstract or strip cartoon. Therefore, when we look at a drawing by Jack Knox, it is not just a matter of recognition – a loaf of bread or a basket of fruit. What should really be involved is an appreciation of how the artist has adapted the most appropriate form of graphic language in order to present the distinctive visual characteristics of his chosen subject. Furthermore, all true artists have their own recognisable vision and personal style of expression. This is what semiologists term their *parole*, where the artist's own individual 'voice' breaks through their chosen form of *langue* and presents us with the unmistakable quality and character of a 'Jack Knox drawing' for instance.

So what is it that gives Knox's pictures their own inimitable personality and engaging manner? If visual artists, like poets, also have a 'voice' then Knox certainly draws with a detectable accent. Of course there is nothing overtly Scottish about his favoured subject matter, (thankfully no haggis or whisky glasses in sight) yet there is still, to use Robert Louis Stevenson's phrase, 'a strong Scotch accent of mind' coming through in all of Knox's work. In their own modest way, Knox's drawings are non-combative examples of MacDiarmid's 'Caledonian Antisyzygy'. They are not where extremes collide, yet much of their inner vitality is generated by the tension of opposites. For instance, although Knox preferred the genre of still life, there is nothing inanimate or moribund about his treatment of his subjects. The objects in his pictures seem to have an internal life of their own, a definite body language, which engages us in a visual dialogue that is not only formal, but personal and social as well. Furthermore, we are made to respond to the pictorial world of Knox as a recognisably 'real' one, not through objective formal correctness, but by our own physical and emotional familiarity with what he presents to us. Following Edwin Muir's account of the split nature of the Scottish psyche, Knox's drawings stimulate with great pleasure and delight the frisson of opposites; between what we think as being correct and what we feel to be true.

This exciting tension between contending forces can already be sensed in an early student life drawing of the late 1950s. In this work Knox immediately demonstrates he has mastered the academic language of drawing, but instead of the pursuit of some idealised form, he seems to be much more concerned here with the search for a graphic equivalent to the sensual experience of the model's physical presence. Rather than placing her on some platonic pedestal, her feet are firmly planted on the ground. Yet for all the well-balanced stability of the pose, this is not a static composition. Knox's line which traces the shapes and forms of the anatomy is continually changing in character from bold to tentative, from descriptive to suggestive, from prosaic to poetic. This leads the eye on a journey of discovery which equally allows intimate investigation of the model's hair and back of neck, as well as detached observation of the mechanics involved in the tactile relationship of the heel, sole and toes with the floor beneath. There is an extremely satisfying, rational beauty at work in such drawing.

When Knox left Glasgow School of Art in 1958 he had already shown that he was a worthy heir to the great tradition of graphic skills which he had inherited from his illustrious predecessors such as Joan Eardley, James Cowie and Muirhead Bone, and which could probably be traced right back to David Allan and the Foulis Academy in the 18th century. As with all ambitious young Scottish artists, since the days of Allan Ramsay, Knox made for Europe to widen his geographical and artistic horizons. He went to Paris and, like a whole generation of Scottish students, he attended the studio of André Lhote, who had previously taught other Scottish artists like William Johnstone and Gillies as far back as the 1920s.

There Knox came into first-hand contact with one of the last remaining original practitioners of the cubist language of modernist expression. By this time however, Cubism had long lost any of its innovative radicalism, and had become just another conventional method of pictorial and graphic practice. Yet Knox did gain lasting benefit from his interest in Cubism. Firstly, the centrality of domestic still life as an inspiration for such an important movement in modern art must have been very reassuring to the young Scottish artist. Secondly, while the likes of Lhote were now merely modernist hacks, Knox's idol, Braque, could still go on, forever subtly refining the cubist language of modern painting. Braque's beautifully wrought masterpieces of harmonious balance and sensual delight echoed all that the French master claimed when he said, 'Objects don't exist for me except insofar as a rapport exists between them and myself. When one attains this harmony, one reaches a sort of intellectual non-existence… which makes everything possible and right. Life then becomes a perpetual revelation'. Even though Knox's next artistic development was to go its own more turbulent way for the coming decade, Braque's example and inspiration would never leave him.

During the early 1960s, the dominant force in modern art was undoubtedly Abstract Expressionism and after seeing a major exhibition of contemporary American painting in Brussels, Knox was bowled over by its raw vigour and dynamic integrity – painting speaking for itself! The safe academic control of his previous work was blown away as he attempted to forge a new multilingual mode of expression for his emerging art practice. This can be seen in such works as *Studio 17-8-64*. This picture is bursting at the seams with energy and movement – a crudely drawn graffiti arrow thrusts its way into the picture, while rhythmic patterns of lines and dashes are smeared across the upper surface and traces of ghostly iconic imagery are randomly scattered over the back wall of the 'studio'. It is as though the artist has many things to say and all at the same time. This is a real babble of a picture, with academic conventions of perspective and chiaroscuro dominating the lower areas, cubistic fragmentation jumping around in the middle band, and abstract gesturing crowning the top. In *Studio 17-8-64* there is an almost deafening cacophony of various types of pictorial voices all simultaneously shouting for attention. Knox, soon felt that he needed to quieten things down.

Throughout the rest of the 1960s Knox set out to control, distil and refine the potent power released by his multilingual pictorial expression. This tempering process can be clearly seen in a work from a few years later, *Studio with Kyle's Swing 1967*. Now everything has found its proper place and the conversation between each element in the composition has become extremely polite, even verging on the genteel. The only disturbing presence is the bit of graffiti writing which has been vigorously rubbed over as being out of place in such respectable company. There is still a suggestion of the original free-flowing 'stream of consciousness', but now the artist is in danger of merely talking to himself. Knowing how important communication always has been to Jack Knox, it is not surprising that, despite their critical success, he became dissatisfied with the works he produced in the late 1960s and early 1970s.

What radically altered the course of Knox's artistic development was truly a 'Road to Damascus' epiphany experience. Having gone to Amsterdam with a group of his students to see a major American abstract colour field exhibition in 1972, he felt so disgruntled with such examples of High Modernism that he sought refuge in the nearby Rijksmuseum. There, as though preordained, he again discovered his deep attachment to the humble still life subject matter; especially in the form of the work of those 17th century Dutch masters, who specialised in the simple 'Ontbijt', or breakfast-type painting with just a piece of cheese and knife, a bit of fruit and egg. Fired up with enthusiasm for such authentic simplicity, Knox now returned to his own northern European artistic roots, with all its Doric honesty. From now on Knox's drawing would not merely be a means to an end, but something in its own right, and central to his art. In fact, you might even say that drawing began to dictate the course of the development of his painting. The first remarkable results of the Amsterdam conversion can be clearly seen in such works as *Study: Apples in a Napkin, 1973* and *Study: Bread with Knife* (1973). These ultra-austere drawings have an almost Calvinistic seriousness about them. There is nothing frivolous or flashy here; in fact they are the result of a deep meditation on the very nature of the art of drawing. They ultimately are asking the disturbing question, where does the truth of such images lie? – is it in the subject matter or how that subject matter has been represented? The later seems to be the case, for as Knox himself said at the time, 'I started drawing, using a thick black pencil, a 6B I think, making it all very sharp and exact, and shading it so that the way in which it was done looked so convincing and so accurate that you were sure it must be so. But of course it wasn't. It's a bit like those architectural drawings you sometimes see of imaginary buildings, which are so positive and convincing you are bound to believe they exist somewhere.'

Fortunately, it is not in Knox's nature to pursue these platonic over-intellectual speculations which quickly can become dour, joyless obsessions, turning art into a set of theoretical statements. As with all the great artists and poets in the history of the Scottish culture, Knox realises the open, communicative value of enjoyment and humour. One of the most distinguishing characteristics of his work since the later 1970s has been its robust, jocular *joie de vivre* which has animated his art ever since. For Knox appreciates more than most, the close parallels between words and images and how both means of communication operate. Delight in verbal and visual language engages us because we are constantly listening and looking for close similarities and subtle differences between one sound and another, (talk/walk for example), or one mark and another. Artists and poets who wish to stimulate and entertain their audience's eyes and ears are continually exploiting this. For example in *Waterfall* (1987), there is very little difference or variation in the manner Knox registers the mountains, the lake, the rocks or the waterfall, yet because of their placement in the overall composition, and the minute, but crucial contrasts between the treatment of directional marks on paper in each area, we can easily appreciate the three-dimensional nature of the artist's subject. Here we have graphic skill and imaginative invention of a superb draughtsman – a visual poet indeed.

Isaiah Berlin in his famous essay *Tolstoy and History* made the distinction between the two basic different types of creative genius; on the one hand, there is the fox, who 'knows many things' and on the other, the hedgehog, who 'knows one big thing'. In modern art this contrast is no more strikingly seen as between Picasso and Braque. The former is the most versatile, quick-change artist the world has ever seen, with as many different styles and approaches to his art as you could possibly imagine. Braque, on the other hand, is positively myopic in comparison, as he relentlessly stalks his sole ambition of getting it 'right'.

Jack Knox has long passed through his 'Picasso' stage of multilingual visual experimentation and has since followed Braque's example to work quietly and steadily to develop his own distinctive personal voice and vision. The perimeters Knox sets for himself may seem to some, rather limited. Compared with all the cornucopia of flashy gimmickry churned out by much contemporary British art, Knox's work may be less than 'sensational'. However, any person with trained and developed senses – an attuned ear and discerning eye – does not need a dissected carcass in formaldehyde to give them some secondhand theatrical thrill. In a world of seemingly relentless crassness, both in high and popular culture, and virus spreading technology, what is desperately needed is to be able to pick up on the still small voice of genuine humanity.

For me, a Jack Knox drawing, such as *Bike* (1996) does allow access to our deeply felt human experiences and desires. Gendered in the feminine, there she stands on her own two wheels; battered, but still trembling with potential movement and expectation, just itching either to transport us back to fond memories of earlier times, or willing to give us the chance to mount up, if only in our imaginations, and make for the distant horizon of exciting opportunities.

This essay was published in *Cencrastus* (issue 62, 1997).

BARBARA RAE

Between Two Worlds – Outer Perception and Inner Vision

That is why I have to put the drawings behind me and keep to a much more simple idea, so that I am not tied to just reinterpreting the drawings. It has got to be different.
Barbara Rae, 1988

FOR THOSE OF us who have had a long interest in, and a deep passion for, the art of Barbara Rae, this new book on her work and career is very welcome indeed. In this beautiful publication we can gain a range of insights into the particular nature of Barbara Rae's distinctive contribution to modern painting. This can be found in her long and revealing interview with Andrew Lambirth for instance, where we can make direct contact with the artist's observations and opinions on a variety of different issues that are pertinent to a fuller and more rewarding understanding of the development of her distinguished career. These topics of discussion touch on a range of pertinent issues, including: the particular character of her training at Edinburgh College of Art in the mid-1960s, the broad biographical narrative of her subsequent successful career as a major British painter in the second half of the 20th century, the various changing influences on her artistic outlook and studio practice, and most of all, her complex relationship with her sources of inspirational subject matter and the ever-evolving technical methods she employs in her endless quest for a more satisfactory mode of pictorial expression. Such a wide-ranging discourse gives some indication of the multi-various nature of Barbara Rae's art.

This book also visually provides for the first time a comprehensive survey of Barbara Rae's painting. Even a cursory perusal of this sumptuous illustrative material reveals, on the one hand, not only the range and diversity of her richly creative output, but also on the other, the sustained commitment and continuous development that Barbara Rae has always shown as the basic characteristic of her artistic practice. This dialectical interplay of opposites runs through all aspects of Barbara Rae's art, but at the core there is always this dynamic tension between the forces of change, variety and innovation on the one side, and those of commitment, consistency and continuity on the other.

With her consistently fresh and undiminished enthusiastic attitude it may come somewhat as a surprise to realise that Barbara Rae's distinguished and highly productive career now spans some four decades. As we all know the last 40 years have been extremely turbulent ones for the contemporary visual arts. Especially with the seismic critical and artistic shift in the 1960s from the previous dominance of high Modernism to its overthrow by the triumph rise of Postmodernism. This important change in 20th century art has taken place

with such rapidity that future generations, looking back to our era, might
find it a little difficult to work out how Barbara Rae and, say Tracy Emin and
Cindy Sherman, for instance, were all successfully working in the same period.
Art history can have a disturbing knack of telescoping together unexpected
juxtapositions. Again, if on the other hand, we look this time at the beginning
of Barbara Rae's career, when she was still at Art College, we may be equally
surprised to find that her contemporaries – of course, from a much older
generation – included painters such as Scottish luminaries as Joan Eardley and
Ann Redpath.

Barbara Rae's relationship to the profound changes that took place in the
British art world in the second half of the last century is as pertinent as it is
revealing. In Scotland for instance, the legacy of the Scottish Colourists and
the Edinburgh School, led by William Gillies, was still surprisingly dominant
in the 1960s. While there were characteristic differences in the modes of
painting between the Edinburgh School and its Glasgow counterpart the
dominant subject matter in both cases was invariably landscape and still life,
usually executed in an expressionist or decorative *belle peinture* manner. It
is notable however, that the next generation of women painters following
on from that of Eardley and Redpath, determinedly moved away from those
traditional subjects assigned to feminine artists by convention. Instead they
turned their attention to the critical re-examination and visual deconstruction
of the representation of the female figure. In marked contrast however,
Barbara Rae, for various reasons, has always avoided this feminist trend
and chosen to continue, but in a highly innovative and personal fashion,
that tradition of Scottish modern painting which she inherited as a student
at Edinburgh College of Art. In this less controversial subject area of artistic
activity she has however, radically expanded the parameters and potential
of that inherited tradition. This is most spectacularly demonstrated in her
ambitions for her painting which is regularly worked out on a monumental
scale never seriously contemplated by her predecessors. Also, her inspirational
subject matter is drawn from such distant and remote areas of the globe that
even the thought of it would have given most of her early mentors a nose
bleed. Furthermore, this ever-expanding range and variety of innovative
studio techniques employed by Barbara Rae is vastly wider and infinitely
more complex than anything envisaged by the previous generation. Thus,
although there is usually some discernible Scottish modern painting traditional
dimension to Barbara Rae's work, with her longstanding commitment to
forever pushing the technical possibilities in her art practice, no one could
justifiably accuse her of either being dependent or complacent. Barbara
Rae may not to be an artistic rebel – we probably have got enough of those
anyway – but she should be seen as a challenging innovator and radical
revisionist in late modern painting.

Turning now to examine in detail the issue of subject matter in Barbara
Rae's art we saw how she refrained from the dominant trend by women

painters to engage with the female figure. Interestingly, while insistent feminist issues seemed to compel women artists to shift their critical attention away from the natural to the social world, many avant-garde male artists moved in the other direction and returned to nature in the form, not of painting, but of land art. Thus if we examine Barbara Rae's attitude towards her chosen subject matter, compared with those of contemporary male landscapists, there are crucial and telling differences which help to distinguish Barbara Rae's own independent position. These male conceptionalist land artists invariably present themselves as new types of artistic explorers of the natural world. Furthermore, their art usually has a narrative framework as they record and document their passage through their chosen landscape. Thus while linear temporal chronology is the basic mode of communication with these male landscapists, the opposite is the case with the approach of Barbara Rae. Ultimately, through the power of intuitive expression, her painterly expression of contact with the natural world reveals to us, in an all-encompassing instant, the ever-present spirit of nature, where temporal chronology is transformed into instantaneous pictorial epiphany. Furthermore, while these conceptualist landscapists usually demonstrate an ideological ecopolitical attitude towards the cultural conditioned significance of their carefully sought-out environments, Barbara Rae more poetic approach, on the other hand, is motivated in her engagement with her inspirational worlds by her own sensual, psychological and highly personal feelings of identity and empathy. In short, these male land artists take an interventionist approach and impose their semantic message, in one form or another, on the environment that they pass through; while Barbara Rae operates in a very different way.

After the opening period of initial contact, through her thoroughly researched historical study of her chosen locale and her analytical examination of her inspirational subject matter, the artist gradually allows her informative experiences to be absorbed into the spirit of the place with all its accumulated collective and personal memories. In marked contrast to the interventionist actions of her male landscapist counterparts, no physical traces of the painter's presence are left behind on the landscape, but much more importantly, an invisible bond of an indelible relationship has been created which the artist will later draw upon again and again whenever the mood is right for further creative development. After this, the next challenge for Barbara Rae in her working process, is to find and develop appropriate ways and means to transform these recorded and remembered thoughts and feelings experienced in front of the natural motif into the expressive language of painting. This process must work in such a way that is both true to the inspiration of the subject and also integral to the formal act of painting itself.

This dialectic between subject, content and pictorial form of course affects the work of all serious and ambitious artists – as it does the art of Barbara Rae. In her case however, this stimulating dialogue is particularly acute and revealing of the vital tensions that give such dynamic power to her work. For instance, as shown in the accompanying interview she deeply dislikes being labelled a conventional landscape painter even though much of the content of her work is drawn from her continual contact with the natural world all over the globe. As she rightly points out, her aim and intention has never been to merely record the topographical appearance of her subjects and present scenic 'views' in a picturesque fashion to an expectant public. Furthermore, her painting also has never been used as an empirical document just to record a particular place and time in a realistic impressionist, metrological manner. Neither typical landscape painting conventions, nor pseudo-scientific tropes, have much to do with Barbara Rae's work.

In her very illuminating account of her working practices it can clearly be seen that Barbara Rae in fact puts more stress on what goes on in the studio than her time in the landscape in front of the motif. It is through the elaborate rituals of her studio practice, where the subject/content of her pictures is subjected to a barrage of painting processes. This is in order to give them the appropriate form of display, which the artist triumphantly achieves through the final effects that she seeks. It is through this demanding physical and mental process that the painting is enabled to take on a distinct life and identity of its own. The artist develops, by experimental trial and error, a way of painting which has little to do with empirical description and is infinitely more connected to the modernist mode of improvised abstraction. It is through the way the artist manipulates her medium that allows the painting in the end, to appear to speak for itself in its final resolved pictorial statement.

Does this then make Barbara Rae a modernist abstract artist rather than say a figurative landscape painter? This is a very difficult, possibly unanswerable question in light of the constant interplay of opposites that seem to operate at the heart of Barbara Rae's artistic practice. For example, although in her studio she freely works her paintings very much in an abstractionist manner, and can creatively utilise the expressive language of abstraction as well as any; her art always seems to require motivation and inspiration from her direct contact with the outside physical world. Barbara Rae's ever-recurring nomadic travel across the globe to seek out sympathetic environments to stimulate her art also are clearly a necessary component to her creative process. Thus although abstraction plays a vital role in the technical stylistics and the aesthetic qualities of her practise it is never used as an autonomous end in itself.

As the wide array of illustrations in this book gloriously demonstrate, Barbara Rae works with a variety of different types of subjects that have a particular pictorial appeal for her and are conducive to her art. Undoubtedly however, the predominant feature of her work throughout her career has been landscape. It is thus necessary for a fuller understanding of the significance of this, to examine contextually the relationship between this central generic theme in Barbara Rae's paintings and the history of Western landscape and the pastoral tradition.

Unfortunately, or fortunately, depending on your point of view, the term landscape is not as straightforward as it might initially appear. Although it may seem on the face of it to be simply the name given to a pictorial view of the natural world, landscape in fact, is an extremely complex, even contradictory, artistic and critical concept. These complexities of contradiction involve the very subject of landscape itself. As with a similar discursive term such as history for example, landscape is both its subject of study and simultaneously, the study of that subject itself. For example, the content of history is of course the past; yet on the other hand, the subject of historical studies is not the past, but in fact, the way the past is represented by the present to itself. Likewise, a similar objective/subjective dichotomy is to be found at the heart of landscape where, on the one hand, the term can simply refer to the subject 'out there'; yet equally, and simultaneously, apply to the representational transcription made by the artist on the picture surface itself. This duality and unstable ontological and cultural status of landscape – with the endless oscillations between the objective, detached subject (usually prescribed by the title on the label) and the artist's interpretive response to, and representation of, that subject, is pertinent, and crucially important, to an understanding of Barbara Rae's relationship to her landscapes – both outside and inside the studio. This oscillating objective/subjective tension which is at the heart of our attitudes to landscape in a post-Romantic era is sensitively developed and subtly articulated by Barbara Rae in her painting.

Another pertinent critical issue involving the theoretical concept of landscape is its academic status. For instance, when Barbara Rae was a young and impressionable student in the 1960s the academic approach to teaching art as a formal discipline, with its array of acquired skills, was in rapid and terminal decline in British art schools. However, because of various factors, but especially due to the long-established and rarely challenged nature of the pedagogical outlook of the staff in the Drawing and Painting Department at Edinburgh College of Art, a strongly academic attitude and approach to teaching still prevailed. This was most clearly demonstrated by the fact that the main emphasis in basic training continued to be placed on observed study through drawing from the model. As can be seen from her interview Barbara Rae has never forgotten the importance of her early academic training and the strong and enduring effect that such a mode of learning has had on the subsequent progress of her art practice. In fact, in many ways it is on that solid basis of formal techniques and learnt skills acquired from those student days that much of her later progress is built – especially in the area of her amazing manual dexterity and painting facility. This will be more fully discussed again later, but in the meantime, it is necessary to return again to the discourse on the particular status of landscape within an academic context.

Landscape as a theoretically defined subject within the discipline of art is one of the five artistic genres that were formulated by the powerful Western academies in the 17th and 18th centuries. These genres were arranged in a hierarchical system of significant cultural importance which forcibly underlined the dominant ideological outlook of the European Enlightenment with its emphasis on humanistic rationalism. This is clearly exemplified by the fact that three upper and most prestigious genres – history painting, portraiture and genre painting deal with the themes concerning human nature and social affairs within a sociocultural context; while lowly, still life at the bottom, is relegated to concerning itself with the world of material or natural objects. Yet what is of particular interest to us is where landscape fits in within this particular scheme of things. Interestingly, landscape seems to hover between the upper and lower echelons of the academic genre league table and acts as a bridge connecting the human and the natural worlds.

This continually evolving, and forever sustaining relationship between the natural and human worlds is at the thematic centre of both, the history of landscape painting, and the pastoral tradition – as it is within the art of Barbara Rae. With the emergence of the distinctive genre of landscape in the 17th century there has always been a crucial division of opposite attitudes and approaches in how to best, and most truthfully, express the bonding relationship between the human and the natural. On the one side for example, the Dutch pioneering landscapists of the naturalist persuasion stressed the physically tangible and socially lived realities of that relationship with their recordings of the mundane factuality and quotidian routine of their native countryside. Such an objective empirical approach however, could never be an end in itself for Barbara Rae who, through the poetics of her art, is ultimately seeking a more profound and metaphysical relationship with the essential nature of her subjects. Looking back to the 17th century again, there is however, to be found another approach to the art of landscape which is in the same mode as lyrical pastoral poetry. This alternative mode is most notably exemplified by the classical landscapes of Claude Lorraine which, although loosely based on his *en plein air* studies of different aspects of the surrounding Roman countryside where he resided, owe infinitely more in inspiration to his visual interpretation of the antique pastoralists such as Virgil. Thus the Claudian landscape does not depict and present an actual landscape of a specific geographical and historical locale; but rather, evokes a poetic reverie on human nature and experience to meditate and ponder upon. Unarguably Barbara Rae's own approach to the interpretation of her own highly interpretative approach to landscape subjects is much closer to the lyrical poetics of Claude than the prosaic naturalism of the Dutch. Like the great 17th century master, but without resorting to the use of the pictorial tropes of classical landscape composition and props, Barbara Rae also successfully seeks to pierce through the veil of fleeting tangential appearances to reveal and bring forth the underlying essence, and eternally recurring features, which forever holds and bonds us to the natural world.

This mediating channel of communication between the human and the natural worlds, which is the central desire of all serious landscape and pastoral art, must also concern the art of Barbara Rae. As she points out herself, in all her work, including her landscapes, despite the fact that figures never, if ever, actually appear in person, traces of the human presence are always being suggested and felt in one way or another. This of course, is most readily discernible in her occasional urban and industrial subjects. With such man-made motifs as visual inspiration – whether it be the towering hull of a great Norwegian cargo ship in Leith Docks, or the rickety structure of a spindly lifeguard tower on a Californian beach – the artist can imaginatively utilise their abstract shapes and their non-naturalistic colours as the basic decorative arrangements for her pictorial compositions. In these land/cityscapes, the human world, in its many different manifestations, profoundly influences the visual reaction and pictorial form of the artist's response to her subject. On the other hand, however, it is usually a very different type of landscape subject – a seemingly untouched, remote terrain, which is most likely to be the characteristic content of Barbara Rae's painting. Everyone who has any interest in and knowledge of Barbara Rae's landscape work knows that it is founded on a continuous quest for inspiring geographical and geological subject matter all over the globe – from as far afield as the southwest desert lands of America to the most southern tip of the African continent; from the western isles of Scotland to the Atlantic coast of Ireland. These continuous peripatetic wanderings, which in the future may even take her as far as the winter wildernesses of the northern Arctic, are literally a thousand miles from the safe and cosy *hortus conclusus* worlds of local nature produced by most of her predecessors in earlier modern British landscape painting. Yet Barbara Rae's determined journeys to and careful studies of distant lands are not in any way retreats from human contact and social culture. She may indeed seek out the isolated and lost lands of our planet in what to many may appear to be godforsaken corners of the globe; still this, however, is never done in order to run away and retreat from human contact. On the contrary, the aim and purpose is, in fact, to reconnect with it in a much more fundamental and avatar form. In such isolated and purified environments as the desert visas of the African Cape or the ancient Pueblo homelands of Arizona and New Mexico for example; the attentive outer eye and the receptive inner spirit of the sympathetic presence of the artist can surely arouse and reconnect with the eternal forces that sustained and guided the earlier human communities in those now almost forgotten lands. As she closely surveys such wild untamed terrains, Barbara Rae is always keenly attentive to any signs – obvious or obscure – that links with the human history of the place. This might take many different forms, from the worked and reworked surface of the land by past and present agrarian communities, through to esoteric symbols, carved on rocks or standing stones as a lasting expression of the religious beliefs that once were a living reality to the indigenous peoples.

As previously suggested the noble art of landscape is never as straightforward as it may appear. Ultimately this is because it is always aiming to engage critically with those ever-shifting relationships between the human and natural worlds. These eternal, unbroken relationships of inter-dependency receded forever into the vast distances of time and space, but at the same time, also project back into our own world of the here and now through a network of multiple framed perspectives. It is these perspectives, particularly in their spatial form that are crucially pertinent to the art of landscape painting. Thus, the earlier mathematical ideal of Renaissance art theory that saw painting as a fixed framed window view on to the world of nature is no longer feasible in our multi-dimensional postmodern era, where nothing seems certain or stable. Barbara Rae's highly sensitive and responsive art skilfully captures these many faceted relational complexities and contradictions in our contemporary situation. As with most modern painters she is acutely aware that the most fundamental compositional relationship at the core of visual representation is that between illusionary depth and actual surface. In the history of art of the past – from the Renaissance to before the emergence of the modern movement, the compositional balance between these two spatial polarities was pretty much controlled by the systematic laws of linear perspective. With the emergence of Modernism however, especially after Cubism, with its revolutionary multifaceted interpretation of visual reality, pictorial depth and manipulated surface no longer could be contained within such a rigid geometrical paradigm. Barbara Rae, of course, is fully aware and conversant with this radically different mode of pictorial representation. Throughout her work she continually utilises various appropriate aspects of modernist design and practice – from architectonic Cubism to gestural abstraction. With such an amenable attitude and flexible approach to the language of visual representation, the artist can, with skilful variation, work and rework the ever-shifting spatial relationships between elusive depth and tangible surface, and so create yet another dialectical tension to give added vitality to her painting.

This dazzling virtuosity of painterly skill, which is one of the distinguishing hall marks of Barbara Rae's art, is however, never purely an end in itself. Ultimately whatever she does on the built-up surfaces of her evolving images is expressive of a parallel process to be found also in the multi-layered structures of the landscapes themselves. Whether it be the broken rock formations of an abandoned quarry or the open terrain of a vast desert plain, all these different types of landscapes need to be read through strata of past histories – from the remote geological through to the contemporary demographical – each of which leaves traces of their presence on the surface of the landscape. In a similar organic fashion, Barbara Rae continuously works over her picture surfaces which are also built up in a layered, overlapping manner – from the raw collaged ground to the thickly encrusted painted surface. Thus with such richly wrought paintings what evolves is hardly a straightforward 'view as seen through a window.' A widely travelled, but deeply empathetic, creative personality like Barbara Rae never allows herself to be content with the passive role of mere observing recorder, cursorily passing through new exotic vistas in order to pick up superficial views as artistic trophies. On the contrary Barbara Rae's works are absorbing and enticing records of an ongoing process which visually parallels the same creative and organic forces that formed the inspirational landscape subjects themselves. Ultimately, the truly committed landscape artist must give up her detached self and merge with the spirit of the place. After that abandonment of separate self, the all-absorbing creative forces that are drawn from sensual experience and meditative memory can integrate and fully express themselves through the intuitive mark-making and spontaneous poring that takes place on the deeply layered surface of the image itself.

Being possessed of such an attitude and approach, Barbara Rae is therefore, by no stretch of the imagination, to be considered a conventional landscape artist. She may need, for whatever inspirational reasons, to search the world for vistas, both new and familiar, to stimulate her creative energies. In the end however, it is not the particular character or individual appearance of these different landscape subjects that is the most important thematic concern of her work. The constant urge to develop and expand ever new ways and means to express her complex and ever-shifting relationship with her empathic environments is the driving desire that fundamentally motivates her art. In the end it is not just the physical link, but the metaphysical bond the artist builds with her subject that needs to find full expression. Therefore, the final image is never solely drawn from the inspirational environment of the landscape itself, but in fact emerges in the creative atmosphere of the studio. Ultimately it is on the painted surface of the finished image itself that the interplay of apparently oppositional strands running through all the work of Barbara Rae's work triumphantly resolves themselves. It is through this long and elaborate process of image-making and display that the constantly sought-after goal of the profoundly 'different' and 'simple' is finally achieved.

This is the appropriate point to move from discussing the nature and significance of the content of Barbara Rae's painting to direct our analytical attention to the distinctive stylistic forms that her painting takes. In short, our focus of critical concern will now shift from *what* she paints to *how* she paints it. Immediately it should, be stressed however, that, as is always the case with all practitioners with powerful creative abilities, the content and form in the work of Barbara Rae is so closely interconnected and interdependent that there is never any discernible break or contradiction between these two components in the making of art. Content and form should always have a mutually compatible relationship with each other. This uniting bond is never something imposed on the work by the artist, but is always at the very heart of Barbara Rae's evolving approach to her art. As we have already seen, the central dialectic in her complex relationship with her subject matter forever lies in the shifting balance between objective observation in the landscape itself and the subsequent subjective interpretation carried out on the worked surface of the painting in the studio. Of course there is always a constant creative dialogue operating throughout the whole elaborate working process.

Barbara Rae experienced her first serious engagement with a systemised working method as a keen and receptive art student at Edinburgh College of Art, which in the radical 1960s, must have seemed, especially from the London art scene, as a back water of outmoded artistic convention. There, at that time, academic training, with its emphasis on controlled observation and visual descriptive recording, through drawing, still dominated. Within such a system of optical analysis lies the rational belief that the academic mode of drawing is the foundation of all visual analysis and understanding of the outside world. Barbara Rae has certainly moved a long way since her basic training as a student, to become one of the most sophisticated 'painterly' artists around; yet the academic ideology that she received back then still has an important relevance to a fuller understanding of her work. As can be seen from her recent interview she was also introduced during her period at Art College, to a wide range of other types of experimental processes in painting and printmaking that were as equally important as life drawing for instance. With these new techniques she quickly learnt to operate on an expansive scale which was rarely attempted by the senior members of the then Scottish art scene, but was beginning to be a favoured mode of practice amongst the emerging younger Scottish painters. This radical widening of creative possibilities, through scale, subject matter interpretation and technical experimentation with new kinds of mediums and materials was the reverse side to the Scottish academic approach. This much more open approach to making art introduced Barbara Rae to the attractive and stimulating possibilities offered by Modernism. Thus from the beginning of her career and consistently running through the long development of her creative practice has been this fruitful dialectic of opposite artistic ideologies. On the 'visual hand, the academic, with its commitment to objective, rational analysis of the visual world; and on the other, Modernism, with its stress on the subjective interpretation of personal experience through technical experimentation and spontaneous improvisation.

Undeniably the modernist approach and practice has increasingly been the dominant tendency throughout Barbara Rae's later career. Yet her academic training has also played an important role in that process and this can especially be noticed in her earlier artistic development. An examination of Barbara Rea's work pre-1980s before she 'discovered' the full potential of using colour in all its kaleidoscopic glory reveals a strikingly different approach to her art from its later manifestations. Her work through the decade or so after Art College is by contrast to the later colouristic developments, almost monochromatic in appearance. In such work the agency of drawing is very conspicuous in the whole construction of the image which appears to focus primarily on an analytical investigation into the architectonics of the geological structure of the landscape. On the other hand, however, there is also a modernist dimension to be found even in the earlier work which is much closer to analytical Cubism with its austere dispassionate investigation into the basic structure of form – both in the subject observed and the pictorial compositional arrangement of the work of art itself. Even the remarkable transformation that came about later with the spectacular use of colour, and the opening out of pictorial design to much wider vistas was still, however, based on a consistent evolution from the solid ground work laid in the previous two decades. That development from the mono to multichromic in Barbara Rae's work can be read in much the same way that, for instance synthetic Cubism – for all its radical innovative use of decorative colour and inventive design – is still clearly a consistent outcome from the previous analytical stage. Another useful analogy might be this: it is as if the artist was studying the landscape as if it were a Gothic cathedral; initially from the outside where the magnificent architectural structures predominate and there is only a mere hint of colour from the tracery windows, but when she moves inside the same building, her whole visual experience is transformed into one of splendid radiant coloured light and souring space. Thus, a complete journey through the elevating art of Barbara Rae can transport us from the analytical to the synthetic, from the monochromatic to the kaleidoscopic, from the material to the mystical, from the world of the senses through the realms of the spirit.

It would be misguided however, to readily assume that the evolving relationship between the academic and modernistic is no longer to be found in Barbara Rae's approach to her art practice – that there is a clearcut chronological development where the former has now been completely superseded by the latter. This is far too straightforward a scenario to explain the evolution of Barbara Rae's complex art. Both the academic, as a sound foundation of rational certainty; and Modernism, with all the exciting possibilities of venturing into the new and the unknown through innovation and experimentation, have always found a dual place in the artist's practice. As with other modern artists, there is no reason why these two modes of artistic creativity, found in Barbra Rae's art, should not coexist in a stimulating and fruitful dialectical partnership. In 20th century modern art for instance, the most striking example of this fruitful coexistence is the work of Picasso who would effortlessly move through a whole range of different languages of pictorial representation – from highly formal academic Neoclassicism to almost out-and-out abstraction to achieve what he required. Barbara Rae's methods of working are of course different, probably much closer to those of Matisse, in her pursuit of 'a much more simple idea.' Similar to the great French modern master, she utilises in her creative practices, both the academic approach of analytical study and the synthesising methods of Modernism to distil down to a unified visual essence her sensual and emotional relationship with her subject. Thus whereas academic discipline provides the primary rational control to keep the outside subject at a detached distance through the early period of contact; there is then a subsequent move to a very different relationship, where the image-making process begins to take over and allows the previous subject/object distance to be brushed aside and become totally absorbed in the act of painting itself. Now the emerging pictorial image is no longer dependent on the original source of inspiration. Something else takes over in the creative process as it evolves through the different stages of additive and reductive technical processes that the artist skilfully applies to the picture surface. It is only at the end of this ongoing, evolving way of working, with its changing rituals and shifting relationships between the artist, her subject and her chosen medium of expression, that Barbara Rae can finally integrate all the various strands in her painting into a harmonious unity of profound simplicity.

It has been insistently argued throughout this discussion of Barbara Rae's work that the power and vitality of her art lies in her ability to resolve, with great skill and creative imagination, a wide range of seemingly opposing forces. This interplay of opposites which are constantly set off against each other throughout the ongoing creative process is finally resolved on the picture surface itself, where the viewer is now able to critically and meditatively engage with the work as it displays its own individual identity. The finished and presented painted image must of course communicate with the viewer through the distinct language of visual communication which, regardless of how sophisticated it can be elaborated upon, basically consists of the two fundamental components – mark and colour. This fundamental visual linguistic duality in earlier academic theory was critically viewed in terms of the essential dialectic between design (as drawing) and colour (as painting) and subsequently in the modern period as the contrast between figuration and abstraction. These perceived divisions in the language of visual representation and communication were in the past artificially and theoretically enforced on the artists and their public alike by influential critics and powerful institutions. Mercifully this type of aesthetic brainwashing carries little authority and credibility today. Thus one of the great strengths and attractions of the multi-various nature of the art and practice of Barbara Rae is that it cannot be readily categorised and is receptive to a wide range of critical responses for those who have their eyes and their hearts wide open.

The work of Barbara Rae is not however, in any way a fashionable eclectic hybrid art form. On the contrary, it should be seen as an exemplary demonstration of a deeply egalitarian approach which shows what can be achieved when there is a sustained commitment to a full integration of all aspects of the visual and the poetic possibilities of painting. With such an all-inclusive and comprehensive attitude it would be antithetical and perversely constricting to control and categorise within any academic genre, or under any specific critical label, such an open and receptive approach as that of Barbara Rae. To call her simply a landscape painter for instance, could easily imply that she passively describes the visual appearances of natural world through the inherited languages and tropes of Western landscape painting. Nothing could be further from the actual case. Barbara Rae, with her endless inventive creativity, actively seeks out and draws inspiration from her deeply sensual and psychological involvement with all lands which she visits. Yet at the end of her long and involved creative process it is not the original natural world that she pictures, but rather, her own visionary one, which has been elaborately constructed out of a range of contending sources – from her direct observations, her lingering memories, her various studio strategies and finally, and most crucially, the act of painting itself. Then all the necessary stages that are involved in the creative process finally integrate and resolve themselves in the harmonious unity of the work of art itself. With such an achievement the landscape artist truly (and literally) transforms into a religious painter. This comes about from the word 'religio' which originally meant to bind together in unified communal and spiritual accord. And this is what the art of Barbara Rae ultimately achieves – a profound expression of the possible, and deeply desired, holy unity between the human and the natural worlds, between individual consciousness and the collective unconscious, between ourselves and our origins in nature itself.

Tragically it seems we are living in a contemporary era of endless worldwide violent antagonisms. Everywhere we can see deep division and strife between peoples and their perceived threatening enemies – between the insatiable greed of those people and the threatened resources of the natural world. Neither political reason nor religious faith seems to have the will or the power to address and resolve the spiralling crises of conflict in which we find ourselves. Yet even in these dark times there are always scattered beacons of hope. In their own silent, but illuminating way, the paintings of Barbara Rae are such rays of enlightenment and reconciliation. On the open and welcoming surfaces of her truly 'simple' paintings all previous conflicting tensions are resolved through the joyous interplay of opposites – between struggle and resolution, between control and chance, between intelligence and intuition, between the pragmatic and the poetic, between the sensual and the spiritual, between the material and the metaphoric, between the physical and the metaphysical, between the earthly and the Edenic, between existence and essence, and ultimately between sight and vision.

This essay was written for the publication *Barbara Rae*, B Hare, A Lambirth and G Wardell (Lund Humphries, London, 2008).

LYS HANSEN
Divided Self, United Vision

'PAINTING IS DEAD' has been the verdict handed down from the courts of fashionable art criticism throughout this – ultimate decade of our century. To be more accurate, it is figurative painting which is now judged to be completely obsolete and redundant. Scottish artists, however, seem not to have got the message and the painting of human subject matter is still the central focus of concern for many of our leading painters. The art of Lys Hansen is a notable example of this determined and continuing commitment to the representation of humanist values in contemporary Scottish art.

If one were asked to single out the most significant trend that has emerged on the Scottish art scene over the last 20 years, in which Lys Hansen has been a leading professional painter, this would have to be the spectacular rise in the number of women artists coming to prominence. What is also remarkable is that a high number of these artists have made the figure, or more specifically the female body, their primary subject. Lys Hansen, along with other women painters such as Gwen Hardie, Margaret Hunter, June Redfern, Helen Flockhart and Alison Watt are a loose but distinctive force in recent Scottish figurative art. Before focusing on the work and career of Lys Hansen, therefore, a brief discussion of the wider significance of this phenomenon is necessary.

In contrast to the history of art in most other countries, the depiction of the nude figure, male or female, is conspicuous by its almost total absence in Scottish painting. In the early 18th century Richard Watt exceptionally presented himself in a self-portrait, painting a rather naïve version of *Venus at her Toilet* (1728). Needless to say, he did not find many takers amongst his prudish patrons for such a risqué subject. Even in the 19th century, when Scottish artists were granted a little more freedom in what they might be allowed to paint, the figure in the landscape was well and truly clothed against the cauld blast of conventional Caledonian morality. JD Fergusson apart, this cultural apartheid against the nude was still forcibly evident as late as the 1950s. When the hapless Joan Eardley, for instance, exhibited her picture *Sleeping Male Nude* (1954/5), now in the National Galleries of Scotland collection, she was ridiculed in the Scottish popular press with such juvenile headlines as 'Oh, He's Got No Clothes On'. Predictably, Eardley never repeated such an exposure again!

In the late 1970s and early 1980s, when Lys Hansen returned to full-time painting after bringing up her young family, the art scene in Scotland was definitely changing. After the predominance of Conceptionalism and Minimalism from the 1960s, raw painting was back with a vengeance. Yet even though Lys Hansen was never part of any specific art movement, her style of painting could readily be linked with what became known as Scottish Neo-Expressionism. There were strong affinities between her depictions of female figures in highly agitated and contorted poses and the dominant characteristics of much of the art of the younger Scottish painters of the 1980s. For instance, the male painters such as Ken Currie and Peter Howson, sometimes called the New Glasgow Boys, also concentrated on the human figure, but usually in an overtly social or even political context. Hansen, on the other hand, as with a number of her fellow Scottish women artists, tended to disconnect her figures from any particular social or domestic environment and instead dealt with much more universal (and at the same time, deeply subjective) themes specifically female in character. For these women artists, and especially Lys Hansen, the female body became the scene for a whole range of disturbing discourses on our physical and emotional condition which the eminent writer and psychologist RD Laing had earlier diagnosed as the 'Divided Self'.

Similar to the dominant characteristic in much figurative painting in 1980s, Lys Hansen's early works tended to have a mythic dimension. This can be found in her version of *Athena* (1980), for instance. Compared with her later free, expressionistic mode of painting, this rather Pop Art-style picture has a strong sense of graphic design in which the female anatomy is subjected to cubistic division and rearrangement in the fashion of Richard Hamilton, for example. Yet, even in such a relatively academic piece of work, one senses that just underneath the surface powerful emotional forces could split apart this veneer of cool controlled anatomical order.

This split immediately occurs in a subsequent work from this period – *One and the Other* (1980). It is almost as if the artist is now rewriting the mythical birth of Athena from a contemporary feminine point of view. In the ancient Greek version the head of Zeus, Athena's father, is split open with an axe and the goddess is created fully formed as the original 'brain child'. Clearly in such a story the emphasis is exclusively on the male intellectual aspect of creativity. With *One and the Other*, however, Lys Hansen wishes to present a very different version of events. Creativity and birth for an artist – who is also a mother – is a very potent topic. Lys Hansen's paintings continually return to different ways of expressing what this means and feels for her. The prevalent characteristic of her treatment of this theme is to emphasise the physical and emotional experiences involved. In *One and the Other*, therefore, it is not the male head, but the female body, which is being split apart. The colour here is much more austere compared with the earlier erotic *Athena*. The spinal area of the torso is torn wide open to reveal a dark chasm, while the rest of the body appears to shudder in great convulsions, with breasts and buttocks quivering with seismic tremors of sensual pleasure and physical pain. That experience of cathartic ecstasy is also most powerfully expressed in *Electric Torso* (1980).

As images of convulsive sensual experiences, these paintings of the early 1980s are very compelling. Yet they still tend to rely on a decidedly graphic mode of representation and so the intrinsically expressive potential of the painting medium itself is still not fully utilised. Throughout the mid-1980s, however, Hansen developed her own distinctive style of painting by concentrating on bridging the gap between form and stylistic expression in her work.

This begins in a relatively tentative manner, as can be seen in a picture like *Woman with Man* (1979–82). Here, colour is no longer restricted to being used in the flat and circumscribed manner of the earlier paintings, but is much more freely applied, with the whole surface of the picture plane being worked over by aggressive brushstrokes. This gives more all-round organic unity to the work, although there is still a sense of a figure firmly placed in front of a fixed background. The figure itself is a commanding presence: like a not-too-distant cousin of one of Willem De Kooning's 'Women'. Lys Hansen's 'Woman', however, represents a more primaeval nature with her gigantic, overflowing breasts recalling the monumental fecundity of the *Venus of Willendorf*. Not surprisingly, the head of the male presence, perched precariously on the woman's chest, looks decidedly uneasy about his predicament. Yet powerful as this painting is, it still tends to have an over-reliance on drawing and graphic outline. In fact, the most resolved painterly area in the picture is the massive right thigh which is a *tour de force* in the use of colour to suggest form and yet at the same time convey sensual energy.

From the mid-1980s onwards, that energisation of the painting medium becomes one of the outstanding features of Lys Hansen's work. The division between medium and message is successfully bridged by the animated manner with which she appears to activate the all-over surface of her canvases. This can be fully appreciated in a group of paintings she produced around 1984–85 in which two human heads seem to be submerging themselves into each other in the manner of Brancusi's *Kiss* (1908). Here the highly charged dialectical conflict, between tender attraction and brutal aggression is underlined in the pictures' titles such as *Licking and Biting*, *Love Bites* and *Agony in the First Garden*. In these works, the rapacious, devouring heads practically fill the whole canvas and so almost eliminate the foreground/background dichotomy which dogged some of the earlier works. Furthermore, there is now a real dramatic conflict involved which has an all-consuming focus of attention, as soft vulnerable tongues or fingers are lured into the gaping trap of the bared-teethed mouth of the ambivalent lovers. In these highly charged paintings, mouths, teeth, tongues, fingers and lips are all sucked into a great vortex of sexual passion which recalls the 'battle of the sexes' work of Picasso and Giacometti of the early 1930s.

Lys Hansen is in fact one of the few Scottish artists who has been able to develop a meaningfully creative dialogue between her work and that of a modern master like Picasso, especially with his surrealist period of the late 1920s and early 1930s, The fruits of this scrutiny of Picasso are further seen in the single-figure pictures, which she was also producing in the mid-1980s, as for example *Allein* (*Alone*) and *Signals*, both 1985. Such works recall the great *Bather* paintings by Picasso, especially *The Swimmer* of 1929. Yet while Picasso's figures feel like giant puppets activated by the Master's outside string-pulling control, Lys Hansen's women are animated by their own disturbing internal, emotional and psychic energy. In paintings like *Allein*, the figure appears to be trapped within the narrow confines of the picture frame. The space that the woman occupies seems less like a physical dimension and more like a psychological one, created by the obsessive mind of the protagonist herself. This results in any room for manoeuvre being reduced almost to the shallow surface of the picture plane, thus forcing the figure into a grotesque posture which powerfully suggests the turbulent mental condition of the woman herself. This figure generates a disturbing presence which, through contorted and displaced limbs, challenges and threatens the viewer's normal attitude to the representation of women within a whole range of artistic, sexual and social contexts.

While at this time many of the women figures in Lys Hansen's paintings are presented with a marked feeling of isolation and entrapment, the artist herself was eager to open out her work to a wider social and political environment. This first came to the fore after she went to Berlin in 1985 as a visiting artist. There she could see for herself not only individual people, but a whole society which was divided from itself and its own recent history. One of the major achievements of her Berlin experience was that she now had the confidence and ability to raise her art to the dimensions of modern history painting. This resulted firstly in the monumental *Berlin Trilogy* (1985) in which the three panels treat human form within the allegorical tale of the Three Wise Monkeys. While the mythical Monkeys deliberately cut themselves off from the outside world around them, the condition of the humans in Lys Hansen's triptych is that they 'Hear Everything', 'See All' but 'Say Nothing' as indicated by the separate titles for each panel. Thus the ironic situation in our contemporary society is that we are ever bombarded with a never-ending stream of sounds and images but, despite all our mass media technology of communication, we are unable, or unwilling, to make any real contact with each other in a one-to-one relationship.

As with much of Lys Hansen's later work, the *Berlin Trilogy* strongly suggests a pervasive atmosphere of suppression which is expressed through the self-imprisoning posture of the figures, acting as a metaphor for the wider context of social discontinuity in the body politic at large. The deep divisions in our society are reflected in the way that the human hands in the *Trilogy* do not act as agents of response to what we see and hear, but instead work against their communicative role to become suppressive forces that enclose us from the world outside. The deeply injurious effect that this internal civil war of the senses can have on us is dramatically expressed in another work of 1985, the appropriately entitled *Divided Self Trilogy*, where the human head and body are literally tearing each other apart.

In *Grip*, the central panel from the *Divided Self Trilogy*, the initial onslaught on the viewer's sensibilities is created by the violent distortions to which the highly mutable face is being subjected. On closer inspection, however one begins to appreciate that these facial mutilations have a strong pictorial authenticity to them as well a psychological one. In the internal narrative of the picture, the fingers of the half-hidden hand manipulate the features to suggest the powerful psychosocial ritual of 'putting on a public face'. While this psychological narrative forcibly impacts on our immediate attention, *Grip* also rewards a more sustained and critical analysis. Here I would suggest that this involves a variety of pictorial languages that are at work within the painting. *Grip* is rich in the multilingual range of modern painting's modes of representation from allusions to cubistic fragmentation and multi-viewpoints, to surrealist biomorphic transformations to expressionist primitivistic distortions – all adding many layers of visual complexities to a haunting image of the human experience. By now Lys Hansen's work has evolved into a highly intelligent and personal version of the language of Expressionism. Her paintings are the product of an extremely articulate artist who is well skilled in the art of picture-making. She is able to communicate the deeply felt realities of her imagination in a manner that attempts, not only to gain the viewer's emotional sympathies, but also their aesthetic sensibilities.

During the 1990s, despite marked changes in taste and fashion, Lys Hansen's commitment to, and faith in, the intrinsic power of painting to express an authentic vision of human affairs has remained steadfast. This is strongly evident in her triptych *Witness with Evidence* (1994), which possesses a truly mythic quality. This work has a strong catastrophic theme, so that the dark ominous threat which stalks most of her work now reaches apocalyptical dimensions. There are obvious biblical overtones, with such panel titles as *Where were you, God, when I needed you?* (1995). Yet, although there is a heartrending despair running through all the panels and the accompanying sculptures, there is also an energy and vitality animating the work. The symbolic imagery may, like Dürer's *Four Horsemen of the Apocalypse* (1498) spell out doom and disaster; yet like the German master, Hansen infuses her vision with such dedication to her painterly craft and such commitment to the grand rhetoric of her theme, that this work expands the viewer's outlook on human life and history.

In her most recent major work, Lys Hansen has attempted to deal with a specific historical and local tragedy that occurred frighteningly close to home. The artist's studio is near the town Dunblane, where 16 schoolchildren and their teacher were murdered by a crazed gunman. Like the rest of the country, Lys Hansen was deeply distressed by this horrendous event, especially as the plight of children is a recurring theme in her work. Despite certain reservations, she committed herself to making a large painting entitled *Day of the Jackal* (1996–97).

With such a subject, which instantly recalls the *Massacre of the Innocents*, a strong biblical theme is again suggested in the painting. In the right-hand panel, two figures look pleadingly to the heavens for an answer to the artist's earlier question, 'Where were you, God, when I needed you?' On the left side of the painting there is the artist's own version of the *pieta*. Above the grieving group is the ominous presence of a threatening black crow, recalling the old Scots ballad, *Twa Corbies*. Appropriately the deadly bird spreads its wings like a black crucifix. Next to the *pieta* group is the giant figure of a child who, like many of the heads in the artist's earlier paintings, is torn between looking out and covering up its terrified eyes with its hands clasped protectively around its face. The central panel seems to look on to a bleak inhospitable landscape, with a vivid yellow escarpment on the horizon. A terrifying skull-like head dominates the immediate foreground while just behind is a figure of a wailing woman etched in bare outline into the dark blue ground. From the woman's arms falls the white silhouette of the innocent dead child, drawn out like a police murder scene diagram. Such a graphic device as a reference to forensic imagery adds to the particular potency of the work in a similar way to Picasso's documentary allusions in *Guernica* (1937). In the *Day of the Jackal*, Lys Hansen has, with skill and sensitivity managed to negotiate the difficult divide between responding to the specific circumstances of the actual event, and at the same time fulfilling the need to elevate this local tragedy onto the level of universal significance.

Day of the Jackal is painted on three separate panels, but unlike the earlier triptychs these are butted together to create a much greater visual unifying coherence for the work. That sense of unity is also felt in the inter-relatedness of the picture's consistent iconography of pain and death which allows the stridently discordant colours to play off against each other in an extremely highly charged fashion. This is what the whole development of Lys Hansen's work seems to have been striving to achieve. She is truly a courageous artist, who is prepared to acknowledge and address the deep and troubling divisions which wrack not only our own physical and mental life, but also the whole fabric of modern society. Yet Lys Hansen the artist, although distressed, is not daunted by what she sees around her. The overall unity of her artistic vision, as evidenced by her major works, gives her the creative power to exorcise her own and everyone else's demons which can terrorise our lives and haunt our imaginations. As with high tragedy, the paintings of Lys Hansen ultimately have a cathartic power, which is able to rejuvenate our senses and revitalise our spirit. Such painting is never dead.

This essay was published in *Passionate Paint: The Art of Lys Hansen*, ed. Giles Sutherland (Mainstream Publishing, Edinburgh, London, 1998).

JOYCE CAIRNS
Witnessing and Warning

I write what I would never dare tell anyone.
Primo Levi

UNLEASH THE DOGS OF WAR! Most people believe that is the most terrible curse inflicted on human history. War is the Four Men of the Apocalypse rolled into one. War spreads devastation and suffering wherever and whenever it rides. Yet, on the other hand, war, ironically, has also been the source and inspiration for some of the most memorable works of literature and art the world has ever known – from Homer's *Illiad* to Picasso's *Guernica*. In this essay I will contend that these inspiring and disturbing paintings of Joyce Cairns yet again bear witness to this continuing contradiction between the destructive force of war and the creative power of art.

By chance while writing this essay on one of Scotland's most remarkable and critically admired contemporary figurative painters, I happened to hear two news items which seemed absolutely appropriate for the thematic significance of Joyce Cairns' epic *War Tourist* series. Firstly, it was announced that the last surviving Australian First War veteran had just died at the ripe old age of 104. Secondly, the Pentagon reported that the death toll of US troops in Iraq had just passed the symbolically significant two thousand mark. Here, yet again, we can see in stark contradistinction the same recurring concern which runs all through Joyce Cairns' work: the fundamental contrast between the war experience of one individual, hero or victim, set against the seemingly endless mass of anonymous human suffering and carnage.

While naturally the Americans wish to play down the immensity of their current war losses, the Australian government, on the other hand, is delighted to honour with a full state funeral, its last surviving combatant of a devastating war, now safely confined to the history books and archive film. No one of course, would oppose this appropriate gesture of public gratitude and remembrance. This is the time-honoured ritual that gives any nation a very tangible sense of its historical identity and plugs into the collective consciousness of its subjects. War by its very nature is a great social coming-together which seeks to involve everyone it touches in its public demonstrations of unity and solidarity, both during, and after, the time of conflict. Joyce Cairns' paintings, however, aim to penetrate underneath this hallowed, self-decorated surface of military posturing and public coherence. In *War Tourist* she sets out to sympathetically explore and critically expose the more private, feminine side of our attitude to the devastating and traumatic impact of armed conflict on the individual human psyche and the collective memory.

Such is the enthralling narrative of these paintings that even someone like myself, who has little interest in military history, is absorbed by their epic sweep of subject matter and their intense pictorial examination of human actions and responses under the most adverse and harrowing circumstances. Monumental in scale, most of these pictures of Joyce Cairns are also bursting with expressive high emotional drama, ranging from deep pathos (*Irma*) to intense outrage (*The Drums of War*). Clearly with such work, this dedicated and highly experienced painter has risen to the highest realms of her artistic ambition and intent. In academic terms such pictures confirm that the artist has now become a contemporary history painter of immense visual rhetorical power and great moral and artistic authority, demonstrated by such 'great machines' as *The Deadly Wars*.

Amongst other things, all history painters need to demonstrate, as Joyce Cairns undoubtedly does here, that they are skilled in rendering every type of subject matter – from epic tragedy to keenly observed still life. She even manages to bring these two dimensions together in *After the Battle*. Furthermore, confronted with such an awesome sweep of the horrors of modern history, the viewer desperately requires a trusted presence to guide them through the seemingly endless physical and human devastation that is presented to their horrified eyes. Mercifully we are provided with the eponymous *War Tourist* who, like some ancient female deity from classical art, acts as our sympathetic champion and medium, reflecting and transmitting our various responses to the heroic actions and deep suffering to be found in these images.

Clearly the artist is fully aware that much of what she presents in her painting is for many people extremely harrowing and profoundly disturbing. This, however, is not shock for shock's sake, as is the case in much of our multimedia age. As a dedicated history painter she is required to confront the dominant historical forces of her time and convey them truthfully to her contemporaries. On the other hand, also being a modern female artist, her attitude and approach will be radically different from that of the male history painters of the past. Then, history painting was highly esteemed because it was expected to express, in the most learned and exemplary pictorial forms, a universal understanding and celebration of human heroic and tragic actions. With the emergence however, of modern ideological and technological warfare, and its awesome capacity to annihilate vast numbers of combatants and civilians alike, the previously held Enlightenment faith in the power of human reason to understand the ways of man and historical progress was severely challenged – as was the authority of conventional academic history painting. Working now as a contemporary history painter, Joyce Cairns here re-examines and reassesses the new role and purpose of this type of painting under very different conditions from the past. Instead of vainly clinging to history painting's earlier, and now redundant, mission of intellectual, moral and religious instruction, Cairns conveys her powerful pictorial themes not through received wisdom and conventional instruction, but with highly expressive emotional impact and passionate empathic reaction. These paintings of Joyce Cairns are not public pronouncements, but open discourses on the moral conditions of our age, where tragically war seems to still be endemic.

Notably in all these works there is a distinctive female response to war, where the more personal and private emotional dimensions operate at a different level from that of the official chronological account of reasonable cause and effect. Here we are more likely to be dealing with memory and myth as the motivating and guiding forces on human actions than documentary fact. Once the reassuring facade of reason and order is smashed, the artist courageously dives into the vortex of the ever-shifting, constantly changing, realm of the human imagination of fear and desire. As with Picasso's *Guernica* for example, nothing is securely fixed, neither in time nor space. In such a pictorial world of fluctuating imagery, as instanced in *They Said the War was Partly to Blame* traumatic personal recollections of childhood domestic incidents merge and overlap with imagined scenes from her own father's war experiences – whether in the blazing sunlit deserts of North Africa (*Longstop Hill*), or the mine-covered beaches of Normandy (*Sword Beach*), or the deadly silent wasteland of Holocaust Central Europe (*Polish Journey*). While all the time this real and imagined fragmented imagery from the war-torn world – both past and present – comes back to haunt and inspire the artist in the mission hall studio of her beloved Footdee village at the mouth of Aberdeen harbour. For even here war invades the lives of this small fishing community, as seen in *Messerschmitt over Footdee*.

Joyce Cairns' multilayered images reveal that, whether we like it or not, we are all touched and involved in some way by the destructive forces of human history. Mephistopheles' chilling observation to Faust that hell is here and we are all in it, seems to be abundantly confirmed today by the global village of mass media communication which is the very stuff of our nightmare electronic age. Now, if we wish we can watch people in previously inaccessible parts of the world being blown to bloody bits, while we eat our TV Dinners. Thus in Joyce Cairns' fractured and multifaceted images the artist's array of highly personal memorabilia is constantly linking, through association and the power of memory, with the relentless forces of history outside the sanctuary of her domestic environment. Thus Joyce Cairns' grand history painting and humble still life jostle and merge with each other. The macrocosm and microcosm overlap, creating a continuous interconnection which binds us all with the ongoing historical process – through past, present and future.

This vertiginous sensation of whirling disequilibrium which gives such powerful vitality to many of Joyce Cairns' pictorial compositions is very much epitomised by the motif of the carousel which appears in two of her works – *The Deadly Wars* and *Irma*. This sensation of concentric spiralling motion, where the centre is barely holding all the disparate parts together, powerfully conveys the schizophrenic experience of a fragmenting reality seen from both the inner and outer worlds. While at the same time, yet another, even more frightening effect of war is also portrayed in these paintings. In marked contrast, both in form and mood, are the works dealing directly with that ultimate modern horror – the Holocaust.

In *Auschwitz Memorial* the whole image is framed within a rigid grid to convey what Primo Levi astutely describes as the 'geometric madness' of the Nazi's Final Solution Programme of ethnic cleansing – or to put it more bluntly, annihilation. With this pictorial paranoia we are starkly confronted with the pitiless process of natural selection, where scientific categorisation is taken to its final insane conclusion – millions of people reduced to mere tattooed numbers. Into this totally alien world of 'primordial mechanism' the artist has valiantly attempted to bring back that most humane of artistic expression – portraiture. Portraiture, from the Latin word *protrahere*, meaning to single out from the mass, is the very antithesis of what was perpetrated on those helpless victims who were turned into a faceless mass of subhumanity by their victimisers. In a compassionate attempt to rectify this monstrous affront to basic human respect, the artist has valiantly attempted, through the life affirming spirit of painting itself, to resist this deadly system of total depersonalisation by giving back to the photographic images of these nameless ones their place in human history. By her painstaking dedication to her art and her subjects, the artist sympathetically strives to restore their fundamental birthright of individual dignity and common humanity.

This total commitment to her seemingly impossible self-appointed task is most borne out by the gigantic still life painting, *Shoes from Majdanek*. Under adverse conditions (working with a magnifying glass to see poor definition photographs that she took in the huts at the camp filled to overflowing with rotting shoes), the artist has unflinchingly confronted the stark logic and pitiless acquisitiveness of the Nazi ideal of the fulfilment of its vision of the Hegelian historical process. As Joyce Cairns' uncompromising picture shows, this perverted vision of Nazi historicism ends in a mountain of silent shoes, stolen from their helpless owners on their last naked, barefoot walk to the gas chamber, in order that these pathetic human artefacts might be reutilised for the further glory of the Third Reich. Here for countless victimised people the process of modern history came to a grinding halt – but the artist defiantly refuses to allow their killers to have the final say.

The contrast in treatment and mood between these concentration camp images and Joyce Cairns' other war pictures, such as the lovingly rendered paintings of her father's highland regiment uniform, *Father's Memorabilia* could not be more striking. Furthermore, in another very different work, *Sword Beach*, the artist fully demonstrates her unique pictorial narrative skills in conveying through a range of disparate means, her imagined impression of what her father might have experienced in the bloody mayhem of the D-Day Normandy landings. Thus, while such paintings are redolent with explosive action and varied incident, her other subjects (whether human or not) in the concentration camp pictures are equally treated with the same degree of obsessive attention. Within these Holocaust images nothing is overtly stressed and so the grotesque nature of the historical reality just behind the surface appearance is infinitely more powerfully conveyed by the matter-of-fact technique employed by the artist. Where we might have expected something more apocalyptic, everything is as silent as the grave. So with dedicated commitment and compassion Joyce Cairns, against all the odds and resisting her natural inclinations as an intuitive narrative painter, has managed to express and convey the essential moribund nature of the concentration camps, where all human personality and emotion and vitality is drained and reduced to a deathly zero.

War Tourist confirms that after those long years of hard work and determined effort – where artistic skills have been honed to precision and the committed search for authentic subject matter has been relentlessly pursued – has now come together to produce some of the most powerful and moving paintings ever created by a Scottish artist. The range of themes and approaches developed in these works is vastly varied: from the celebration of the human spirit under the most catastrophic conditions through to the unflinching depiction of acts of monstrous barbarity. Yet, at the same time, all this is expressed and conveyed with a deeply personal and sincerely committed seriousness and compassion. In these very challenging works the artist shows us that even in the face of the most incomprehensible and inexplicable acts of man's inhumanity to man, the empathic power of the human spirit and the sympathetic imagination can survive, and even triumph, over all the evils that are carried out in the name of war. With the constant reassuring female presence of the *War Tourist* to sustain and guide us through the horrors of recent and current human affairs, we, as individuals and as a society of kindred spirits, might still be able to survive in a war-torn world that even now has to learn the lessons of history. In the end it will only be when we are both able to follow the way of the *War Tourist*, and also readily heed the voice of the survivor ('that it is always preferable to witness than to judge') that we may hopefully look forward to a war-free future. By facing up to what we might all wish to avoid seeing, it is ironically, through our confrontation with the disturbing images of Joyce Cairns' war-torn paintings that we witness a means to this cherished ideal.

This catalogue essay was published for the exhibition *Joyce Cairns, War Tourist* shown at Aberdeen Art Gallery in 2006.

DOUG COCKER

A Servant of Two Masters

IF YOU GO to George Square in Glasgow, as with most other city centres, you will hardly notice the numerous public statues to the great and the good of the past. If, however, you put your ear to the ground you might still hear the faint receding sounds of a celebration which only a short time ago was all the rage. You may just remember it, it was known as the Triumph of Scottish Painting. Of course, much has changed on the Scottish art scene since those heady days, full of vim and vigour back in the early '80s. Today, for instance, any with-it artist or trendy gallery who desires to be regarded as being at the cutting edge of avant-garde Postmodernism must avoid being associated with painting 'like the plague' – unless of course to parody and mock its assumed pretentiousness.

Yet, like the parrot in the famous *Monty Python* routine, painting may have been pronounced dead by some, but there are others who refuse to believe it. This is very much the case in Scotland, where despite all the evidence of painting's demise, most galleries will still show the stuff, most people who buy art still want the stuff, and most critics still write articles and books about the stuff. Therefore, it may be hip to be a young installation artist. Making sculpture is the sexy thing to do; yet despite all this, if you seriously wish to contemplate a long career as a full-time professional sculptor in this country you are either very brave and/or extremely foolhardy. Speaking to Doug Cocker I still get the strong impression that even he has not fully made up his mind on this matter, as his attitude to his working situation can fluctuate between hope and despair.

In 1990 Doug Cocker quit his job as lecturer in sculpture at Gray's School of Art, Aberdeen to become a full-time sculptor – almost as rare a species in Scotland as the golden eagle.

However, this was not a decision made on sudden impulse, but by an artist, who, then in his mid-career, had a strong proven track record of impressive exhibitions, major commissions and most importantly, a distinctly creative voice as evidenced by an impressive body of work. This he had slowly and painstakingly established over the previous decade or so, before he finally decided to cross the Rubicon.

As the title of my essay implies, I feel that the strength of Cocker's sculpture (and, incidentally, the frustrations that he experienced as an artist) lies in a whole range of oppositional tensions within the work itself. There is a procedural parallel to this in the context of his practice as a professional sculptor working within the public domain. These contradictory pressures have changed in nature over the last ten years, but remain one of the main driving forces behind Cocker's artistic development. Never complacent, he is motivated by an ongoing urge to re-examine and requestion both his work and the society he wishes his sculpture to serve. So there is a fundamental dilemma in Cocker's situation, through his dual ambitions of wishing to be a professional sculptor, relying very much on public and corporate commission patronage; and yet at the same time, desiring his work to retain its challenging, even disturbing, social critical edge. He is conscious of the dangers of biting the hand that feeds, while at the same time being true to his own self-imposed criteria of artistic validity.

At the outset of his career, there was little to indicate from the early work the sociopolitical direction Cocker's art would take. In the late '70s and early '80s, landscape was the main inspiration for the form and imagery of his sculpture. This is not surprising since Cocker is from a rural Perthshire farming background, and continues to live outwith the urban environments where most of his public sculpture is located.

Cocker's early sculptures took two very different forms. Firstly, there were a series of 'box sets', with titles such as *Responses to a Farmyard* and the *Perthshire* and *River Series*. These works seem to act as repositories for his autobiographical investigations through the associative power of landscape and natural objects, such as stones, wood, bark, etc which were placed within a pictorial framed arrangement. Using a 'discovery and response' procedure not dissimilar to that of Richard Long, but on a much more modest scale, and more preoccupied with rediscovery than discovery, Cocker chose to use the objective eye of the camera as the controlling factor in these 'box' sets. The photographs acted as stimuli for the configurations which ensued, often involving a prolonged process of contemplation and distillation.

There are a number of similarities in the work procedures between these box sets and Cocker's latest wall reliefs in this exhibition, but what is so striking about these earlier works is the private and intimate nature of their unassuming presence. Yet, they also clearly demonstrated an awareness of and response to many of the issues in British sculpture of the '70s, which were being formulated by a group of young English artists who were strongly reacting against the dominant Caroesque modernist Formalism of the time.

It was surprising then to find the next development in Cocker's work in the early '80s was a swing away from the process-based imagery of the enclosed box sets to an open, constructivist abstract style of sculpture. This is most clearly seen in the free-flowing wall pieces like *Bridges* and *Fast Landscape*. These finely made pieces of intricate sculptural engineering indicated how important to the artist was the sensual and aesthetic pleasure aroused by manual skill and ingenuity of craftsmanship. Yet on the other hand, this open display of technical virtuosity was imbued with an honesty of making which invited scrutiny from a non-specialist public. Cocker acknowledges that this awareness of different levels of public response is always present, though not necessarily helpful, in his approach to making. Yet, maybe this is one of the contributory reasons why he has been so successful in winning and carrying through such a comparatively high number of major publicly sited works.

Although the early box-series and later abstract pieces were very different in construction and appearance, they were basically linked by a narrative approach. Both types of sculpture suggest the notion of progression, through either time or space by the power of metaphorical association and stimulation. However, a number of circumstances in the mid-1980s coincided to generate a new impulse in his work output. In 1984 Cocker had made an extended teaching visit to Philadelphia, which provided fresh insights into large scale sculptures. He had moved back to live in Scotland two years earlier, thus eliminating the subconscious stream of distanced 'memory' imagery which had largely fed his work output up to this point. On a broader front the multifarious social iniquities of Thatcher's programme had by now become clear, fully operational and, for him increasingly difficult to ignore.

These factors, fortuitously combined with opportunity to work on an ambitious scale, provided ground and perceived need to reject the pictorial and formal complexities of his previous work in favour of a sculpture aspiring to monumental public presence, and which could challenge attention through the power of a 'singleness of image'. What immediately followed, were large, outdoor temporarily sited works such as *State of a Nation, Boss, One of Us* and *Song of Sisyphus.* These were quixotic but unavoidable 'follies' imbued with mock grandeur and demanding, through collaboration of scale and title, some sort of pause on the part of the viewer – consideration as to how such a purposeless artefact could relate to how we live now. Cocker's targets had become transposed from his consciousness as citizen into the realms of his work.

If one looks at *Coda,* which presents a collection of Cocker's iconic sculptures in model form, one can see that after the mid-'80s his work becomes, in one particular way, much more conceptional, employing visual and verbal metaphor to intrigue and stimulate speculation. The space which now gives access to his sculpture is not only the physical one between forms, but also the cognitive gap between the work and its title. It is somewhere in the semiotic no man's land, between the sign and the signified, that a possible 'meaning' for each piece is likely to be found. Enigmatic titles, with a poetical beauty of their own, such as *Persian Whispers,* or *Beneath the Screaming Eagle* engage our attention, as much as the physical formulation of the sculptures themselves. In these works there is a striking contrast between the self-contained iconic nature of their construction, and the open, elusive nature of possible meaning through metaphor, metonymy and association, at his best Cocker evades the Modernist's need for the author's 'presence' to be felt through total attention to aesthetic craftsmanship. With his desire also to address social and moral issues, the power of Cocker's art does not solely lie in the autonomous purity of its formal perfection; but also in its ability to stimulate a sociopolitical critical awareness in the spectator.

Over the last ten years Doug Cocker has found his own individual voice where he can, when appropriate, use his distinctive sculptural expression to address important contemporary social experience. Like the work of the best of his peers, such as Cragg and Woodrow, Cocker's sculpture is political in the broadest sense of the word. By that I mean that it is not escapist, esoteric or purely aesthetic, but aims to raise awareness of the underlying contradictions in late 20th century capitalist society. For example, in an earlier work of the mid-'80s *Beneath the Screaming Eagle,* the ultimate symbol of material status and security, the house, is enclosed from above by an encircling barrier that throws a protective, but ominously imprisoning shadow on all below. In this very powerful piece, Cocker echoes the dire warnings of Noam Chomsky that we put our trust in false gods to secure us from our worst nightmares, only to find that they heighten our sense of insecurity and further imprison us in our increased fearful state.

Many of these works also have a strong satirical edge to them. For example, the artist employs bathos to underline the vacuousness of much political rhetoric, where the visual and the verbal mock each other. This is most acutely observed in one of Cocker's major works, *State of a Nation,* where hollow chauvinism is undermined by the unstable rocking-horse base on which the classical temple of social order and national pride is precariously placed.

Yet despite the humorous vein running through Cocker's work, there is also a dark undercurrent of despair, as a number of these sculptures appear to suggest dominating, imprisoning forces in operation. Many of his sculptures seem to allude to the profound struggle taking place in modern society between the aspirations to individual creative freedom and the deadening effect of institutionalised power and corporate consumer imperialism. This takes on a particular personal significance in one of Cocker's most successful pieces, *Eyeless in Gaza.* In this work, it is the artist who is enthralled and threatened by the blind philistinism to be found at all levels of public life which places the actual and ideological pursuit of things material above those cultural.

Since the mid-'80s the theme of social and ideological restriction has been a recurring one in Cocker's sculpture. It can be readily perceived in such recent works as *Flock* and in some of the pieces in this exhibition such as *2 Tribes – 40 Shades. Flock* was created during his tenure of the first Essex Fine Art Scholarship in 1991–92. A two-ton sycamore construction, standing over 13' high, the sculpture consists of 16 fairly crudely carved, schematised human figures tightly corralled into a raised sheep pen. These figures are jointed together and lifted high off the ground so that although they can slightly sway back and forwards their freedom of movement is very limited and to little purpose. In *Flock* the issue of control and uniformity is dealt with in a broad generalised manner. By contrast, similar thematic concerns are given a specific historical, ideological context in *2 Tribes – 40 Shades.* Here Cocker discourses on the religious sectarianism in Northern Ireland. He sees this endemic tribalism, whether in Ireland or elsewhere, as one of the main internal, self-deluding and self-destructive forces which suppress freedom of thought and action. Such blind bigotry can only countenance differences not commonality, and so prevents the development of organically coherent communities in a multi-ethnic world.

The theme of confinement and control which Cocker so passionately addresses in many of his works is also something which he experiences himself as a sculptor who wants to see his work sited. As he points out, working for public art commissions almost inevitably closes down the artist's room for personal creative expression. Thus the long process of translating the initial spark of inventive imagination to the finished product can turn out to be a disheartening one. What can become lost in the long fabrication and bureaucratic processes is the original authenticity, which, for the artist, is to be found in the outflowing of initial ideas created by his first drawings. Drawing, for Cocker, is very close to the surrealist's practice of automatism, where the artist freely allows forms and images to body forth onto the page with little or no rational restraint or control. These spontaneous sketches are the testing ground where he rejects or begins to develop his ideas for possible sculptures. In the most convincing of Cocker's work this flexibility is continued right through to the finished piece and its enigmatic title. The power of his most successful sculptures lies in their truly metamorphic nature, which keeps their shifting significance and allusive meaning continually open to interpretation.

When, however, Cocker's original ideas are to be utilised for presentation in the public arena, another skill is required of his sculpture, that of spatial politics. Then the original openness can be closed down, turning the sculptures into emblems of corporate and institutionalised power. This restricting process narrows the sculptor's options and thus metaphor can turn into symbol, symbol into emblem and art becomes stylish design. Ironically, most public art by the very nature of its circumstances (that is, it has to say something of a very general and usually banal character, but at the same time not draw attention to itself as a work of art) quickly becomes invisible. As Robert Musil observed, 'There is nothing in the world as invisible as monuments. Doubtless they have been erected to be seen – even to attract attention; yet at the same time something has impregnated them against attention' – like being 'Eyeless' in George Square, Glasgow!

There is nothing 'invisible', however, about Cocker's own creative work; it commands attention, stimulates thoughts and discussion and then renews enquiry. Much of the power of his work lies in the inner tensions of those very opposing forces which find in his sculpture a focus for formal and philosophical debate. This has been the ongoing source of artistic energy which has motored the development of Cocker's work as a sculptor. Such as dialectical tensions of opposites, between nature and culture, private and public, spontaneity and manufacture, freedom and conformity, expression and silence; all are actively present in the work created for this exhibition. Just look at *Calvin's Tools,* for example.

This catalogue essay was written for the exhibition *Doug Cocker, Sculpture and Drawings 1987–1995* shown at the Talbot Rice Gallery, The University of Edinburgh in 1995.

JOHN KIRKWOOD

Pie in the Sky – the Edinburgh War Photomontages

The notion of a world free of nuclear weapons is pie in the sky!
Margaret Thatcher, BBC radio interview, March 1985

IN A RATHER gloomy catalogue introduction to an AIR Gallery exhibition which featured the work of four young Scottish artists, including John Kirkwood, Alexander Moffat bemoaned, amongst other things, the fact that, at that time (1977) there was so little figurative painting to boast about in Scotland. All has changed – *Ars Longa, Vita Brevis*? Life may still be brief but fashions on the contemporary art scene can be as short as the life expectancy of a butterfly. What we have witnessed recently is not so much a return to the expressionistic figurative in painting, as a positive stampede, especially amongst younger artists. As Peter Fuller observed, during the 1970s, when Formalism and Minimalism were all the rage, art galleries had the immaculate appearance of a hospital operating theatre. Now with Neo-Expressionism holding centre stage, most galleries look as though hamfisted operations have actually been carried out there.

In Scotland, as elsewhere, the walls of our art colleges and young contemporary art exhibitions are currently strewn with violently coloured paintings of angst-contorted figures. The international art scene, and closer to home, the persuasive influence of Alexander Moffat and Alan Bold, along with the powerful vitality of John Bellany's work, have stimulated the massive response amongst younger painters to break with the traditional decorative character of much earlier Scottish modern painting and take up the challenge of the figurative and the narrative again.

Needless to say, there are a few good, and many not so good practitioners in every mode of artistic expression. Each mode presents its own advantages and challenges, and it is the manner in which the individual artist capitalises on these advantages and resolves the challenges that his or her success is judged. For example, representational painting, especially on the large scale which is practiced at the moment, presents a platform from which it is possible to 'say something' – with all the concomitant benefits and problems that that incurs. Of course, all art, by its very nature, is in the business of communication, but some forms of expression, as for example abstract painting, rely more on the evocative than on the cognitive. As the abstract painter, Albert Irvin, stated in a recent interview, 'my painting is about the world rather than of it in the descriptive sense. I think it is possible to make a painting about how a human being feels without putting nose holes and big feet in'. Figurative painting, however, dealing with some kind of recognisable subject matter, should be experienced in a more specific context than that of abstract art. To misquote the Gospels, 'when two or three figures are gathered together on a canvas, there are the beginnings of narrative' and, if on a large scale, history painting. Much recent figurative art does aspire to this status, simply through scale and the incorporation into its pictorial vocabulary of a veritable cornucopia of bits and bobs from the historical, mythical and primeval past. In these cases, presumably it is hoped, if there are enough visual quotations and stylistic references, that a work will draw to itself the profundity of meaning usually associated with history painting.

With less pretension, but much greater panache, Sir Joshua Reynolds, PRA used to pull a similar trick when he wished to raise 'mere' portrait painting a few rungs up the ladder of 18th century cultural status. He would throw in a couple of antique busts and have his sitters togged out in some fancy dress attire, '*a la Grece*', much to the delight of his patrons and learned admirers. However, the French revolution and 19th century industrialisation put an end to much of that! The modern world realised, with a mixture of joy and dread, that history was not encased in the past, reserved for the privileged few. In fact, history was now perceived as a continuing process whose true reality could only be understood in the light of present experience, as expounded in the writings of Baudelaire. Only those who addressed themselves to the real nature of the historical process as it manifested itself in contemporary events could affect in any way its future course. This applied to artists – Goya, Gericault, Turner, Courbet, and Manet for example – as well as political philosophers and their followers. One such political philosopher was Thomas Carlyle who wrote at the beginning of the modern Age:

> We too admit that the present is an important time, as all present time necessarily is. The poorest Day that passes over us is the conflux of two Eternities, it is made up of currents that issue from the remotest Past, and flow onwards into the remotest Future. We were wise indeed, could we discern truly the signs of our own times, and by knowledge of its wants and advantages, wisely adjust our own position in it. Let us, instead of gazing idly into the obscure distance, look calmly around us, for a little, on the perplexed scene where we stand. Perhaps, on a more serious inspection, something of its perplexity will disappear, some of its distinctive characters and deeper tendencies more clearly reveal themselves, whereby our own relations to it, our own true aims and endeavours in it, may also become clearer.
> *Signs of the Times*, 1829

Unfortunately, as has been the general rule in the past, much contemporary Scottish art seems to be 'gazing idly into the obscure distance' – with much neo-expressionist figurative painting usually turning to history and the even remoter realms of ancient mythology. The reasons for this learned escapism are understandable in an age of crass commercial and political exploitation, inhuman technology and potential nuclear annihilation. Fortunately however, there are a few artists who are courageous enough to look 'on the perplexed scene where we stand'. Today, these are our history painters and in his photomontages, John Kirkwood – despite using the 'wrong' medium – is one of them.

If modern art can be thought of as a diverse, but broadly homogenous family – with Modernism as its highly admired offspring – then photomontage is very much the poor relation. An unruly, truculent tear-away, with uncertain parentage. It burst on to the scene, street-wise, sharp as nails, and looking for a fight! Unlike its very respectable bourgeois elder relation, Cubism, photomontage was not conceived within the bounds of an artistic marriage such as that of Braque and Picasso. Not for photomontage the loving, careful upbringing in the rarefied and pampered atmosphere of a Parisian studio. As you might have expected with a childhood devoid of the cultivation of finely tuned aesthetic taste and little art historical education, photomontage wanted nothing to do with *les beaux arts*. As Raoul Hausmann put it – 'We called this process photomontage because it embodied our refusal to play the part of artist'.

The abstract, neoplatonic philosophising of Cubism and its followers, along with the reactionary, self-indulgent individualism of the Expressionists, were despised and dismissed as irresponsible escapism by the early practitioners of photomontage in war-torn, revolutionary Europe. Some cubist techniques and expressionistic exaggeration were pillaged by photomontage in its mission to engage and do battle with the worn-out European establishment it wished to overthrow, To achieve this, its main weapons of visual and intellectual assault were drawn from the modern world of mass communication. Hans Richter explained the method of photomontage thus:

> They cut up photographs, stuck them together in provocative ways, added drawings, cut these up too, pasted in bits of newspaper or old letters, or whatever happened to be lying around, to confront a crazy world with its own image.

From the start photomontage was a political animal to the core, bursting with all the vigour and pent-up resentment of a youth who quickly comes to the conclusion that he has no respect for the social or cultural values of the older generation, and is raring to kick them over. Two early practitioners, George Grosz and Wieland Herzfelde put it this way: 'our mistake was to have concerned ourselves with art at all… We saw then the insane end-products of the prevailing social order, and burst out laughing…'

During the 1920s and 1930s, photomontage was certainly in its element. Europe was a battleground of contending political ideologies all bent on ruthlessly sweeping away the 'prevailing social orders', and propagating utopian visions of inhuman magnitude. During the period of immense political turbulence, photomontage was in constant demand, lambasting the inherited aesthetic values, moribund subjects and clapped-out modes of expression of the academic art establishment. Ironically, because of its power of visual impact, photomontage was also being recruited by both the extreme political right and left to promote their rival propaganda and leaders as the true protectors and guides of mankind's destiny.

Not surprisingly, photomontage's association with this era of political turmoil and catastrophic military conflict has done it little good since then. (The recent Royal Academy 20th century German art exhibition, for example, chose not to include the work of the great genius of political photomontage, John Heartfield). Since the Second World War, modern art has shed all traces of its youthful radicalism and gratefully moved to the relative safety of the village politics of the art gallery scene, leaving photomontage to fend for itself where it may – mostly in the market place of commercial advertising. Despite the example of superb practitioners of the medium, such as the dadaists, Max Ernst, John Heartfield and El Lissitzky, photomontage has pretty well been ignored over the past 40 years; the occasional exception being when some artists, such as a few of those associated with the Pop Art movement of the late 1950s and 1960s, turned their attention to the sub-cultural world of commercial art and technological communication and examined the mass media's manipulation of our response to modern reality. Recently however, photomontage has been employed by artists connected with the peace movement campaign. Worthy in intent, and occasionally witty in content, these CND (Campaign for Nuclear Disarmament) photomontages because of their specific aims, show a limited use of the medium's potential.

The photomontages of Kirkwood sometimes incorporate fragmented elements from the hard-sell world of sexploitation and commercial and military promotion. However, his adaptation of such types of glossy imagery as compared to, say, a Pop artist, such as Eduardo Paolozzi and Richard Hamilton, has much less concern for sophisticated exercises into the semantics of commercial art techniques and stylistic improvisations. There is more axe grinding than nail-paring in Kirkwood's work. This is not in any way to belittle Kirkwood's skill in handling the photomontage medium, but to distance him from the more recent developments. In the end, his work is much closer in spirit to the original intentions of the pioneers of photomontage. Kirkwood is much closer to Raoul Hausmann who described the practice thus:

> Photomontage in its earliest form was an explosive mixture of different points of views and levels... with its contrasts of structure and dimension, rough against smooth, aerial photograph against close-up, perspective against flat surface, the utmost technical flexibility and most lucid formal dialects are equally possible.

Kirkwood combines stunning 'technical flexibility' with 'lucid formal dialects' to create the highly potent scenes in his photomontages. These

scenes dramatise and illuminate the recurring central theme of his work –
the interconnection and seemingly unbreakable interdependence of ruthless
economic exploitation and military domination, which, unless there is a
radical change of heart, will surely absorb all of us into the apocalyptic
scenario which Kirkwood's photomontages play out. Yet it would be wrong
to regard them simply as science fiction prophecies of doom. Although set in a
nightmarish, not-too-distant future, the photomontages concentrate as much
on the historical and contemporary causes of our possible annihilation. For
that reason, to appreciate fully the complexity of the artist's vision and the
strength of his conviction, it is necessary to relate Kirkwood's photomontages
to a wider European and Scottish historical context.

It goes without saying that the invention of photomontage was only
possible in the age of photographic reproduction. Yet, if photography had
been available to one particular previous era, say the Reformation, it would
surely have been employed in a similar way as in the 1920s and 1930s.
During the Reformation, the first age of mass communication, the visual arts
were likewise in the forefront of the raging political and religious schismatic
struggles which sought to capture and recapture peoples' minds and souls. A
powerful instrument in this battle was the machine-produced broadsheet and
print. Through these new channels of communication, vicious satirical attacks
could be launched against the Church and its leaders. The manipulation,
distortion and reinvention of images for didactic purposes of popular
persuasion has its democratic origins here. Since then similar methods have
been continued by most politically conscious artists, such as Hogarth, Goya,
Daumier, the early photomontagists and certainly Kirkwood himself.

The major concern of the protagonists during the Reformation struggle
was to secure the spiritual and political allegiance of the European princes
and their subjects. Towards the end of the 15th century there was, as today, a
widespread sense of foreboding that the final collapse of civilisation was nigh,
and Divine Judgement was imminent. The work which reflects this outlook
most intensely, and which is an illuminating comparison with Kirkwood's
photomontages, is Dürer's 15 woodcut series *Apocalypse*. Dürer's publication
of illustrations to St John the Divine's visionary *Book of Revelation* appeared
in 1498 – just before what many expected to be the Second Coming on the
stroke of 1500 AD.

Dürer published the *Apocalypse* series himself, keeping maximum control
over the whole operation by cutting out as many middle men as he could. His
aim, to reach as wide an audience as possible, is reflected by the fact that the
accompanying Biblical text is printed in German as well as in Latin. As for the
famous images themselves; they in no way merely illustrate and were in fact
presented separately from the text which was placed on the back of each print.
This allowed Dürer's own choice and interpretation of the visions of the Saint
to be studied and appreciated for their own sake. The prints are not servile
accompaniments to their literary source: they stand for themselves with all the

strength of identity of emerging Protestant individualism.

Produced in an age of rhetorical hype and super-hype, Dürer's *Apocalypse* series is one of the most powerful works created by a European artist. At the time of their making, these prints were a means by which Dürer could express his profound reaction to the political and spiritual troubles of contemporary European society. In later centuries, however, they transcended their historical origins. This is shown for example, by their strong influence on William Blake, and can still carry fearful implications for our own age. We, too, know, or should know, that human nature and imagination are capable of anything. Dürer shows us that the divine, the real and the grotesque, are all aspects of the same continuing process. In one print for instance, St Michael and his angelic storm-troopers can be seen clashing with monstrous satanic dragons above a tranquil landscape; and, in another, descend to that same landscape to mete out bloody punishment to popes, priests, princes and the like. As with Kirkwood's photomontages, what we are being presented within the *Apocalypse* series is not self-contained, finished illustrations, but continuous dramatic action in which all aspects of experience, celestial and earthly, biblical and contemporary, are inseparably interlinked. Dürer may be using a biblical source, as Kirkwood sometimes employs art historical material, but both aim to engage their own contemporary world.

The great German art historian, Panofsky, very much credits this achievement of Dürer to his ability, through his mastery of technique, to reconcile the need for 'factuality' with the presentation of 'miraculous event'. According to Panofsky, to 'realise' a vision in a work of art – that is, to make it convincing without the aid of conventional signs or inscriptions – the artist has to fulfil two seemingly contradictory requirements. On the one hand, he must be an accomplished master of 'naturalism', for only where we behold a world evidently controlled by the laws of nature can we become aware of that temporary suspension of these laws which is the essence of a 'miracle'. On the other hand, he must be capable of transplanting the miraculous event from the level of factuality to that on an imaginary experience.

As Panofsky more succinctly points out, 'every increase in verisimilitude and animation strengthens rather than weakens the "visionary effect".'

It would now be useful to study briefly Kirkwood's own methods in the presentation of the 'visionary effect' within the photomontage medium, in the light of what Panofsky writes about Dürer. Broadly speaking, there can usually be found three layers of 'reality' in Kirkwood's photomontages. The mundane: Dürer's terrestrial landscapes are matched in the modern artist's work by the use of 'grainy' documentary styled photographs of the less distinguished 'unhistorical' areas of Edinburgh (although occasionally he does include more recognisable features of the city for a specific purpose). These are in neutral black and white and can be seen as being at Panofsky's 'level of factuality' – the here and now of the ordinary and the everyday. The second aspect of 'reality' – the celestial dimension in Dürer's prints – is the dramatic introduction of high-quality glossy coloured images from the 'dream world' of consumer advertising and military technology. Again using Panofsky's terminology, these constitute the 'miraculous event(s)' which transform the ordinary into the extraordinary, the present into the 'brave new world' of tomorrow. Finally, Kirkwood may occasionally employ a symbolic presence in his photomontages. These are not taken from religious iconography but from the history of art, for example, Delacroix's *Liberty on the Barricades* (1830) or Landseer's *Monarch of the Glen* (1850). The artist, however, never incorporates the whole of a famous painting into his work as does Peter Kennard, for example. In that way, in Kirkwood's method the art historical source is altered and at the same time its presence comments on its new environment. The 'painterliness' of these art historical images gives them a status, both artistic and social, which sets them apart and above their photographic surroundings. These painted images embody values as much as portray events. The values themselves, be they liberty or nobility, may be timeless, but their artistic presentation is rooted in their own time. Thus these cultural symbols from the past contribute a historical perspective which adds to the complexity of meaning involved in the apocalyptic nature of the photomontages. For what is ultimately being presented is the explosive moment when our historical heritage collides with our possible future rather than sustains and compliments it.

In the *Apocalypse* series, Dürer similarly deals with the catastrophic collision between historical consequences and future speculation, but in the form of Divine intervention. With the presence of the Divine, Dürer retains an overall unity of vision which the later 20th century artist cannot share. This sense of unity is firstly created by Dürer's style and technique which controls and concentrates every line on the printed page. By contrast, Kirkwood's collaged use of disparate images emphasises the discontinuity of modern experience which in his photomontages is heightened to the near-total breakdown of man's mind to make sense of the world which he has taken over from God and tried to run himself.

The events in Dürer's prints may be as violent and epic as in Kirkwood's work, but they do have a rationality and a purpose – the punishment and destruction of evil and the acknowledgement and reward of Faith. In *The Seven Trumpets* for instance, the trumpet-blasting, heavenly hosts bring down burning destruction on the cities below. God, the eternal judge, takes the sins of mankind deadly seriously. In Kirkwood's *Surveillance and Control* (1986) by contrast, the gun barrel of one of the attacking flying machines over Edinburgh literally blows raspberries at Scotland's premier city. It was Georg Lukacs who said that a good photomontage has the effect of a good joke. Here, however, the humour is very black and grotesque like the photomotage's advancing American Mommas, who for us, with their grossly exaggerated air-hostess smiles, are infinitely more fearsome than Dürer's classically inspired avenging angels. These De Kooning's 'Women', in the context of this work, are more menacing to us because they are rawer and much closer to home. The photomontage expounds, with cutting humour, on our great American ally's economic, military, and cultural domination, in the guise of offering material prosperity and protecting our cherished political and artistic freedoms. The traditional Mother figure, who should bring life and joy, is here revealed as a female monster of greed and destruction – the four horsemen of the Apocalypse rolled into one. As with Stanley Kubrick's *Dr Strangelove*, Kirkwood's photomontages 'confront a crazy world with its own image'.

Despite the title and the almost non-stop celestial punishment ladled out to mankind in the *Apocalypse* series, Dürer still manages in the end to break through in the last print to utopian optimism. The visionary saint is taken up to a high place and given a glimpse of the New Jerusalem, while Auld Nick is safely locked away in the bottomless pit.

If St John the Divine was only allowed a wee keek at the perfect city, the men of vision of the 18th century Edinburgh Enlightenment set out to build it – just north of the Nor Loch. Turning their backs on the Sodom and Gomorrah of the Auld Toun, they aimed to raise on classical pillars of stone, the new Athens of the North.

Not surprisingly, this new age of reason wished to put behind what they regarded as the dangerous religious extremism and political radicalism of the previous era. However, as Goya pointed out in his print *The Sleep of Reason brings forth Monsters* (1799) the forces in human nature that, to quote the Scottish Augustin poet, James Thomson, 'barbarise an age', could not be easily laid to rest beneath the foundations of the neoclassical buildings erected along 'Apollo's sacred walks' around the Edinburgh's Calton Hill. Futhermore, despite all the efforts to paper over the social and cultural cracks during Scotland's subsequent history – 18th century anglification, 19th century sanctified economic exploitation, and 20th century false promises and political duplicity – all have failed to keep Robert Garioch's 'Brither Worm' from… 'pokin' his heid, if he had yin, up throu a hole in the New Toun'.

In Kirkwood's *Edinburgh War Photomontages*, the cracks have finally split asunder into yawning chasms. Dunedin, 'the fortress of the hillside' is about to be overthrown and the volcanic foundations of the city seem to have broken their bonds of geological, architectural and historical imprisonment and are claiming the Heart of Midlothian for their own again. Yet Kirkwood is not a prophet of doom any more than Dürer. His speculative vaticinations are catastrophic rather than terminally pessimistic. Certainly destruction and mayhem abound in these photomontages of his, but what we see, to use a frequent phrase of the artist, is the 'flux of things' – not necessarily the end of things. It is the 'flux of things' between order and chaos in the historical process which ultimately concerns Kirkwood. His is a creative awareness of history, and in his *Edinburgh War Photomontages* series he focuses on the particular Scottish dimension.

Finally, let us raise our gaze to the distant *Monarch of the Glen*. In Landseer's famous painting, the attention is squarely set on the eponymous royal stag. This is as it should be, as the *Monarch of the Glen* is the last triumph, not to say the last trump, of aristocratic portraiture. Landseer's subject can trace its long royal lineage back to at least van Dyck's equestrian portraits of that equally famous, but doomed Scottish royal exile, Charles I. Undoubtedly, the *Monarch of the Glen* is the portrait which Landseer would have liked to have produced for his own monarch had they both lived in an earlier, nobler age. Painted in a Highland mist, on the mid-stroke of the 19th century, this king of all he surveys stands proudly over his domain; as Her Imperial Highness, Queen Victoria was to do the following year. However, the focus of attention at the *Great Exhibition* of 1851 was on the tribute-bearing Empire, whereas the 'Glen' in Landseer's painting is conveniently excluded from view: for in truth, all the 'Monarch' can actually survey is a desolate land, bereft of human communities, and fit only for sheep and shooting parties. All have gone – or all that were able to do so – driven off their land in the name of economic progress by those who put profit before the people who, historically, always looked to them for protection.

The 19th century rural and human desolation which Landseer chooses to avoid is taken over by an up-to-date replacement in Kirkwood's photomontage *Monarch of the Glen-USAF Warthog, as D. Gray Watches On* (1985). Set in Edinburgh, and placed against the blackened ruins of Scotland's industrial graveyard, the 'Monarch' returns – like Banquo's ghost – to witness the tragic end of another epoch in Scotland's history. Whether the beast with all the protection of painterly status and popular myth can be destroyed by a mere black and white photograph of an assassin's bullet is open to question.

There is no doubt however, that in the distance, St Andrew's House, the present 'guardian' of Scotland's welfare, is certainly under serious attack. By whom, in all the confusion, it is difficult to say. Then that is the nature of things in a post-Orwellian Newspeak world. Is the USAF guardians of our democratic liberty, or protectors of American investment and military installations? Does the shiny, all-American face of consumer promotion really mean that sustained economic growth is just around the corner with cake for everyone instead of the usual privileged few? Or does it seem more likely, as is suggested by Kirkwood's metamorphic flying machines, made out of succulent roast meat and crisp, baked pastry, that the unholy partnership between commercial exploitation and military domination will make it yet again – just pie in the sky?

This essay was published in *Alba* (issue 1, 1986).

STEVEN CAMPBELL

Campbell at the Crossroads

I WOULD ADVISE anyone who has seen the Steven Campbell exhibition *On Form and Fiction* (1990) at the Third Eye, Glasgow to also pay a visit to the National Gallery of Scotland. While the former Second City of Empire turned European City of Culture mounts a fanfare of media attention for the triumphant return of the most celebrated of the New Glasgow Boys, Edinburgh by contrast has mounted a low-key, if rather apologetic exhibition of the work of one of its own artistic sons, David Scott. The contrast between Campbell and Scott is entertaining and enlightening.

David Scott (1806–49) and Steven Campbell face each other over that vast cultural chasm we now historically call Modernism, running from roughly the mid-19th century to mid-20th. However, despite such a separation, these two painters are curiously connected – in fact, they are almost mirror images of each other. Much of Campbell's art sets out to parody most of the stylistic characteristics of the high Victorian Romanticism that is the stuff of Scott's work. In Campbell's hands the high vaunting themes of Scott's work usually invoking epic voyages by the likes of Ulysses or Vasco da Gama, with accompanying grandiose titles such as *Death and Life-in-Death Dice for the Crew,* are turned into farcically mock-heroic slap-stick parodies as witnessed in *The Hiker in a Landscape Turned into a Marsh Overnight.* Yet, despite these similarities and others (such as a shared inability to master convincing anatomical draughtsmanship), Campbell enjoys the critical attention which Scott craved, but failed, to attain. Why should this be; why should these two Scottish artists have been treated differently?

The reason is as much to do with historical circumstances as artistic ability and personality. Scott was a casualty of the cultural collision of old and new values, which was taking place in a rapidly changing 19th century industrial society. Unlike Manet and the Impressionists for instance, he refused to read the signs of the times and tried to voyage on in the leaking ship of academic history painting. The crashing waves churned up by the newly launched SS *Modernism* swept away the likes of Scott. Yet by the time Steven Campbell was leaving Glasgow Art College, Modernism had also completely run out of steam and was disappearing over the far horizon of contemporary art.

Throughout the 1980s, there was a ground-swell of reaction to the now aridity of late Modernism, with a triumphant return to such things as figurative painting, literary and socially concerned subject matter, which many had feared had been lost forever. In Scotland, where there was a return to 'New Image' painting, created around the Glasgow School of Art, Campbell's work led the way, his style and success stimulating many younger Scottish artists to emulate his example.

So why did Campbell succeed where Scott had failed miserably? Firstly, the Glaswegian – unlike his Edinburgh counterpart – initially gave his fellow countrymen the body-swerve. While Scott continuously banged his head against a brick wall trying to sell his work to his own country, Campbell was quick to pursue the success abroad – especially in New York and London – that was impossible at home. Secondly, Campbell achieved this ironically by appearing to be an archetypical Scottish artist to the Americans and English in the mould of a successful Victorian artist like Landseer (Landseer is not Scottish, of course, but foreigners – and most English – don't know that). Furthermore, at the same time Campbell's paintings have the audacity to deny most of the things that Scottish painting is traditionally meant to stand for – good drawing, atmospheric colour, naturalistic landscape. Thirdly, whereas David Scott was by temperament mind-numbingly serious, Steven Campbell is pure Glasgow gallus. While David Scott's work exemplifies the rigid criteria of history painting as laid down by the likes of Shaftesbury, rejecting 'whatsoever appears in historical Design, which is not essential to the Action, (this) serves only to confound the Representation and perplex the mind'. Campbell is in the business to do that very thing — 'confound and perplex'. As he pointed out in an interview in the first issue of *Alba*:

> if the picture is filled with all these unimportant details you see the most obvious thing, and then the least obvious thing and because the latter are the most surprising things in the painting they take on great importance – chickens, eggs, plants, etc. The cage becomes a completely ridiculous vehicle for something else. Hide as much possible with the image and all these little things come out of the cupboard.

The Lord Shaftesbury quote comes from his instruction to a Neapolitan painter how pictorially to present correctly *Hercules at the Crossroads,* a subject with which I am sure, Campbell could have a field day. However, there is a dimension to the mythological episode which Campbell might just wish to reflect on. His career, like that of the ancient Greek hero, seems to have come to a crossroads and like Hercules he is confronted, if not strictly by Vice and Virtue, then by a choice of options for his future development.

The success of his earlier work has been based on a very perceptive awareness of how to turn the structuralist concerns with the languages of representation into visual parodies by treating history painting (a la David Scott) in the mode of a comedy of manners. In this way, he has been able (as seen in the Third Eye exhibition) to continue delighting the critics with a play on a whole range of art historical conventions and intellectual whimsy concerning visual signs and pictorial significance (or lack of it).

Despite the determinist and reductive tone of the supporting essays for the catalogue of *Forms and Fictions* – 'Where art can only deal with the same old subjects' – I would argue that a broader look at the history of art would not preclude the highly imaginative painting of Campbell from opening out from this current self-referential practice. The most obvious method for someone as witty and intelligent as Campbell is through satire. Campbell is known for his admiration of Hogarth and Goya. The Spanish master is a good case in point; he too, like Campbell, began as a rococo painter of social manners, but developed his highly critical art to search below the surface appearances of Spanish society to a deeper investigation of historical and psychological reality.

In his latest exhibition there are hints of a more cutting edge to Campbell's outlook, especially in the area of gallery/ museum presentation and art market status of what constitutes a 'masterpiece'. On the whole, the exhibition does give the impression of a shift in Campbell's attitude, in that the spectator – as he/she surveys the 150 accompanying sketches to the 10 selected paintings – is at least now being allowed to be party to the creative process. Yet, despite this freer approach, Campbell still seems to remain an entertaining salon painter.

David Scott, by contrast, continually aspired to elevate his paintings to the monumental dimensions demanded of High Public Art, despite continual knock-backs which must have left him feeling completely isolated. It is not surprising then that one of his most passionate works should be *Thilocetes Abandoned on the Isle of Lemnos* (1840). Scott could only feel that he, like the wounded Greek warrior, had also been abandoned and left behind by the tide of history.

By coincidence Campbell also has a maritime subject in his latest exhibition: *Two Men in Pursuit of Simplicity*. As the title suggests, the painting is a postmodernist parody of the romantic sublime, with two figures in a small sailing boat battling, none too convincingly, against the open sea. The sails are as blank as a minimalist canvas. It seems time now – if he is not to end up as a minor master of temporary fashionable ideas – for Campbell to nail some new and richer colours to the mast.

This essay was published in *Radical Scotland* (issue 44, 1990).

KEN CURRIE
The Sleep of Reason

IN TRULY GOYAESQUE fashion, the British electorate has been caricatured by one of our best cartoonists, as a blood-spattered headless chicken racing across a desert landscape towards a setting sun. The fear of change and the pursuit of ruthless self-interest seems to have reached suicidal dimensions. North of the border however, there still seems to be a little social sanity left. Even the English national newspapers have noticed the fact that Scotland is a different political society to the Home Counties. The *Guardian*, for example, observed, 'Scotland, we know, is different. Scotland is more instinctively communal of attitudes'.

On the art scene in Scotland that 'communal attitude' is most likely to be found in the various artists workshops which have been set up all over the country in the last 20 years or so. In particular the printmakers' workshops have been extremely successful in encouraging a whole range of different types of artists to develop the creative potential of that great art medium. Scotland, of course, has a distinguished record in printmaking, especially in this century. The celebrated names of Scottish printmaking, such as Muirhead Bone, James McBey and DY Cameron were skilled exponents of that craft. They were master printmakers. Now, however, much of the best work produced in the workshops, is through the collaboration between visiting artists, who are not necessarily proficient in all the technicalities of the various printing processes, and the assisting members of the workshop staff. These powerful etchings which Ken Currie has produced for this year's Mayfest exhibition at the Glasgow Print Studio are a result of such a collaboration between the artist and the printmaker craftsman.

To those who are familiar with Ken Currie and his work, it will not come as a surprise that he is also a remarkable maker of prints. He has only recently turned his hand to the art of etching, but already shows strong indications that he has exceptional powers to make this particular type of printmaking into another medium for his own form of artistic expression. The main reason I think is less to do with skilful facility (although that, of course, is there) and more to do with the fact that Currie has something important to say, and the etching is an ideal medium for what Currie urgently wants to express. By this I mean that I do not see Currie setting out to innovate new technical potential for the art of etching. Rather he consciously works within the long-established European tradition of great printmakers whose work, like that of Currie's, is a critical response to the politically turbulent times in which they lived. Looking at the prints in this exhibition, I do not feel it is too difficult to view Currie's work in the same perspective as some of the renowned printmakers of the past – Dürer in the 16th century, Rembrandt in the 17th, Hogarth in the 18th, Goya in the 18and 19th, Daumier in the 19th, and Dix in the 20th century. As Sandy Moffat has observed, Currie is 'a Scottish artist with a world view' and his work, both in painting and printmaking, is permeated with his deeply felt admiration and knowledge of the great masters of the past. Yet if there is any one particular creative influence contributing to these etchings by Currie it must be Goya.

The parallels between the development of Currie's artistic career and Goya's are in fact quite revealing, if one remembers that whereas Currie has accomplished so much in a relatively short time, Goya only began to realise his awesome potential as a creative genius in his later life. Both artists began with strong, idealistic outlooks. Goya, for instance, was an enthusiastic supporter of European liberalism as promoted by the enlightened monarchs and aristocracy of the 18th century; while Currie, after his initial youthful existentialism, became a committed communist. Early in their careers, both artists expressed the support of their political beliefs in major works – for instance, Goya's designs for the royal tapestries and Currie's murals celebrating the history of the Scottish Labour Movement for the People's Palace Museum in Glasgow. Both also produced fairly eulogistic representations of the people they socially admired. Goya painted flattering portraits of the intellectually progressive members of Spanish society, while in the mid-80s, Currie worked on a series of idealised images of the self-educated, politically motived Scottish working-class. I draw attention to the earlier work of Currie, because I feel, as with Goya, that a good degree of the satire which motivates their later more mature art, is not only directed against the human stupidities and social injustices which they deplore, but also in some ways mocks the misplaced faith of their own early ideological idealism.

As with the Spanish master, the strength of Currie's development as an artist, is the painful, but heroic response, they both show to their changing historical and political times. Goya's belief in the beneficial effects which liberal ideals should bring to European society after the French Revolution was swept away with the invasion of Spain by Napoleon, and the later restoration of the arch-reactionary Bourbon monarchy to the Spanish throne. Likewise, Currie has had to reconsider seriously his beliefs, both political and artistic, in the light of the great upheavals in Eastern Europe which led to the total collapse of Soviet communism.

Interestingly, both artists responded to the turbulent events of their times in a similar way. They began to question and forsake their earlier idealistic beliefs by shifting their work, stylistically, to a much more realistic form of expression. Goya abandoned his initial flirtations with Neoclassicism and Currie has publicly admitted that he no longer feels that classic Modernism, as found in say the work of Leger for example is appropriate for the development of his art in a post-communist western world. Like Goya, who had access to the Flemish paintings in the Spanish royal collection, Currie has been seeking out, for close attention, the work of the great Northern European masters – such as Bosch, Breughel and Rembrandt. It may be that it was the example of Rembrandt more than any that inspired both Goya and Currie to become serious printmakers. Goya owned about a dozen of the Dutch artist's engravings, and in this exhibition Currie pays full homage to the master with his aquatint *Rembrandt's Carcass* (1991), after the famous painting in Kelvingrove Gallery. With the general development of Currie's career outlined as above, it then should not come as a great surprise that he has turned to printmaking. The more specific reasons for this could be accounted for as follows.

Firstly, because of his strong socialist beliefs, Currie has had certain intellectual difficulties with the place his paintings should take within a capitalist art market; although he is now firmly convinced that 'art has to be effective within capitalism.' However, no such moral dilemma need arise with printmaking. In Walter Benjamin's terms, prints are not contaminated with the sin of 'unique aura' as is painting. Most easel paintings within the capitalist system will always have the burden of being a desirable object for the privileged few, while with prints it is the content of imagery which is available to be possessed by many.

Secondly, Currie has consistently been critical of the crippling anti-intellectualism of much of 20th century Scottish painting. Printmaking on the other hand, even in Scotland, has been a vehicle for philosophical and social debate. It is not without significance, for example, that two of the most intellectual of contemporary Scottish artists, Eduardo Paolozzi and Ian Hamilton Finlay, use their prints to encourage the public to reflect on important social and ethical issues which can have universal significance.

Thirdly, Currie's working methods would seem to be particularly suited to printmaking. As with the aquatint and etching processes, Currie develops his ideas and imagery over an extended period of time. For example, a particular observation, say a down-and-out figure seen on the streets of the depressed area of Glasgow where he has his studio, might lead to speculation on a universal human type like 'The Wandering Jew', which then might connect with previous interpretations of such themes by earlier painters, such as Breughel or Courbet. This particular social-inflected kind of realism which Currie gives to his imagery, which is not naturalistic, but more interpretive, tending towards the allegorical, is very much suited to black and white printmaking, and goes back to the religious propaganda prints and broad-sheets of the 16th century Reformation. Thus the evolving process of Currie's intellectually didactic art can be continued throughout the printing process with its continual reworking of the plate and the re-editing of the printed image.

Turning now to the prints in this exhibition, I think it is again possible to continue to draw parallels between them and the work of Goya. As with the great Spanish master, Currie has moved from an optimistic philosophical outlook which had strong positive dimensions, to one characterised by what he has termed – 'rational despair'. Although Currie's work may not quite match the deep, almost terminal pessimism of Goya's print *Nade* from his *Disasters of War* series, there is a similar fatalistic view about human nature where Currie says, 'Some things seem incurable'. Yet, as Goya triumphantly proved with *Los Caprichios* (1799) and the later *Disasters of War* (1810–20) and *Proverbios* (1815–23), such dark thoughts seem to find their most effective means of expression through the black ink on the etched plate. More than any other artist working in Britain, Currie's art reflects 'The Dark Times' the present world is living through – his titles alone give warning of this. Such darkness, both physical and socio-psychological is even more expressed in Currie's prints than in his paintings. Now that his work has become less overtly propagandist, Currie is much more concerned to create 'atmosphere' rather than a straight political message. As with Goya, specific meaning becomes more elusive, more poetic in a profoundly tragic sense. Thus the enveloping blackness of the printer's ink can suggest even more than paint the underlying profound hellishness of human actions and the human mind. Thus in many of Currie's prints we begin to realise what Milton meant when he described Hell as having 'no lights, but darkness made visible'.

The prints in this exhibition seem to fall into three main groups. To begin with there are the works which were inspired by Currie's reaction to the Gulf War, such as *Covert Operation* and *Collateral Damage* (both 1991). In many cases, the moral outrage of the artist is further emphasised by the satirical use of the military 'newspeak' employed in the titles. The superabundance of destructive high technology employed during the Gulf War is ironically contrasted with the dearth of information, especially about the casualties of the conflict. Thus, Currie mocks this devious secrecy of the modern news media, by his identification with the honourable tradition of open debate which has characterised the democratic nature of printmaking since the Reformation. Also connected with the *Gulf War* series are the studies of human heads such as *War Worries, Memory of Conflict*, and *Battlefield* (all 1991). Here the actual etching process is fundamental to the creation of the image; the ink seems to eat into the paper to reveal the terrible state of mind of those who are traumatised by the awful human destruction that war causes.

The second group of prints in the exhibition are more theatrical in narrative presentation than the *Gulf War* series; for example. *That Time of Year Again* and *In Praise of Learning* (both 1992). The origins of such enigmatic interior scenes probably go back to Currie's student work of the early 1980s, such as *This Had to Happen*. There is a strong existential feel to these prints and they create a similar menacing claustrophobic atmosphere that one associates with the plays of Beckett, the films of Bergman and the paintings of Bacon. However, these prints of Currie, express such a raw, visceral edge so that they never fall into the trap of merely being scenes from intriguing little mystery stories.

The last group of prints, such as *The Cold City* (1991), *The Shape of the*

People (1992) and *The Constructors* (1991) links quite closely with a number of Currie's recent monumental *Street* paintings. These express the artist's response to his own personal experience of the collapse of the communist regimes in Russia and its former Soviet empire. Apart from the imagery itself, much of the power of such prints lies in the ironic contrast between Currie's depiction of the crowd scenes and the conventional presentation in the history of painting. Traditionally, such scenes of great crowds are a triumphant celebration of public order and civic unity, as exemplified, for instance, in the work of Veronese, Rubens, David, or the Soviet Realist artists. In Currie's depictions, however, the crowd has turned into a mob, a frightening 'many-headed monster', where individuals terrorise or are terrorised by their fellow citizens. As though to mock the idealism of his earlier paintings which were inspired by the likes of Leger and the Mexican muralists, in these recent prints we are presented with a human society much closer to Breughel's *Netherlandish Proverbs* (1559), Hogarth's *Gin Lane* (1751) or Goya's *Los Caprichios*, where the blind lead the blind and man's inhumanity to man seems to know no bounds.

In these troubled, blood-stained times, we need strong critical artists like Ken Currie. In Scotland we are fortunate then that the present art scene has produced such an artist and that he is not a lone voice; only the most successful of a number of socially conscious and politically aware artists working here.

The great curse of the Scots is cringing 'inferiorism'. However, I believe that artists such as Ken Currie are now producing work of such significant intellectual and artistic importance that in the area of politically orientated art, Scotland is unquestionably a world leader. Of course there are always those who will be critical and dismissive of such art. To those on the right, art should be above politics; to those in the liberal centre, artists are in danger of exploiting the plight of the victims of injustice for their own artistic ends; while to those on the left, political art, which is commercially successful in the capitalist art market, must have its critical edge blunted by such success. I do not believe that any of these accusations can be validly levelled at Ken Currie. On the contrary, I feel his uncompromising critical eye is sharper than ever.

This catalogue essay was written for the exhibition *Ken Currie: The Age of Uncertainty* shown at Glasgow Print Studio in 1992.

PETER HOWSON

Drawing the Line

The Scotsman, that guardian of our nation's cultural life recently investigated the state of the arts in this country with a series called 'The Flowering of Scotland'. It kicked off with a look at the visual arts by the newly arrived supremo at Kelvingrove, Julian Spalding. Coming from south of the border into a top job here, he may have felt it behoved him to draw a favourable distinction between Scottish and English art, which he made on the grounds of the adage 'the English can draw, but the Scots can paint'. I was a little surprised that, in essence, he agreed with this, despite the obvious painterly qualities of the leading names in the English school – Bacon, Freud, Auerback and Kossoff. While, furthermore, in Scotland, the graphic style of the leading young Scottish artists Currie, Howson, Wiszniewski, for example – has dominated the Scottish art scene over the last decade. (Still, that may be London/Glasgow distinction rather than a wider English/Scottish one).

To return to the three Scottish artists mentioned, drawing is crucial. In Howson's case especially, drawing is not merely a means to an end, a preparatory stage before painting, a hidden structural framework to his pictures. It is infinitely more. Drawing, for him, is a triumphant display in everything he produces, it is the breath of life of his art, his *raison d'etre* as an artist. By this I mean that with Howson you feel that it is not just what he can draw that he wants to present to the spectator, but that he wishes to show us that somehow he has been singled out, blessed with a rare, almost magical gift; I draw therefore I am.

To appreciate this basic human enthusiasm for the power of self-discovery through art you have to cast your mind back to your school days and remember the awe in which anyone in the class was held if they seemed to have some special accomplishment. I don't mean being 'clever' which is usually regarded with a mixture of envy and contempt. No, I'm referring to a one-off talent, usually possessed by the non-academic individual; the kid who has the ability to mimic the teachers for example and so mock their authority, or the person who can play the latest hit tune on any instrument, without being able to read a line of music, or simply the guy who can draw! Of course, most youngsters who are touched by this divine quality quickly lose the power of their magical talent and become ordinary mortals like the rest of us, simply because they never find a satisfactory answer to the awesome question – *What* should I draw?

Howson's pictures are his answer to that question, but even he seems to have gone through a brief period of creative crisis during his time as a student at Glasgow School of Art in the late '70s. He left college in a state of disillusionment for a couple of years, serving a year in the army and then doing a number of dead-end jobs. However, he returned to his studies and with the encouragement of his tutor Sandy Moffat, discovered a renewed purpose and, through his recent experiences, fresh subject matter for his art; the dark, violent underside of modern life, particularly associated with the city of Glasgow. By his prodigious output of innumerable scenes of urban low-life over the past ten years, Howson now seems to have become the unofficial visual recorder of the other face of the newly cleaned-up City of Culture.

Since the Romantic era, as a reaction against the rapid increase of urban living, urban artists and art lovers have made nature and landscape a major focus of moral and aesthetic concern. Despite this, however, the celebration of the city, arguably, still remains the high point of achievement in Western culture. The artist is essential to the pursuit of this ideal – Phidias and classical Athens, Michaelangelo and renaissance Florence, Bernini and baroque Rome, Rembrandt and republican Amsterdam, Raeburn and Enlightenment Edinburgh, Manet and bourgeois Paris, and now Peter Howson and Ken Currie in post-industrial Glasgow.

The reasons why these great towns should come to prominence at certain points in European history are obviously complex in each specific case. Broadly speaking, however, these cities' finest hour usually occurs as a new self-confident social order or class emerges into a dominant position when there is a progressive development from one economic state to another (eg agricultural/feudal to commercial/capitalist). New patrons take over, with new demands for a new kind of art from a new type of artist. This applies to the recent 'flowering' of Glasgow. Some people may be more than a little surprised at the breath-taking transformation of the former second city of the Empire from a run-down, planner-blighted urban mess into European City of Culture. However, this spectacular transition has come about by the perceptive realisation of its leading political, commercial and artistic citizens that the city could be successfully negotiated from its rapidly redundant historical condition into a new sense of self-confidence and contemporary relevance. Glasgow has transformed itself sooner and more quickly than any other equivalent city from a heavy engineering, supply-led metropolis into a post-industrial, multiproduct, consumer society; where the look of a thing is as important as its use.

Before discussing Peter Howson's art and the treatment of his urban subject matter, it may be useful briefly to look at the historical relationship between the artist and his chosen city, by asking the question what service is demanded of him by his fellow citizens? Broadly speaking, the artist can serve the demands of the progressive sections of his society in two ways. On the one hand he can celebrate the triumphant fulfilment of the group achievement of the new dominant class by giving them the 'look' that they feel is appropriate – for example rendering the grave seriousness of the participants on the Parthenon frieze, the swaggering confidence of the Officer of the Dutch Militia Companies, or the self-conscious informality of the Parisian bourgeoisie's Sunday afternoon at the Tuilleries Gardens. Glasgow, in its heyday was, unfortunately, handicapped as a subject for self-congratulatory portrayal because of the non-picturesque industrial nature of its power base – pictorially, aristocratic sail is infinitely preferable to proletarian steam. Working-class, urban subjects were all very fine for the low art of music hall song, but in the serious business of painting they become problematic as William Gilpin, influential spokesperson for the picturesque movement, pointed out: contrary to real life, in painting 'the loitering peasant is always preferable to the industrial mechanic'. It is only then, in situations of extreme national crisis – during the two world wars, for example – that Muirhead Bone and later Stanley Spencer were asked to record the heroic communal efforts of the Glasgow working population. Belatedly Ken Currie has valiantly been attempting to rectify this gaping void in the city's visual and social history.

Peter Howson's work, on the other hand, can be placed in the alternative type of art which a new dominant urban class demands for its social/ psychological needs. This usually entails a portrayal of the way of life which has been overtaken by the recent traumatic economic changes. The newly upwardly mobile city types can look back at typical representatives of this dying way of life with a mixture of rose-tinted nostalgia and reassuring superiority. In 17th century Holland, the low-life comic scenes of Steen and Teniers served this purpose, as later did the elegiac poems of Francois Millet of gleaning or praying peasants in 19th century France. In real life, of course, peasants and farm workers were never so docile and sanitised, nor Howson's Glasgow down-and-outs ever so heroic, but as they move into a more and more extinct condition 'nothing becomes them in life like the leaving of it'.

At this stage I should quickly point out that I do not wish to imply that Howson's art is necessarily untruthful. He is not dealing in literal truths. In many ways his work pursues a deeper reality than that which the ordinary recording eye can see. This can be at a level of experience where the physical and the spiritual meet. At his best Howson can capture the profound tragedy and human suffering of urban existence, as expressed by William Blake in his poem 'London'; 'and mark in every face I meet/ Marks of weakness, marks of woe'. At other times, however, his treatment of his subjects is more problematic and he could be accused of some degree of misrepresentation for imposed effect. Howson deals in a highly sensitive area of social and potential artistic exploitation which undoubtedly makes his work difficult for certain people – including myself, I have to admit. Throughout the '80s Howson's work has grown in popularity and critical stature. His success with certain art buyers may not be unconnected with the romantic idea of the artist 'going native' (Howson's studio is in the poorest area of Glasgow, in Gallowgate) and sending back exotic trophies from the Heart of Darkness. Furthermore, from an intellectual point of view, his non-political view of subjects can allow critics to regard the people in his paintings more accommodatingly as 'existential heroes of modern life'.

It has to be pointed out that it would be inappropriate to compare directly Howson's relationship with his subjects in exactly the same way as other artists with similar themes in the past. Howson is an artist of the 1980s, and the justification for such subjects, if any is needed of course, may more likely lie with the postmodernist interest in the peripheral, whether it be geographical, cultural or social. Furthermore, stylistically, Howson's treatments of his Glasgow hard-men and dropouts are far from straightforward reportage. With his natural drawing ability, his figures and scenes are filtered through a range of stylistic adaptations from art history and popular visual culture in line with the contemporary critical taste for eclecticism. Howson can use this over-laying of an image with stylistic references for intriguing effect, and can set up all kinds of ambiguities in, for example, his *Heroic Dossers* series.

An artist, of course, is ambitious for his work and attempts to develop a more complex vision of his subject. That expanding complexity can be based on increased intensity of observation, as well as the widening of range of references and quotations. For me, Howson's most powerful work still lies with his single figures and portrait heads, which he continues to produce. There the immediacy and directness which his drawing can readily convey is most evident. In such studies Howson's draughtsman eye for the characteristic look, the revealing posture, allows him not only to describe individual appearances but suggest personal histories. However, it is when he broadens the dimensions of his field of focus to wider situational settings for his pictures that his work becomes less convincing for me. This has little to do with any lack of technical ability. Visually, Howson's large scale work, his 'grand machines' such as his modern crucifixion in *Death of Innocence* (1989), shown at Glasgow's Great British Art Show, have a very powerful impact. Where they fail for me is that the protagonists within these violent crowded dramas slip over the very fine dividing line (suggested by Hogarth) between characterisation and caricature. Although both these artistic approaches may treat their subjects on a metaphorical or allegorical plane, characterisation, unlike caricature, never loses contact with the individuality of the people involved (never treating them as merely puppet-players). Furthermore, although both caricature and characterisation may use the grotesque for effect, the latter does not allow its morbid attraction to detract from its ultimate commitment to revealing the deeper reality of the vicious circle of cause and effect in human affairs.

Finally, in his latest epic drama *Stairway to Heaven* (to be seen at Glasgow Print Studio), Howson deals with the Hogarthian theme of the moral corruption and progressive destruction of innocence. The painting takes the form of a three-part Gothic horror narrative in which we follow the downfall of a young girl from her arrival in the big bad city to her ultimate suicidal despair in a *'The Idiot'* moon-lit cemetery. Despite using all kinds of compositional virtuosity and atmospheric lighting, *Stairway to Heaven* (1990) fails to rise above the mawkish trivialisation found in the worse kind of Victorian moralising pictures.

When Cezanne began his career, pictures like *Stairway to Heaven* were all the rage. In fact his early work deals with violent themes similar to Howson's, but gradually he forced himself to move away from these high-flown melodramas to a more direct contact with much humbler subjects. Late in life Cezanne felt confident enough, because of the experience of his own artistic development, to warn a young artist that painters should give the body-swerve to all literary subject matter. Looking at a picture like *Stairway to Heaven*, I have to admit I can see what the old Father of Modernism meant.

This essay was published in *Radical Scotland* (issue 45, 1990).

HENRY KONDRACKI
A Scots Flaneur

MORE THAN ANYTHING, the Scottish Victorian landscape painters gave
most people their idea of how they thought Scotland should look and be
identified. Works by the likes of Horatio McCulloch, who manufactured those
unforgettable Caledonian images of wild rugged scenery, are indelibly etched
on everyone's heart as they speed along the M9 through that great picturesque
theme park in the north – The Scottish Highlands. Yet back in the 19th century
the Scottish genre painters of the everyday routine in rural life were even more
successful than McCulloch and his ilk. None more so than the Faed brothers,
who managed to take over the illustrious mantle of Sir David Wilkie, especially
after they moved down to London in the 1860s. Despite their popularity (or
maybe because of it), these painters were never taken very seriously in High
Art circles. In such a class-conscious country as Britain, genre painters and
their lowly subjects were merely tolerated as long as they knew their place and
stayed there. Their main function was to amuse and entertain a new industrial,
urban audience with highly illustrative, sentimental or comic scenes from a
rapidly disappearing rural way of life. In Scotland this kind of populist art is
called 'kailyard' (cabbage patch), and was expected to have about as much
intellectually challenging content as our present day soap operas.

One only has to stand before Courbet's monumental *Burial at Ornans*
(1848–50) or van Gogh's moving *The Potato Eaters* (1885) to realise such
limiting attitudes to this kind of painting are not universal. In Britain however,
genre painting has suffered greatly from its Victorian reputation, and only
fairly recently has begun to be regarded seriously as an important aspect of
contemporary painting. This critical attitude emerged most spectacularly in the
1980s with the return to figuration in painting. It has been Scottish artists in
particular who have re-established genre painting as a major force – notably
Ken Currie and Peter Howson in Glasgow and Henry Kondracki in Edinburgh.

The most striking thing about such genre painting today, compared with
last century, is the marked shift to urban subject matter, concentrating mainly
on the street life of our post-industrial cities. In fact the contemporary artist
has become a bit of a Baudelairian 'flaneur' in the portrayal of contemporary
urban life. Yet, although the subject of interest in Scottish genre painting has
radically changed, some of the same problems of critical credibility persist. Aside
from the perennial issue of the endemic illustrative nature of such painting, the
accusation could, and has, been made that, whereas the Victorians tended to treat
their subjects in a sanitised, sentimentalising fashion – ignoring the harsh realities
of life – contemporary genre painters equally exploit their subjects for sensational
or ideological ends. Instead of bringing the viewer to a closer, more sympathetic

and compassionate understanding of other people's lives, such paintings emphasise the gap between 'us and them', and turn 'them' into threatening, or victimised creatures from the lower depths of another darker underground world.

After seeing his new work, I maintain that such critical accusations cannot be held against Henry Kondracki. In fact the contrary is the case. For Kondracki's pictures bring us infinitely closer to the lives of other people as social beings, rather than caricatures and stereotypes. Much gentler and more lyrical in his approach than some of his Glaswegian counterparts, Kondracki's paintings of Edinburgh street life and working people positively radiate with strong affection and deep empathy. Each person, whether real or fictional, seen or imagined, is presented with their individual identity intact. This attitude is further emphasised by the number of his single-figure compositions, some of which are on a large scale in the heroic fashion of Beckmann and Courbet. However, Kondracki also adds the subjective introspection of Romanticism to this realist expressionist tradition. This is especially true, for example, of the isolated figure of a wee lad gazing out to sea, surveying the horizon with far-away yearning; or the weary worker, finishing his shift, lost in the comforting world of his own private dreams and memories.

Kondracki's world is a complex one where the real and the imagined intermingle, and you are just as likely to come across the Minotaur or Batman as a lollypop-man or a punk-rocker. To emphasise this persuasive duality, many of Kondracki's compositions play off interior and external spaces. Nowhere is this more successfully achieved than in his picture, entitled *Museum*, where our standpoint is from inside a reptile display-case, looking out at the seemingly gigantic face of a fascinated schoolboy. In his own way, but worthy of Robert Burns, Kondracki grants us the power to see the world from many other points of view besides our own limited outlook.

To return to the question of the illustrative burden of genre painting, Kondracki tackles this in his characteristically sensitive and intelligent manner. As I suggested, one of the great strengths of his paintings is the concerned affection which he demonstrates towards his subjects. This equally applies to his medium of expression as well. Not only are the people in his paintings freed to express themselves and their own way of life, but so are the colour-stained and painted surfaces of his pictures. In his work paint and people have equal voice. Subject and surface matter are totally integrated and mutually supporting. Such a delicate balancing act between pictorial content and appropriate style could only be achieved by a highly alert and experienced artist. As with all great genre painters, Kondracki transforms – by keen observation, sympathetic imagination and skilful technique – the ordinary into the extraordinary in everyday life. Furthermore, Kondracki, through his exhilarating mixture of 'High Art and Low Culture', succeeds in turning his seemingly parochial genre pictures into a rich and rewarding cosmopolitan experience.

This essay was published in *Contemporary Visual Art* (Issue 13, 2010).

PAUL REID

Return to Arcadia

Poetry is more serious than history.
Aristotle, *Poetics*

PAUL REID IS a rare phenomenon in today's art world; he is an academic
history painter. Most of his contemporaries are either unaware of, or
uninterested in, this artistic genre. That however, was not always the case.
In the 18th and 19th centuries, when the art academies were by far the most
powerful culture institutions in Europe, artists with high ambitions would
invariably aspire to the elevated status of history painter. This required, not
only outstanding technical skill in drawing and painting, but also, an in-depth
knowledge of the classics from which to draw upon for appropriate subject
matter. For the only legitimate source of pictorial subjects for a true history
painter was sacred or classical texts. As can be seen Reid continues to follow
this convention by searching through ancient myths and the writings of
Homer and Ovid for the inspiring subject content of his paintings.

What particularly attracted academic painters and their patrons to history
painting was the epic and universal themes that their art addressed. Always
at the thematic core of genuine history painting, was the elemental conflict
between good and evil. This eternal struggle was played out between the same
basic protagonists – the stalwart protagonist and his dastardly monstrous
enemies. On the side of virtue and order stood the hero who, from Hercules
onwards, always had to be physically and morally strong and unflinching in
his single-minded determination to fulfil his divinely appointed destiny. On the
other side, in marked contrast, was his multi-facetted adversaries who could
take on many different aggressive and seductive forms – from male or female,
to animal or even plant. These mutant creatures were truly protean beings.

While the pictorial depiction of the hero in history painting remained
relatively constant right up to the end of the academic era in the 19th
century, his combatant markedly changed from era to era. In Antiquity,
monsters, as depicted on vase paintings for instance, were either aberrations
of the natural order, or malformed offspring of the gods themselves – such
as the cyclops Polyphemus, son of Poseidon. Moving into the Christian era,
with its obsession of eternal redemption and condemnation, monsters were
conscripted into the role of satanic devils, forever tormenting the Damned in
Hell. By contrast, the classically minded artists of the Renaissance were far too
much taken up with idealising the heroic male figure to show much interest in
portraying his monstrous counterpart.

With the Romantic era however, comes the return of the repressed.

Monsters are now back with a vengeance as a reaction to the Enlightenment's triumphalism of human reason; most famously depicted by Goya's *The Sleep of Reason Brings Forth Monsters* (1797–9). The monster has now become a creature of the disturbed imagination responding to an ever increasingly oppressive and inhuman society. This fearful situation is most exemplified at the beginning of the modern age by Kafka's harrowing novella *Metamorphosis* (1915). There, both hero and monster, become as one, equal victims of an inscrutable bureaucratic system. While in modern painting the Surrealists, under the influence of Freud's theories of the human mind, set out to release the monstrous from the deep unconscious as a cathartic outcry against the manifold horrors of the 20th century. Nothing in art however, could match the ultra-horrendous actions and deeds of our own adored monsters in their smart military attire, who were determined to reduce culture and civilisation to 'a handful of dust'. Ironically this 'brave new world' of ours has now become infinitely too monstrous for Reid's archaic monsters, who have wisely retreated back to the relative peace and safety of their original Doric arcadia.

In his history paintings Paul Reid does adhere to most of the conventions of that particular genre, both in form and content. He renders his classical sources with a high degree of mimetic idealism, and a great deal of research, study and painterly skill has clearly gone into the making of his 'grand machines' of pictorial excellence. In one crucial area however, the artist deliberately transgresses. This is in the manner in which he treats the presentation of his mythic narratives contrary to the expected conventions of history painting.

Back in the era when history painting was highly admired a great deal of theoretical discourse was concerned with the issue of what particular incident painters should select from the chronology of their literary sources. In 18th century England for instance, Lord Shaftesbury in his *Notion of the Historical Draught or Tablature of the Judgment of Hercules* (1713) proposed the highly influential idea of the 'pregnant moment'. This concept directed history painters to seek out that vital 'moment' in their visual narrative when the past circumstances, the present drama and the future consequences of the story-line could coalesce and simultaneously reveal their inter-relationship within the layered complexities of a unified pictorial meaning.

In striking contrast, Paul Reid's paintings are less concerned with rendering action, and much more focused on stillness and reflection. The pregnant moments of violent high drama have long past, leaving a poetic mood that is elegiac rather than epic. Set against a Scottish landscape version of Arcadia, Reid's figures – whether human, monstrous or divine – seem to gaze not at the surrounding scenery, but inwardly on their own meditative thoughts and memories of past glories. They, like the history paintings in which they now find themselves, are no longer deemed relevant to the contemporary art scene; nor to our electronic virtual worlds, where monsters, in every conceivable mutant form, can be supplied for mass entertainment at the press of a computer button. Illustrating yet again that each age gets the monsters it deserves.

Finally, it is interesting that the word 'monster' comes from the Latin 'monstrum', meaning a warning, an omen. Keeping this in mind, when we look at Paul Reid's fascinating and intriguing Arcadian scenes, we might, like the figures themselves, ponder on what we have lost over the centuries and, what we have put in their place.

This catalogue essay was written for the exhibition *Monstrous Art* shown at the University of Reading in 2023.

IAIN ROBERTSON
Talking Pictures

*Painting, or art generally, as such, with all its technicalities, difficulties and
particular ends, is nothing but a noble and expressive language.*
John Ruskin, *Modern Painters*, 1843–60

THE ISSUE OF language has been a vitally crucial one to the modern art
movement, and although this may come as a surprise to many this equally
applies to the visual arts as it does to literature. Yet there are those, cultivated,
well-read people, who still fail to appreciate that the language of painting, for
instance, the means of expression is as important as what is being painted.
For such people the act of painting is either so dominated by subject matter
that the main purpose of the artist is merely to record objectively what he or
she sees or thinks; or so taken up with the subjective expression of the artist's
'feelings' that a painting is viewed as some raging battleground of emotional
conflict. These two alternative attitudes are what you might call the `sense' or
'sensibility' approach to art appreciation.

Even a brief examination of the history of art would reveal that since the
Renaissance at least, most serious artists have been involved in choosing a
particular language of expression as much as an inspiring subject to paint.
For example, in the early 17th century, Guido Reni was advised by a critical
patron that it would be better if he painted his subjects in a classicising
manner rather than following the current fashion of Caravaggistic realism. In
Reni's case he chose to take the advice, so decorum won out. It is however,
with the modern movement in art, after the decline of the near monopolistic
power over the genre classification of appropriate style to subject which the
Academies had dictated, that the choice and relevance of expressive language
became central to artistic practices and critical debate. In fact, so important
was this argument involving the language of modern art that as far as the
avant-garde was concerned, 'it ain't what you say, it's the way that you say it',
now held sway.

With this in mind I would like to look at the paintings of the Scottish
abstract painter, Iain Robertson. However, before that, I think it is necessary
to analyse what is meant by language as it is applied to painting in general and
to abstraction in particular.

I would suggest that there are at least four recognisable levels of language
operating when we look at a painting. Firstly, there is what you might call
the subliminal level of language, the 'language of lines' as Ruskin calls it, but
which would also include the language of colours and shapes. (In literary
criticism, TS Eliot's theory of the auditory image of poetry deals with a

similar issue). The early abstractionists, especially the transcendentalists like Kandinsky and Mondrian, staked their faith on the power of non-representational art to 'plug' into the innate language of profound significance, and spiritual communication. Formalists such as Roger Fry and Clive Bell, share similar views. They believed that abstract art would have much deeper psychological power and infinitely greater universal appeal than the less 'pure' representation of figurative painting.

Language at its secondary level is the more recognised notion of that term. This is how we note different languages – French or English for example. In the history of art the same applies. It is the way we can identify a specific kind of painting; for instance, an impressionist from a cubist one. At this secondary level, I admit that abstract painting is more problematic. Yet I would argue despite the earlier sweeping claims that have been made for abstraction: for instance, that through the psychologically expressive power of lines, shapes and colours in themselves, it would become the universal language of emotive communication that has not occurred. Abstraction has not turned out to be the Esperanto of artistic language, but rather it has proved to be another specific means of expression. Abstract art, although admittedly it does appear to operate to a greater degree at a subliminal level than other kinds of painting, has also developed its own particular conventional systems of expression. Thus, because many people are so accustomed to looking at paintings in a 'representational' frame of mind ('C'est une pipe' attitude), they dismiss abstract art as a foreign language, the work of barbarians as the early Greeks saw anything that was non-Greek. Yet this widespread ignorance and misunderstanding does not invalidate my point as to abstraction being predominantly a second level language.

The third and fourth levels at which languages operate are much more particular than the two just discussed. What I am referring to here is the actual lived experience of a communally shared language, with all its distinctive characteristics. English, for example, is spoken all over the world but it has evolved a whole variety of different forms and dialects within individual communities. So that Glaswegian English is a very different animal to that which is spoken in say in the Deep South of the United States. With regard to art this is how we can recognise the various local schools of painting – for example, Flemish from Dutch or Florentine from Sienese. Within the discipline of abstraction different types of practice and sub-languages of expression have evolved; for instance, gestural Expressionism as opposed to geometrical hard-edge. A painter is therefore drawn towards a particular language of painting through the traditions he or she inherits and the impact of artistic influences and the community of fellow practitioners with whom he or she keeps company.

Finally, the fourth level of language is the most particular and the most specifically individual. Now we are dealing with personal speech patterns or the specific 'handwriting' of each individual person. In painting it is here that the artist's own recognisable style emerges as he or she attempts to speak with his or her own voice. It is that finely tuned distinctive quality which allows us to appreciate, through the practice of critical analysis, the crucial differences in means of expression and technical skills, say between a Monet and a Renoir or between a Rothko and a Newman, or in Scottish painting between a Ramsay and a Raeburn or between a Fred Pollock and an Iain Robertson.

To call Iain Robertson a Scottish abstract painter might cause a few eyebrows to be raised even now in some modernist circles. The objection to such labelling would be on the grounds that the nationality of an abstract painter was irrelevant. On this point Jackson Pollock once observed that it was as ridiculous to talk about American abstract art as it was to discuss Czechoslovakian mathematics. That argument is one which is based on the premise that the language of painting at the first level, the subliminal one, is exclusive to abstract art. Such a view sees abstract painting as being an autonomous entity, solely addressing, on the one hand, the intrinsic problems involved in the craft of painting itself, and on the other, dealing exclusively in universal concepts, untouched by any local or historical considerations. For the modernist champion, like Clement Greenberg, this is the language of painting operating at the first level, but speaking at the highest.

There is, however, an alternative to this ideal formalist interpretation of the history and objectives of the modern movement in art, which proposes that all genuine creativity is dependent much more on the other three levels of expressive language. Art must therefore firstly grow out of the local, the social and the personal experiences of the artist, before it can take on universal significance. This view is very much the basis of earlier progressive Romanticism and was succinctly expressed by Blake in his famous epigram, 'To see Eternity in a grain of sand'. This alternative approach to the idealist one was further developed, and so continues to be so, by a hard core of modern art practitioners, including many Scots artists.

The best of 20th century Scottish painting is very much a part of this northern European romantic/modern movement, as is the work of Iain Robertson. To give an example of this, William Gear, one of Scotland's best post-war abstract painters, was involved with the early activities of the COBRA – a modernist group from five northern European capitals, whose very name spells out a deep sense of local and national identity. As can be seen from certain stylistic similarities, Robertson greatly admires the work of William Gear as well as these Scandinavian artists. This is not surprising as he came into contact with William Gear as a teacher, when he was a student at Exeter College of Art. Even in a 'foreign' country abstract artists tend to seek each other out, and form loose networks of communication to share professional gossip and exchange ideas, experiences and influences.

Through his own painterly dialogue with the history of Scottish Expressionism from William McTaggart to Alan Davie, and his connections with like-minded abstract painters, who share the same inclinations towards expressive gestural painting, Iain Robertson's work is clearly connected with this romantic expressionist tradition. It is not surprising then that he has been invited to exhibit in Denmark for example, for his work speaks in a similar expressive language to that of Asger Jorn for instance.

Like such Northern European modern masters, Iain Robertson's paintings openly declare the internal mechanics of their compositional construction, revealing through the very human process of trial and error the gradual building up of the underlying themes which hold each work together within an organic unity of form and content. Even a superficial inspection of his work would show that Robertson's paintings are never a mere expressive vehicle for the release of pent-up personal angst. What motivates Robertson is the ongoing challenge of the possibilities of the language of painting itself. His paintings first and foremost speak about painting as a physical act which more than anything else involves controlled movement. They, like people, use body language and gesture to communicate their individual features and personality. Yet each painting develops out of other paintings previously made, which in turn give birth to something new, but which is also related and dependent. In doing so, as with all artists who have a consistent commitment to their creations, Robertson has built up a recognisable body of work with its distinct family appearances and communal visual language.

The most striking characteristic of Robertson's paintings is their material presence, their physical honesty. As with Cezanne and the cubists, it is optical depth rather than picture surface which holds his compositions together. Depth in the pictorial realm is like conversation in the human one, it is the stuff of life. It creates free dialogue. It allows the eye to enter and move freely or tightly between, and around the gestural marks, the accidental drips and the primitivistic shapes which constitute the evolving internal history of the painting. The act of painting, of making marks and to arrange them into some kind of meaningful order, is fundamental to human creativity that it is accessible to all of us. Robertson's paintings are open to discursive dialogue and are thus truly democratic. As with all healthy democracies, his paintings are not an illustration or a model of a theoretical concept, but a lived experience, which is continually renewed and revitalised for anyone who seriously approaches them with a sensitive eye, an investigative mind and an open heart. Robertson's paintings arouse the viewer's respect, for they can stand up for themselves. They are not 'windows on the world' or surrogate spokespersons for someone else's ideas about what painting should be.

The shape of his paintings tends to be, like ourselves, in a strongly vertical format which adds to their actual material presence as beings in their own right. They stand up and talk directly to us. Furthermore, the raw, robust manner of application, through the use of thick succulent pigment, gestural mark-making and textured coagulated surface, also gives an immediacy which stresses the actuality of their physical being. Yet, as with all art which genuinely deals in such a concrete manner with the tangibly real, there is also a strong sense of a metaphysical dimension to Robertson's work which predominately operates at the first level of creative language. How this occurs is for each discerning viewer to perceive, but it must involve that truly transcendental element in painting – colour, the angelic force in modern art. For as Cezanne pointed out, colour is 'the place where our brain and the universe meet'.

The only literary connection that the artist makes with his paintings is through their titles which celebrate their wonderful sense of shared pleasure and conviviality. The value then of each painting lies in the sum of what the artist puts into it and what the viewer takes out. Yet with paintings so rich and vital in expressive language and poetic mystery – 'the mystery of making' as Francis Bacon called it – this dialogue should never be exhausted. Confronted with such paintings I feel like echoing the words of Sydney Greenstreet in *The Maltese Falcon*, 'I'm a man who likes to talk to a man who likes to talk.'

This essay was published in *Cencrastus* (issue 52, 1995).

DOUGLAS GORDON

Motion and Emotion – Walking a Tightrope

Cinema is truth 24 times a second.
Jean-Luc Goddard

Narrative should have a beginning, a middle, and an end, but not necessarily
in that order.
Jean-Luc Goddard

Film is like a battlefield... Love... Hate... Action... Violence... Death...
In a word Emotion.
Sam Fuller in Goddard's *Pierrot le Fou* (1965)

When a man is astonished at what he knows, it may be proof that he has
merely stood on the brink of science, but it is also proof that he has not
discovered it to be boundless and unfathomable.
James Hogg

If you want your art to be able to disrupt, or cause people to think twice
(or more) about assumptions, or just be 'effective; then I reckon you need to
provide a space for time.
Douglas Gordon

IN A PREVIOUS issue of this magazine (vol3 no2) I contrarily wrote that the
only unifying feature that you could claim for contemporary Scottish painting
was that it is so various. I also think the same could be said of Scottish artists
working in other mediums. This certainly occurred to me when I went to see
the *Spellbound – Art and Film* exhibition at the Hayward Gallery, London
(1996). The Scottish 'presence' was well represented by Eduardo Paolozzi
and Douglas Gordon, but what was so striking was the fundamental contrast
between the work of these artists, coming from different generations and art
historical/theoretical backgrounds. A brief comparison between the two, will
I feel bring out some of the essential characteristics and qualities of Douglas
Gordon's art and aesthetic attitudes.

As Martin Maloney suggested in vol3 no3 of *Contemporary Art*,
Spellbound was a rather disappointing exhibition on the whole. It had
high ambitions which in the end it failed to fulfil. What it lacked was a
comprehensive and imaginative investigation into the mutual areas of interest
which connect the work and ideas of artists and filmmakers. For example if
we link the art of Paolozzi and Gordon with significant cinematic parallels,
revealing comparisons might be made between them and the great giants of
the early Soviet cinema, Eisenstein (1898–1948) and Vertov (1896–1951).

Paolozzi's work, for instance, with its total commitment to collage in all its forms as the essence of modern fragmentary experience, and its obsessive investigation into the process and ideology of myth-making, very much echoes Eisenstein's recreation of history through the power of film montage and epic cinematic narrative. Thus the Paolozzi room in *Spellbound* was like a great sprawling film-set, with multi-props and pieces of costume scattered everywhere, like a cast of thousands ready, at the director's command, to be called into action.

If Paolozzi was full of baroque exuberance, Douglas Gordon's presentation of his solitary exhibit, 24 *Hour Psycho* (1993) was as pared down and austere as the interior of a Scottish Presbyterian kirk. All one got was a darkened room, a screen suspended from the ceiling, a projector somewhere in a corner, and a few large bean-bags scattered on the floor. Ironically however, in such a Spartan environment one is made more acutely aware of one's immediate surroundings. Gordon is very keen that this should be the case.

Like Vertov, Gordon sees his work as a complex psychological relationship, between the strategically staged environment and controlled presentation of an unfolding series of images, and his physically aware and emotionally involved audience. Vertov, for example, begins his classic documentary *The Man with a Movie Camera* (1929), by showing us the whole mechanical ritual of cinema viewing – the empty auditorium, the fold-up seats awaiting their audience, the curtained screen, the public arriving full of expectation, the projector being switched on, etc. All this is vitally necessary before the film can begin in the new Soviet State. Yet, this very public, collective viewing experience of the early cinema is no longer appropriate for the late 20th century audience which Gordon's work addresses. Instead of uniform rows of seats, there are now scattered bean-bags, into which people can flop as though they were at home. Thus the conditions under which one views Gordon's work is unclear and ambiguous, hovering between some kind of public formality and casual domestic intimacy.

Another pertinent link between Gordon and Vertov, besides the strong audience awareness in both their work, is their mutual commitment to the open presentation of the image-making and display process. The 'hero' of Vertov's films is ultimately the camera itself, and its presence is not only keenly felt, but continually revealed. Gordon too wishes his audience to be fully aware of the physical immediacy of the technical machinery and manipulation which creates the artifice and ritual of film viewing. His audience is . encouraged to walk around his subtly cinematic installation, even going behind the suspended screen and viewing the film in reverse mirror-image. For what is crucial to Gordon's Brechtian approach is that the audience should not become disembodied, as in the normal 'Saturday night at the Movies' cinema-going habit. The immediate physical environment should be as much part of the aesthetic experience as the audience's emotional involvement with the dramatic narrative of the film itself. The 'seductive surface' of the silver screen has to be shattered if the true mystery of the cinema is to be released.

Vertov was the great pioneer of documentary film. Unlike Eisenstein he did not make his subjects, they were already there for him. They were everywhere – on the streets, in the houses and factories of the modern city – a 'ready-made' on a grand scale. Gordon too uses material made for him, but usually by someone else. As such he is not a documentarist, or even a filmmaker in the traditional sense of the word. In fact, he does not even use video in the same way as his contemporaries. He came to video only through the circumstances of his development as a multimedia artist.

Gordon was born in Glasgow in 1966 and studied at Glasgow School of Art and the Slade School of Art, London in 1984–90. Since then he has developed his artistic career through various media, such as text-based art, installation, performance and video. As is the case with many of the younger Scottish artists, he has worked and shown abroad as much as in this country. However, more recently, his work has become better known in Britain through his shows at the Lisson Gallery in London and the Tramway in Glasgow, and through his inclusion in *The British Art Show 4* and *Spellbound* exhibitions.

Gordon's film work developed out of his earlier interest in performance and text-based installation work. He also became involved in video, but even here he is not typical. He does not make films like other 'Brits', such as Steve McQueen or Damien Hirst who were also in *Spellbound*. As with his text-based work, where Gordon tended to use names, quotations and popular clichés; his films are found material, 'temporal ready-mades', whether medical documentary films such as *Hysteria* or *10ms-1* (1994) or classic popular films as in *24 Hour Psycho* (1993). In fact, the originality of Gordon's film work lies not in the way he constructs something 'new', but in the manner he deconstructs and re-presents something already in existence. With such an approach he opens up his carefully chosen subjects, and releases a whole variety of previously hidden sub-narratives, which frees his audience to speculate on much more than the imposed ideologically dominant one. As he points out himself, the more one tries to deconstruct through slowing down a film for formal analysis, the more 'boundless and unfathomable' it becomes.

So, whereas Paolozzi is fascinated by the iconic construction and continual reconstruction of myth, Gordon, especially through the influence of Roland Barthes, is drawn to the deconstruction of myth through the reassessment and reinvention of narrative. This can be seen both in his film and performance/installation work. For instance, with the latter type of work, Gordon has used the tightrope walker on more than one occasion, almost as a metaphorical manifestation of the narrative in action. Such a figure is placed in a truly existentialist context, where narrative past, and future, are completely taken up with the all-absorbing present action. Gordon uses this real, yet allegorical figure, in two of his most successful installation pieces, *Trust Me* (1993) and *Practice Tightrope* (1994–95). In *Trust Me*, where the performer walked above the heads of the audience as though on an invisible ceiling/floor, Gordon was keen, as indicated by the title, to draw attention to the audience's deeply ambivalent attitude to what they saw. Their projected narrative onto this performance could either be the continued safety of the man above, or their secret, malicious desire to see him fall – or a mixture of both. In the other work *Practice Tightrope*, the audience were confronted with a rope strung across the gallery, but merely 12 inches above the floor. However, on the wall facing was a large colour photograph of the Niagara Falls, half obscured by spray. The audience were, as with all of Gordon's work, left to fill in the narrative connections between what appeared to be a present practice session, and the grand future project. Present safety and future danger playing off each other.

At the Lisson Gallery (London), where *Practice Tightrope* was shown, there was also a companion piece, its 'mirror-image' in a way, entitled *10ms-1* (1994). This was another of Gordon's temporal ready-mades, a piece of medical archive footage, which Gordon had recently found. There was a screen casually propped up against a pole, and a film was shown on it, without any sound or commentary, of a man, in seemingly good health, struggling to stand up. Every time he attempted to walk his legs gave way under him. Unlike the tightrope walker, this man could not even place one foot in front of the other without falling over. Again Gordon's audience were left to make of it what they could. Who is he? The bare, hospital-like room suggests he might be a soldier, although he only wears a pair of trunks. He might be a shell-shock victim. He appears the opposite of the man on the tightrope, who is motivated by his future ambitions; whereas the 'soldier' is deeply traumatised and paralysed by his past (combat?) experience. Yet both are locked in their present condition, the one forever suspended over the roaring abyss of his future imaginings, the other crawling around the no man's land of his dreadful past. Yet, as with all of Gordon's work, it is also the audience's own emotional reaction which is equally under scrutiny. What we feel towards the tightrope walker, a mixture of admiration, envy and malice is mirrored in reverse by our sympathy, curiosity and repulsion for the crawling man. Thus we have to ask ourselves, are our emotions the touchstone of our moral condition? Or are those feelings and desires of our imagination safe indulgences, just personal catharsis, completely separate from our socially responsible behaviour?

These were questions which also fascinated Alfred Hitchcock, and so it is not surprising that Gordon should have chosen *Psycho*, that great myth of our time, as a subject for his major work to date – *24 Hour Psycho*. Like Hitchcock, Gordon is not in any way a moralising artist; he takes, like the Master himself, a very cool and detached approach to his emotionally charged subjects. Both are more concerned with the mechanics of narrative construction and presentation than any morally educating message. As Gordon has indicated in a number of interviews, the choice of *Psycho* was as much influenced by the fact that the film has now acquired mythic status, so that his audience would be pretty familiar with the film's narrative. Thus by slowing down the running of the film to two frames per second over a 24-hour period, people can come in on it at any point and relate what they see to the overall story-line of the film. Initially many would be bemused, regarding it as a pointless exercise; however, once enthralled by its mesmerising quality, they would become fascinated by what they saw, which in many ways is a fundamentally different experience from their original contact with the film.

The essential ambiguity which surrounds Gordon's 24 *Hour Psycho* begins, as I have indicated, with the 'art gallery' presentation context. Firstly the audience is invited to have a different kind of physical relationship with this film compared with seeing it either in the cinema or in their own home. Secondly, this sense of ambiguity is contained within the actual image on the screen, which is so slowed down that it hovers between still photograph and slow-motion. Like the tightrope walker, the audience is in a kind of limbo between an immovable static state, and simultaneously being imperceptibly nudged forward by the invisible, but inevitable unfolding of the film's overall meta-narrative. Thirdly and finally, the audience is unsure as to what it is seeing on the suspended screen above their heads. With its purely visual (the dialogue and music now gone) presentation reduced to a snail's pace, the original story-line connections are lost and the audience is forced to find significance in that which they have never noticed before. The hidden, subconscious character and action of the film begins to emerge, and these, like the 'punctum' in Roland Barthes' analysis of photography defy conventional narrative explanation. We are into the realm of Hogg's 'boundless and unfathomable'.

What now holds our attention are the movements and unconsciously made by the actors and cameraman, which neither they nor the director were aware of at the time. They come floating to the surface of the screen and into our consciousness, holding and hypnotising our meditations. The relentless drive of the original, preordained, scripted narrative, from the past into future, is now held back, and the present is allowed to break through and luxuriate in its newfound freedom. Such freedom can only be gained in a Barthian sense by the death of the author. The controlling, all-powerful, hand of the omnipotent master/creator has to be prised away. The controlling power that he has over his audience, through the bondage of narrative suspense (always concerned with the future), has to be broken in order to allow the audience to pursue, in Gordon's words their own 'desires and investigations'.

At present Gordon is, amongst other things, hoping to work out two projects. One is to extend the original running time of John Ford's archetypal epic western *The Searchers*, of 113 minutes to the actual length of the film's narrative – 5 years! Meaning that one second of film time would be turned into 6.46 hours of real time. That should provide plenty of 'space for time'. Narrative has now become spectacle.

Gordon's other ambition, which he has been working on for some time, is to make a very personal adaptation of James Hogg's classic study of Calvinist fanaticism, *The Private Memoirs and Confessions of a Justified Sinner*. That such a text should fascinate Gordon is significant. The whole dialectical debate which runs through Hogg's novel, between the dictates of predestination, and personal, moral freedom and responsibilities, are also fundamental to Gordon's concerns with visual narrative and audience response. As with Hogg, Gordon openly presents his subjects for investigation, allowing his audience not only to find out new things about what is presented to them, but also more about themselves. We, the individual members of the audience, through the power of Gordon's work to stimulate the questioning imagination, can break down the imprisoning tyranny of conventional thought and representation and move to a higher plane of intellectual and emotional experience. Both Hogg and Gordon in their different ways take us over 'the brink of science' to 'discover it to be boundless and unfathomable'.

This essay was published in *Contemporary Visual Art* (Issue 3/4, 1996).

Timeline

1945 Hugh MacDiarmid opens New Scottish Group exhibition in Glasgow.
Society of Scottish Artists exhibit a major group show of contemporary French art.

1946 Paolozzi makes his first series of collages.
Arts Council of Great Britain formed.

1947 The first Edinburgh International Festival.
Royal Scottish Academy shows *Scottish Art from 1900*.
SSA exhibits *Modern Scottish Painting*.
Paolozzi's first exhibition at the Mayor Gallery, London.
Paolozzi moves to Paris.

1948 Turnbull moves to join Paolozzi in Paris.
Eardley elected SSA; travels to Italy.
Davie shows for the first time in Venice during the first post-war Biennale and meets Peggy Guggenheim.

1948–9 William Gear exhibits with cobra group in Amsterdam.
Paolozzi and Turnbull visit Giacometti and Brâncuşi in their Paris studios.

1950 SSA exhibit a group German Expressionist show.
Paolozzi and Turnbull return to London.
Davie's first solo exhibit at Gimpels Fils in London.
Paolozzi and Turnbull show at the Hanover Gallery in London.

1951 Paolozzi designs a fountain sculpture for the Festival of Britain, the South Bank, London.
Gear controversially wins a prize for his abstract landscape in the Festival of Britain exhibition *Sixty Paintings for '51*.
Eardley visits Catterline for the first time.

1952 Paolozzi and Turnbull selected for Herbert Read's group exhibition *New Aspects of British Sculpture* shown at the British Pavilion in the Venice Biennale.
Paolozzi presents his *Bunk* slideshow at an Independent Group lecture at the ICA in London.

1953
Davie, Paolozzi and Turnbull hired to teach in various departments by William Johnstone, Principal of the Central School of Arts and Crafts in London.
The Independent Group, including Paolozzi and Turnbull, mount *Parallel of Life and Art* exhibition at the ICA in London.

1954
Eardley shows at the Parsons Gallery in London.
Davie creates a studio and house at Gamels, Hertfordshire and shows regularly at Gimpel Fils in London.

1955
Eardley shows her controversial *Sleeping Nude* at the Royal Glasgow Institute.

1956
Paolozzi and Turnbull contribute to the Independent Group's exhibition, *This is Tomorrow*, at the Whitechapel Art Gallery in London.
Paolozzi stars in Lorenza Mazzetti's film *Together*.
Tate Gallery shows the abstract expressionist exhibition *Modern Art in the United States*.
Davie awarded the Gregory Fellowship in Painting and has his first American exhibition at Catherine Viviano Gallery in New York where he meets Pollock, Rothko and de Kooning.

1957
Foundation of the artist-run 57 Gallery in Edinburgh.
Turnbull has his first major solo exhibition at the ICA in London.
Joan Hills and Mark Boyle meet in Harrogate.

1958
Davie has a work bought by the Tate Gallery and has his first retrospective exhibition at the Whitechapel Gallery in London.

1959
Scottish National Gallery of Modern Art at Inverleith House is given government approval.
Davie has a number of major exhibitions abroad and wins several awards.
Craigie Aitchison has his first solo exhibition at Beaux-Arts Gallery in London.
Jim Haynes opens Paperback Bookshop in Edinburgh and becomes a centre for avant-garde activity in the arts.

1960
The Scottish National Gallery of Modern Art is opened by Kenneth Clark.
Paolozzi moves to teach in Hamburg.

1961
Ian Hamilton Finlay and Jessie McGuffie found Wild Hawthorn Press.
Boyle and Hills make their first assemblages.

1962   Scottish National Gallery of Modern Art show *Contemporary British Sculpture*.
Paolozzi begins making screen prints at Kelpra Studios in London and works with CW Juby foundry in Ipswich.

1963   Traverse Theatre Club, with the Richard Demarco Gallery, opens and shows the Boyles' junk reliefs in the restaurant.
The EIF's International Drama Conference in the McEwan Hall stages the Boyles' happening *In Memory of Big Ed*.

1964   *Joan Eardley* memorial exhibition.
Mark Boyle and Joan Hills make their first replication of a section of ground surface.
John Bellany and Alexander Moffat show their paintings on railings outside the RSA.

1965   Bellany and Moffat again show their paintings outside the RSA.
Boyle Family begin the resin earth studies with their *Shepherd Bush Series*.

1966   Ian and Sue Finlay settle at Stonypath, Lanarkshire, and start working on their neoclassical garden, later to be known as Little Sparta.
Demarco opens his gallery in Melville Crescent, Edinburgh.
Auto-Destructive Art event staged by Ivor Davies in Edinburgh.

1967   Scottish Arts Council established.
Edinburgh Printmakers set up.

1968   Compass Gallery in Glasgow opens.
The random selection of sites for Boyle Family's *World Series* held at the ICA in London.

1969   Bellany finishes at the Royal College of Art and takes a teaching post at Winchester School of Art.
Boyle Family launch their *World Series* with the object of replicating 1,000 sites around the globe.

1970   Richard Demarco and Joseph Beuys organise *Strategy: Get Arts* at Edinburgh College of Art.
The Talbot Rice Art Centre is opened at the University of Edinburgh

1971   Eduardo Paolozzi's retrospective at the Tate Gallery in London.
Scottish Realism exhibition, including the work of John Bellany and Alexander Moffat, a Scottish Arts Council touring show.

1973 Collins Gallery, University of Strathclyde, opens.
Glasgow Printmakers Studio founded.
William Turnbull: Sculpture and Paintings, Retrospective, Tate Gallery in London.
A View of the Portrait: Portraits by Alexander Moffat 1968–1973, Scottish National Portrait Gallery

1974 Peacock Printmakers founded in Aberdeen.
Aspects of Abstract Painting in Britain 1910 1960 at the Talbot Rice Art Centre in Edinburgh.
Joseph Beuys: Three Pots Action exhibition and Oil Conference, Forrest Hill in Edinburgh.

1975 *Edinburgh Ten 30 Works of Ten Edinburgh Artists 1945–75*, Scottish Arts Council exhibition.
Glenshee Sculpture Park founded.
Third Eye Centre in Glasgow founded.
Fruitmarket Gallery in Edinburgh founded and run by the Scottish Arts Council.

1976 MacLaurin Art Gallery in Ayr opens.
Graeme Murray Gallery in Edinburgh founded.
Paolozzi touring ACGB touring exhibition.
Mark Boyle and Ian Hamilton Finlay feature in the group exhibition *Inscape* at the Fruitmarket Gallery.
Paolozzi commissioned to design doors for the Hunterian Art Gallery, University of Glasgow.

1977 Crawford Arts Centre founded at the University of St Andrews.
Workshop & Artists Studio Provision (wasps) founded in Glasgow, Edinburgh, Aberdeen and Dundee.
Stills Scottish Photography Gallery founded in Edinburgh.
Four Abstract Artists, including the work of John McLean and Fred Pollock shown at the Fruitmarket Gallery in Edinburgh. Clement Greenberg writes the foreword in the catalogue.
Joan Eardley exhibition at the RSA.
Expressionism and Scottish Painting, Scottish Arts Council Collection exhibition.

1978 369 Gallery founded in Edinburgh.
Scottish Sculpture Trust founded.
Boyle Family represent Britain at the Venice Biennale.
Painters in Parallel: 76 20th Century Scottish Artists, a Scottish Arts Council exhibition at Edinburgh College of Art.

Scottish Arts Council Travelling Gallery established.

1979   The Pier Arts Centre, Stromness, Orkney opens.
Alan Davie: Magic Pictures shows at The Scottish Gallery in Edinburgh.

1980   Scottish Sculpture Workshop opens at Lumsden, Grampian.
City Art Centre reopens in Edinburgh.
William Johnstone ACGB retrospective exhibition comes to the Talbot Rice Gallery in Edinburgh.
Watermarks an exhibition of work by Robert Callender and Elizabeth Ogilvie at the Fruitmarket Gallery in Edinburgh.
Paolozzi commissioned to design mosaics for Tottenham Court Road Underground Station in London.

1981   *Contemporary Abstraction: Younger Scottish Artist,* New 57 Gallery in Edinburgh.
Scottish Sculpture Open at Kildrummy Castle, Grampian.
Jock McFadyen appointed Artist in Residence at the National Gallery, London.

1982   *Federation of Scottish Sculptors* founded. Bill Scott is Secretary.
Expressive Images (Group show including Steven Campbell) at the New 57 Gallery in Edinburgh.
Scottish Art Now (Group show including John Kirkwood) at the Fruitmarket Gallery in Edinburgh.
Steven Campbell moves to New York.
Steven Campbell, his first solo show at Barbara Toll Fine Arts in New York.

1983   Artist-run Transmission Gallery opens in Glasgow.
Ian Hamilton Finlay's First Battle of Little Sparta with Strathclyde Regional Council.

1984   Scottish National Gallery of Modern Art moves to John Watson's Building, Belford Road in Edinburgh

1985   June Redfern appointed artist-in-residence at National Gallery in London.
New Image-Glasgow (Group show including Steven Campbell and Ken Currie) at the Third Eye Centre in Glasgow.

1986   Paolozzi appointed Her Majesty's Sculptor in Ordinary in Scotland.
Ken Currie commissioned to paint murals for the People's Palace in Glasgow.

Boyle Family have a retrospective exhibition at the Hayward Gallery in London.
John Bellany exhibition at Scottish National Gallery of Modern Art in Edinburgh.

1987   *The Vigorous Imagination: New Scottish Art* exhibition at SNGMA.

1988   *Ken Currie* exhibition at the Third Eye Centre in Glasgow.
Joan Eardley exhibition at the Talbot Rice Gallery in Edinburgh.

1989   *Contemporary Scottish Painting* at 369 Gallery in Edinburgh.
Scottish Art since 1900 opens at Scottish National Gallery of Modern Art in Edinburgh and goes on to Barbican Art Gallery in London.

1990   Glasgow is nominated European City of Culture.
Steven Campbell exhibits *On Form and Fiction* at the Third Eye Centre, Glasgow.

1992   *Alan Davie Works on Paper*, British Council International Touring Exhibition of Europe and South America.

1993   Douglas Gordon's *24 Hour Psycho* shown for the first time at Tramway in Glasgow.

1996   Douglas Gordon is the first Scottish artist to win the Turner Prize.
Glasgow Museum of Modern Art (goma) opens.
William Turnbull: Sculpture and Paintings, retrospective exhibition at the Serpentine Gallery in London.

1997   Douglas Gordon represents Great Britain at the Venice Biennale.

1998   The Modern Institute opens in Glasgow.
Ingleby Gallery opens in Edinburgh.

1999   Dundee Contemporary Arts opens.

2000   *Alan Davie* retrospective exhibition at the Scottish National Gallery of Modern Art.

2001   Martin Creed wins Turner Prize with controversial *Work No. 227: The lights going on and off*.
Doggerfisher Gallery opens in Edinburgh.

2002   Callum Innes wins the Jerwood Painting Prize and later has major solo show at the Fruitmarket Gallery in Edinburgh.

2003   *Boyle Family*, retrospective exhibition at the Scottish National Gallery of Modern Art.

2004   The biannual Glasgow International Festival of Visual Art is launched.

2005   *William Turnbull. Retrospective 1946–2003* opens at the Yorkshire Sculpture Park.

2006   Douglas Gordon's *Zidane: A 21st Century Portrait* is premiered at the Cannes Film Festival.
Alison Watt appointed artist-in-residence at the National Gallery in London.

2007   Bill Scott becomes the first sculptor to be appointed President of the Royal Scottish Academy.

2008   Luke Fowler wins the inaugural Derek Jarman Award for experimental artist film.

2009   · Martin Boyce represents Scotland at the Venice Biennale and wins the Turner Prize.

2010   Susan Philips is the first sound artist to win the Turner Prize.

2011   Martin Creed's multi-marble *Work No. 1059. Scotsman Steps* is opened in Edinburgh.

2012   David Shrigley's solo show *Brain Activity* opens at the Hayward Gallery in London.

2013   National Galleries of Scotland mount major John Bellany retrospective exhibition in the Royal Scottish Academy.

2014   *Generation: 25 Years of Contemporary Art in Scotland* opens in venues all over Scotland.

2015   Tramway in Glasgow hosts the Turner Prize.

2018   Rachel Maclean shows her film *The Lion and the Unicorn* at the National Gallery in London.

2019   Edinburgh Printmakers moves to a new venue at the Castle Mills Complex in Edinburgh.
Joyce Cairns is appointed the first woman President of the Royal Scottish Academy.

2023   Gary Fisher is appointed President of the Royal Scottish Academy

2023   The National Galleries of Scotland open their new Scottish Galleries
       on the Mound, Edinburgh

Select Bibliography

Essential publications on Scottish modern art

Gage, E, *The Eye in the Wind: Contemporary Scottish Painting since 1945* (London, 1977)

Hardie W, *Scottish Painting. 1937 to the Present* (Glasgow, 1990)

Hare, B, *Contemporary Painting in Scotland* (Sydney, 1993)
Scottish Artists in an Age of Radical Change: 1945 to the 21st Century (Edinburgh, 2019, 2022)

Hartley, K, *Scottish Art since 1900* (London, 1989)

Hartley, K et al., *The Vigorous Imagination: New Scottish Art* (Edinburgh, 1987)

Macmillan, D, *Scottish Art in the 20th Century* (Edinburgh, 2000)
Scotland and the Origins of Modern Art (London, 2023)

Patrizio, A, *Contemporary Sculpture in Scotland* (Sydney, 1999)

Richardson, C, *Scottish Art since 1960: Historical Reflections and Contemporary Overviews* (London, 2011)

Strang, A, *A New Era: Scottish Modern Art 1900–1950* (Edinburgh, 2018)

General publications on Scottish art

Birrell, R and Finlay, A, *Justified Sinners: An Archaeology of Scottish Counter-culture (1960–2000)* (Edinburgh, 2002)

Campbell, M, *Line of Tradition: Watercolours, Drawings and Prints by Scottish Artists 1700–1990* (Edinburgh, 1993)

Cornish, S, *Stockwell Depot: 1967–79* (Greenwich, 2015)

DCA, *Here and Now. Scottish Art 2000–1* (Dundee, 2001)

Dewey, A, *New* (Edinburgh, 2002)

Edinburgh Review, New Scottish Painting (Edinburgh, 1986)

Edinburgh Review, Art and Scotland, Issue 91 (Edinburgh, 1994)

Elliot, P, ed, *The Concise Catalogue of the Scottish National Gallery of Modern Art* (Edinburgh, 1993)

Finlay, I, *Art in Scotland* (Oxford, 1948)

Firth, J, *Scottish Watercolour Painting* (Edinburgh, 1979)

Fruitmarket Gallery, *Scottish Art Now* (Edinburgh, 1982)

Goudie, L, *The Story of Scottish Art* (London, 2020)

Harris, P and Halsby, J, *The Dictionary of Scottish Painters 1600–1960* (Edinburgh & Oxford, 1990)

Macdonald, M, *Scottish Art* (London, 2000)

Macmillan, D, *Scottish Art 1460–2000* (Edinburgh, 2000)

Normand, T, *The Modern Scot* (London, 2000)

Pearson, F et al., *Virtue and Vision: Sculpture in Scotland 1540–1990* (Edinburgh, 1991)

Scottish Arts Council, *Scottish Realism* (Edinburgh, 1971)

Third Eye Centre, *Built in Scotland* (Glasgow, 1983)

Third Eye Centre, *New Image Glasgow* (Glasgow, 1985)

Third Eye Centre, *Scatter, New Scotland* (Glasgow, 1989)

Van Raaij, S, *Glasgow Gallery of Modern Art: The First Years* (Glasgow, 1996)

White, N, ed, *New Art in Scotland* (Glasgow, 1994)

Wishart, A and Oliver, C, *The Society of Scottish Artists: The First 100 Years* (Edinburgh, 1991)

General publications on British post-war art

Garlake, M, *New Art/New World: British Art in Postwar Society* (Yale, 1998)

Harrison, M, *Transition: the London art scene in the Fifties* (London, 2002)

Hughes, MM et al., *Blast to Freeze: British Art in the 20th Century* (Wolfburgh, 2002) Buck, L, *Moving Targets: A User's Guide to British Art Now*, Vols 1 & 2 (London, 1997, 2001)

Hyman, J, *The Battle for Realism* (Yale, 2001)

Massey, A, *The Independent Group* (Manchester, 1995)

Morris, F, *Paris – Post War Art and Existentialism 1945–55* (London, 1994)

Royal Academy, *British Art in the 20th Century: The Modern Movement* (London, 1987)

Selected publications on the individual Scottish artists featured in this book

Abbot Hall Art Gallery, *Alison Watt A Shadow on the Blind,* (Kendal, 2018)

Abrioux, Y, *Ian Hamilton Finlay: A Visual Primer* (London, 1993)

ACGB, *Craigie Aitchison: Paintings 1953–1981* (London, 1981)

Andreae, C, *Joan Eardley* (London, 2013)

Ascherson, N, *Sandy Moffat: Seven Poets* (Glasgow, 1981)

Bowness, A, *Alan Davie* (London, 1967)

Brown, K, *Douglas Gordon* (London, 2004)

Carrell, C, ed., Cocker, D., *Sculpture and Related Works* (Glasgow, 1986)

Cohen, D, *Jock McFadyen: A Book about a Painter* (London, 2009)

Collins, I, *John McLean* (London, 2009)

Collins, J, *Eduardo Paolozzi* (London, 2014)

Davidson, AA, *William Turnbull: The Sculpture of William Turnbull* (London, 2005)

De Luca, C et al., *Paolozzi at Large in Edinburgh* (Edinburgh, 2018)

Elliott, P et al., *William Turnbull: Sculptures and Paintings* (London, 1995)

Elliott, P, *Alan Davie: Works in the Scottish National Gallery of Modern Art* (Edinburgh, 2000)

Joan Eardley: A Sense of Place (Edinburgh, 2016)
Elliott, P & Hare, B, et al., *Boyle Family* (Edinburgh, 2003)
Fruitmarket Gallery, *Alison Watt: Fold (New Paintings 1996–97)* (Edinburgh, 1996)
Hall, D et al., *Alan Davie* (London, 1992)
Hare, B, *Ken Currie: Age of Uncertainty* (Glasgow, 1992)
  Alan Davie: Channels of Communication (Harrogate, 2006)
  Paul Reid: The Art of Mythmaking (Harrogate, 2014)
  Facing the Nation: The Portraiture of Alexander Moffat (Edinburgh, 2018)
Hare, B et al., *Joyce Cairns: War Tourist* (Aberdeen, 2006)
Hare, B et al., *Alan Davie: Works on Paper* (London, 1992)
Hartley, K et al. *Douglas Gordon: Superhumanatural* (Edinburgh, 2006
Hartley, K et al., *John Bellany* (Edinburgh, 2012)
Haste, C, *Craigie Aitchison: A Life in Colour* (London, 2014)
Hayward Gallery, *Beyond Image: Boyle Family* (London, 1986)
Hendry, J, ed. Ian Hamilton Finlay issue in *Chapman No.78/9* (Edinburgh, 1994)
Locher, JL, *Mark Boyle's Journey to the Surface of the Earth* (Stuttgart, London, 1978)
McEwan, J, *John Bellany* (Edinburgh, 1994)
Macmillan, D, *The Paintings of Steven Campbell: The Story So Far* (Edinburgh, 1993)
  Jock McFadyen (Edinburgh, 2001)
National Gallery, *June Redfern: Artist in Residence* (London, 1986)
Normand, T, *Ken Currie: Details of a Journey* (London, 2002)
  Ken Currie: Paintings and Writings (Edinburgh, 2023)
Oliver, C, *Joan Eardley* (Edinburgh, 1988)
Pearson, F, *Joan Eardley* (Edinburgh, 2007)
  Eduardo Paolozzi (Edinburgh, (1999)
Spencer, R, ed, *Eduardo Paolozzi: an anthology* (Oxford, 2001)
Sutherland, G et al., *Lys Hansen; Passionate Paint* (Edinburgh, 1998)
Sykes, D ed., McLean, J, *Recent Work in Context* (St Andrews, 1998)
Thomson, A ed., Paolozzi, E. *Edinburgh Review No.104* (Edinburgh, 2000
Wardell, G et al., *Barbara Rae* (London, 2008)
Wiggins, C et al., *Alison Watt: Phantom* (London, 2008)
Woods, A, *Douglas Gordon Transcript, Vol 3, Issue 3* (Dundee, 1999)

Acknowledgements

THIS SECOND VOLUME of my essays and commentaries on Scottish art and artists covers over 40 years of my writings. This occassion gives me an opportunity to thank all those people – in a range of different capacities – whom I have had the privilege to work with over the past four decades.

More specifically, for this publication, I would first and foremost, like to express my gratitude to all the artists who are featured in this book. Furthermore, I would like to thank all the various obliging people who have published my writings. Over the years I have been fortunate to be asked to write articles for a number of publications. This gives me the opportunity to express my gratitude to all gallery owners, exhibition curators, art magazine editors and publishers who have allowed me to express my critical opinion and air my aesthetic preferences in print.

Lastly, I must thank those who were involved in the production of this book; Ralph Hughes for the photography, Sebastian Boyle for supplying the Boyle Family cover image, Sandy Moffat for writing the Foreword, Jennie Renton for her input and the Director of Luath Press, Gavin MacDougall, for again agreeing to publish more of my writings.

Luath Press Limited

committed to publishing well written books worth reading

LUATH PRESS takes its name from Robert Burns, whose little collie Luath (*Gael.*, swift or nimble) tripped up Jean Armour at a wedding and gave him the chance to speak to the woman who was to be his wife and the abiding love of his life. Burns called one of the 'Twa Dogs' Luath after Cuchullin's hunting dog in Ossian's *Fingal*. Luath Press was established in 1981 in the heart of Burns country, and is now based a few steps up the road from Burns' first lodgings on Edinburgh's Royal Mile. Luath offers you distinctive writing with a hint of unexpected pleasures.

Most bookshops in the UK, the US, Canada, Australia, New Zealand and parts of Europe, either carry our books in stock or can order them for you. To order direct from us, please send a £sterling cheque, postal order, international money order or your credit card details (number, address of cardholder and expiry date) to us at the address below. Please add post and packing as follows: UK – £1.00 per delivery address; overseas surface mail – £2.50 per delivery address; overseas airmail – £3.50 for the first book to each delivery address, plus £1.00 for each additional book by airmail to the same address. If your order is a gift, we will happily enclose your card or message at no extra charge.

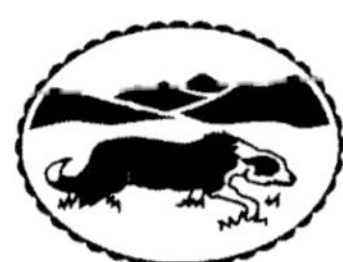

Luath Press Limited
543/2 Castlehill
The Royal Mile
Edinburgh EH1 2ND
Scotland
Telephone: 0131 225 4326 (24 hours)
Email: sales@luath.co.uk
Website: www.luath.co.uk